A HISTORY OF DU CANE COURT:

LAND, ARCHITECTURE, PEOPLE AND POLITI

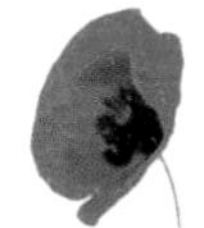

Contents

DISCLAIMER:
The author has made earnest attempts to credit his sources, and to make payment for pictures on the rare occasions when it was required. In the unlikely event that there should be any outstanding problems, he would be happy to take reasonable measures to find a solution.

Any picture in the present work which is owned by the Land Registry is crown copyright, and is reproduced with the permission of the Land Registry.

The author reserves the right to alter this work for future print runs or editions.

ACKNOWLEDGEMENTS

*

I am indebted to the many people whom I interviewed for this project, who regaled me with innumerable anecdotes, as well as personal accounts of their lives and of how this building has been significant to them. As I go to press, some of my interviewees will have moved on to pastures new, or (beyond human horizons) to the Elysian Fields, but what is written was at least accurate, to the best of my knowledge, at the time of recording.

It was a brief presentation in 1998 by Jeremy Jessel, the Chairman of the Balham Society at the time, which inspired me to take up my pen, and I have since spoken with a whole galaxy of residents: Duncan Scobie, Derick Mallett, Sylvia Say, who related some delightfully funny stories to me; Pat Grimshaw; Dolores Maia Bingham; Betty Campbell; Lois Hadley; Audrey Barry; Marjorie Loter; Ms Hockman; Suzanna Hughes (deceased), who came here in 1953; Jessie Boran (deceased); Ruby Thomas, who has since reached her century – before passing away; Edward Kay; Corrie Hutchings; Richard Pobjoy, who had some unusual hearsay; and Alan Bartlett, who was interested in my book from the outset, and who - with Chrissie True - would encourage me when my confidence was flagging.

My conversations with comedian, Arthur Smith, and actor-come-director, Christopher Luscombe, furnished me with an intimate view into the world of radio, music hall and theatre; while the following residents had interesting family backgrounds, which highlighted how times have changed: Louisa Wheway (who arrived in 1944), Claire Macdonald-Ross, and May Arkell (deceased). May also supplied me with a copy of the original brochure for the building, including a menu for the restaurant, which had once been among its most prominent features.

For general information on Wandsworth – and especially Balham – serving as background to my story, the following were good points of reference: Wandsworth Museum; Graham Gower's book, 'Balham: A Brief History'; and certain historical drawings of the neighbourhood, thanks to fellow resident, Brian Gostick (deceased).

I must here mention Neil Mills, the amiable owner of a local hairdressing salon, who enlightened me as to how all other avenues of Balham's local history seem to lead back to Du Cane Court; and Neil Gray, the porter, who entertained me with sad, yet bizarre, tales about those of advanced age who were losing their minds.

Marion Hopkins (deceased) gave me an insight into life in Balham in the 1920s; and clearly recollected David Suchet, who played Agatha Christie's fictional detective, Hercule Poirot, during some filming at Du Cane Court in about 1990. Both she, and a gentleman named Howard Narroeway, even remembered Du Cane Court being built.

I should express warm thanks to Robert Addington, a relation of Doctor Taylor, who inhabited a residence of grand proportions which was removed to make way for the building which is the subject of this history. My conversation with him revealed a way of life which is gone forever.

An article from The Builder for October, 1937, contained a crucial list of companies involved in the construction of the block; whilst Companies House attempted to trace them all for me, as well as sending me microfiche records of the Central London Property Trust, which purchased the underlying parcel of land from Charles Du Cane.

For a marvellous picture of 'work in progress', and for general information, I must acknowledge Noella Morton in our Estate Office; while Patrick Loobey (deceased) – and, again, the aforesaid office - kindly provided me with photographs of the completed building. Mention should also be made of Neville Chuck, Michael Leader, Max Tyler and Doremy Vernon, who all supplied photographs of celebrities; and of Glen Mitchell, for what he told me about the musician, Jim Bray.

Trevor Todd, of the Royal Institute of British Architects, and Ms Valls (I hope I have recorded her name correctly) contributed to my understanding of building methods and architectural style; and the knowledge of Charles Jones was also useful. But I feel especially privileged to have made the acquaintance of Charles Kay Green, who, like so many who are mentioned in these pages, has now gone the way of all flesh. He supplied me with invaluable information on the architect's family background, private life and career from an insider's perspective, for he was his son. In addition, he lent me a complete set of architectural drawings for 'the Court'. Mr McKeer, former manager, took me on a tour of the roof and basement; while Graham Middleton and Adrian Van Rensburg clarified some points on the features thereof; and as for our delightful courtyards, my meeting with Jill Raggett of the Japanese Garden Society was pleasant and instructive.

Regarding life at Du Cane Court in the 1930s and the Second World War, the following assisted with first-hand accounts: Mrs Borris, Jean Evans, Mrs Beerman, and Mr Van Gelder - whose parents received an honorary memorandum from the queen for remaining true to each other for 50 years.

In the hope of confirming the myths and superstitions surrounding Du Cane Court during the war, including that old 'chestnut' about Hitler having his eye on a flat here, I contacted Mrs Klauk, a librarian in the German Historical Institute. Regrettably, she was unable to substantiate anything. But my interview with Emily Quarman may partly explain why the rumours arose in the first place.

For stories of general interest in the 1940s and 1950s ... there was the material from the Times Index, sent to me by Sarah Ash of the Guildhall Library (Corporation of London); and the Reference Library for Associated Newspapers in Kensington was also a useful source. Furthermore, John Brown of the Streatham Society sent me photocopies of various articles relating to the block.

My interviews with the Renak family gave me an insight into what it was like to be a child growing up at Du Cane Court in the 1950s. And for general information on the 1950s and beyond, thanks are due to Hilda Middleton (who has lived here since 1957), for her excellent memory of specific events, and her incisive comment. I am also indebted to Jennifer Whelpton, for speaking to me about the most famous member of staff from the early days - her own mother - who, in the fullness of time, has become something of a legend. As for the best-known resident of them all, Tommy Trinder, I have Ray Vincent to thank for a fine summing-up of his comic routine; and I should mention Ray, again, and Isobel Thompson for their helpful opinions on the manuscript.

Ron Crayden conjured up an arresting portrait of the table-tennis maestro, Ernest Bubley, who lived here after the war; whilst from the Local History Library, at Lavender Hill in Clapham, I discovered which apartments have been occupied by well-known residents, and the years they resided there, – as well as other memorabilia. While we were at the library, Alan Bartlett notified me of a few amusing names of voters (which I later employed in my section, 'The Preece and the Porteus'), and so transformed a dry and dusty, if necessary, afternoon spent in the company of the prolific 'Register of Electors', into a source of light entertainment. May all of those people whose names fed our grey matter with oxygen not turn in their graves, nor their wheelchairs, with angry conceit in the face of some harmless banter ... but laugh with us. Yet naturally, the demographics of such a palatial residence as Du Cane Court extends far beyond a handful of famous or comical names, and, in a wider context, data from the Office of National Statistics proved to be quite revealing.

I am also grateful to the London Metropolitan Archives for information on land transactions within the Du Cane family; to Rosamund Du Cane, for her correspondence on the subject of her illustrious relations; and to Anthony Batho at the Land Registry, who apprised me of the owners of our building, over the 70 or so years since its inception. And with respect to how the management has changed hands, and various intimate events and controversies over the years, I am indebted to the Residents' Association for allowing me access to their archives; and to Wandsworth Council, for its extensive microfiche records.

Sadly, Graham Decor of the Fire Services could find no historic information, or pictures, relating to the various fires which have occurred here over the years. (The fire services had, however, been informed of a fire in the building the very day before my conversation with him.) Nor could the London Police Pensioners' Magazine shed any light on crime at Du Cane Court, although my conversation with a resident policeman named Stan Hardes was of general interest.

Luckily, with the aid of Danny Ashton at Rentokil, my enquiry into the infestation of pharaoh ants on the premises was much more fruitful; as were my dialogues with Gloria Blackhurst and Kulbushan Chopra, who enlightened me with regard to other extraordinary happenings.

One final point: if I have been so remiss as to overlook someone important, may I apologize in advance, and simply say 'thank you' to all of those whose time and patience has made this history possible.

INTRODUCTION

*

A Window on the World

'Chrissie, tell me what you see?'

'I can see foxes from my living room window; and Earl's Court to the right, and Wandsworth Prison too ... and, did you know? There's a red-light district in the inner courtyard!'

When I asked her what she meant, she referred to a red light switched on in one of the flats, where resided a man in a dressing gown.

Mrs Beerman once had an outward-facing flat on the same floor as Chrissie. She praised the breathtaking views of sunsets, which she could gaze at in admiration for 10 minutes at a time.

'And Alan, what do you see?' I asked the ever-sociable Mr Bartlett, who, like them, lived on the sixth floor (before he moved).

'Well, from my flat I can see the Houses of Parliament and Big Ben; the London Eye and St Paul's Cathedral - as well as the Empress State building for the MOD.' Truly, a room with a view.

The vista from the *top* of Du Cane Court is even better. There, you can take in Millbank Tower, the London Eye and the BT Tower - with Hampstead Heath rising in the distance. And there's more ... the House of Lords, Tower Bridge and Canary Wharf - with Canada Square, sporting three red beacons and one white flashing light – and, of course, the gigantic NatWest Tower. These days, only a privileged few are allowed on the roof, although occasional tours have been conducted by the manager.

There are even a couple of penthouses up there, and a bungalow at the back of the estate, referred to as 'The Lodge'. As for the ground floor flats around the side of the building, they give on to tiny plots of land - which are not literally the possession of the flat-owner, but try telling him that!

The front of the building is very pleasant, with two lush, green courtyards – which you would expect to be fully utilized throughout the summer. Perhaps people don't like to be overlooked, although this shortcoming has never bothered me.

The rear of our massive residence is less remarkable, except on a bright summer evening when one turns a corner - and, suddenly, there it is ... looming out of the near distance with a fiery orange glow like Ayer's Rock. Having an 84 foot foyer, Du Cane Court has also been compared to a luxury liner which has come to berth near Balham Station. One day, in a thousand years time, perhaps the remains of this monolith will be venerated, just as a crumbling temple is today.

The Inner World of Du Cane Court

In spite of complaints to the contrary, Du Cane Court is, on the whole, surprisingly quiet for such a large and populated space. On a good day it has the remoteness of a lighthouse, or the battlements of a castle, and one of the security guards once quipped that he might favour the creation of a moat with crocodilians, for which unsuspecting intruders could become a hearty meal! In reality, there is a warning against trespassing, backed up by Closed Circuit Television and a guard dog patrol – with a carnivore only slightly less hungry than a crocodile.

Peter Austin-Hunt, an erudite (former) resident who used to work in the film industry, once observed to me what a delightful mosaic exists in each courtyard at night: with the windows lit up by variegated lampshades, and framing tiny parts of the composite whole. Apparently, after 10pm, the mosaic has more light pixels now than in days gone by, when everyone would hit the proverbial sack by a sensible hour. Such a change fires a degree of consternation in the old if they anticipate a raucous party to be imminent ... for it must be said that the courtyards have their own peculiar sound world: full of effects borne through the air like illegitimate phantoms (for no one will take any responsibility for them), and travelling upwards in a kind of vortex, amplified first by nature, and then by rumour and complaint. One moment, the theme of 'Coronation Street' may hold sway, fortified by a rich vein of Italian opera; the next, perhaps a melody from the big band era, followed by the rhythms of rap and garage music – all serving to remind the perspicacious occupant of what era his residence hails from, and which era it has now arrived at; and let us not forget the occasional percussion of plates and cutlery being scrubbed in a nearby sink, punctuating the speech of a hostess chatting amiably to her guests ... and all finally rounded off, if too loud or too prolonged, with an enraged request from another window to 'be quiet!'

There are parallels with the Hitchcock movie, 'Rear Window', for you occasionally witness things you never wanted to: scantily-clothed residents wandering nonchalantly through their rooms (exposed by windows as naked as they are themselves), and the sounds of lovemaking when you are trying to get to sleep. Were the windows left open out of vanity or ignorance? Either way, my friend Lois has the right words for the moment ... for she will stick her head out of the window and brazenly call out, 'We can heaaaaar you!' A succeeding silence could answer the outstanding question.

And there are sounds which should be irritating but, in the fullness of time, become homely and reassuring, like the chattering of the cleaners in one of the rooms that are allocated to them. In my old studio flat, they would act like an alarm call, as surely as the dawn chorus, - for there are plenty of birds in our trees, and the estate is their home too.

The Size of the Building

The scale of Du Cane Court is truly something to be reckoned with. It sits on about 4.5 acres of land, and has been variously estimated to contain four or six miles of corridor (although I feel that *two* miles would be nearer the mark), so it is hardly surprising that there are problems with the post. Every home is clearly labelled, but I suppose the odd postman with a bad sense of direction just gets tired of walking around! And those who address the envelopes do not always help matters, scrambling the letters and digits with protean inventiveness, even to the point of re-christening the location as 'Du Cann Court' or 'Du Cave Court'! Occasionally, the name of the place might even be omitted altogether ... as if the apartment for which the letter was intended had been excised from the womb of the building by some fantastic caesarian section, and, afflicted by separation anxiety, had thence crawled down the high road to attach itself to the nearest row of houses.

Taking an aerial view, the building is laid out in ten contiguous 'blocks', labelled 'A' to 'K'. Strangely, none is labelled 'I', unless it exists in another space-time continuum (perhaps offering a final resting place for the dearly departed souls who have lived out their lives under the other letters). Often, I will speak of the parts collectively as one block, which, incidentally, crosses various postal districts - as one anecdote clearly illustrates. When Pat Grimshaw moved from the first to the second floor, she was surprised to find that the cost of her contents insurance fell. This is in spite of her new home having two bedrooms, and her previous home having only one. Apparently she now has a better postcode!

The sheer dimensions of what surrounds you here can have a powerful effect on the psyche ... for there is a peculiar sensation in having your front door some way above the ground and along a corridor - ensconced in a building which is already set back from the busy road. Indeed, there are moments when you may enjoy a sense of absolute privacy, even isolation.

An Unusual Miscellany

If one were to select a suitable subject for a history from the oversized dwelling places of the concrete jungle, one's attention would naturally settle upon Du Cane Court. The ample gardens complete with pond and with memorials; the large and welcoming foyer, and the internal mini supermarket; and (formerly) the restaurant and social club; not to mention the sounds of church bells on a Sunday morning emanating from the adjacent place of worship ... all conspire to create the charm of a village.

It has been compared to Dolphin Square in Pimlico unfavourably, for its rival has 1250 flats, plus a whole series of shops in its environs – as well as a restaurant which looks out onto a private swimming-pool. Yet Dolphin Square is a series of blocks rather than one composite whole, and caters for the aristocracy (for even Princess Anne has resided there); while 'the Court' has a broad client base, made up mostly of the common stock of mankind, and is perhaps better maintained.

Samuel Johnson once said of London, 'All of life is here'. Indeed, it has even been argued that the development of a small conurbation reflects the nation which contains it [J.H.Bloom] – and I wonder if Du Cane Court might inspire the same sentiments. In support of such a claim, this work is a strange medley of art deco architecture and Japanese gardens, of famous people and commoners, of landlord and tenant disputes, - all wrapped up in what has become a place of legend for local people.

In December, 1999, a resident from New Zealand was about to embark on an affiliated project of grand proportions. His intention was to document, through pictures, the architectural, residential and social aspects of the building as it stands today. He even wanted to photograph each resident and the interior of every flat. I imagine that a universal wish for privacy (which is acutely felt at Du Cane Court) would have thwarted his progress; and he has now, in any case, gone back to his homeland.

Many aspiring writers have taken up their pens with tales of this block on their agenda, but none have succeeded in completing a work of literature larger than a newspaper article. To the best of my knowledge, all have suffered from the same Achilles heel. For everywhere one looks, it seems, no records have been kept.

Obstacles Encountered During My Research

Various interested parties with whom I have spoken imagine that researching a landmark like ours should be straightforward. Yet even such a venerable institution as the National Monuments Record could only reward my labours with one unexceptional photograph from 1952, which I have no need for. Of course, there are times when public records can be quite rewarding, when a researcher may digress and find answers to questions he did not ask, although he often receives no answers to the questions he came with. The subject of Du Cane Court is so elusive, one feels rather like an ornithologist peering through binoculars, for no sooner does a rare and fleeting thing come into focus than it disappears again.

I contacted Professor Richard Overy, of the Department of History at Kings College; and Adrian Forty, Professor of Architectural History (Bartlett School of Architecture, University College, London), - but neither of them knew our building.

To begin with, I could find nothing on the architect, George Kay Green, for he was not a member of the aforesaid institute, nor had he any letters after his name. Then finally, one day, as I was looking through the Times Obituaries, I stumbled across one 'George Green', who died on July 22nd, 1940. I became momentarily excited, but my heart quickly sank to its previous level of despair when I saw that this particular gentleman was a swimming-pool attendant! Around the year 2000, I visited Wandsworth Council and asked for the original plans of Du Cane Court. I was told that I must have permission from the architect. As he had passed away at about the same time as the swimming-pool attendant, I had to explain that this would prove difficult - but I can only hope that the presiding spirit of our very own Mr George *Kay* Green has since conferred permission through his son, from whom I eventually obtained the architectural plans, and who came across as a most amiable man. (In the end, I got a contact telephone number for him through Directory Enquiries! How quaint that after all of the convoluted lines of enquiry, a solution could be so simple.)

I have pursued photographs and other reproducible memorabilia with the passion of a hunger, especially in relation to the old restaurant, bar and games rooms ... but in the end I must be satisfied with what I have. Like a diamond prospector, I begin to cut and polish, and nature often reveals unusual connections and striking insights that may seem to the casual observer who does not share my passion to be no more than mud and rough stones; but the hope is that fortune will give me readers less casual, who will appreciate what I am trying to do; for in my better moments, I have felt like a private investigator, and I hope that, by venturing into unchartered territory, I may give

'... to airy nothing
A local habitation and a name.'
Shakespeare, 'A Midsummer Night's Dream'

SOME PHILOSOPHICAL REFLECTIONS

*

Natural Selection in the Recording of History

As I scoured the shelves of public libraries to no avail, a persuasive idea came into my mind. There seems to be an implicit assumption that the only buildings worth documenting for the annals of history are those constructed or adopted by official bodies. Thus parliamentary buildings, palaces and castles, stately homes and National Trust gardens, are history's winners in the record-keeping stakes. And one accepts that it should be so. But the principle far exceeds a handful of well-established treasures, to encompass any large object with a public face, or that becomes a template suitable for duplication by the state. Numbered among such productions are the underground stations designed by Charles Holden. Established opinion marks them out as architectural wonders ... an opinion the present author questions, although it is undeniable that the new crop of Northern Line stations in the 1920s opened up south London, and without them Du Cane Court and other blocks in the vicinity might never have been built.

The renowned architectural critic, Nicholas Pevsner, who writes about listed buildings, would have little interest in Du Cane Court. As for houses with beautiful frontages and stained glass windows in private roads nearby, we are expected to delete them all from our consciousness, and be aware of only what is plain and utilitarian.

On a more general level, so much of the history that we study in school relates to the exploits of sovereigns and military leaders, rather than to ordinary people; so it is not surprising that the homes which are bequeathed to us from past ages are palaces rather than cottages - especially as palaces were built to last. In this way, the common man has been robbed of his heritage. The last century has turned this somewhat on its head, and it now seems that no subject is too small for scrutiny. Of course, we understand that as the human race travels from one epoch to the next, we cannot take everything with us; but it is possible to overlook some rare gems whilst panning for gold.

Patrick Loobey, a notable recorder of local history himself, once remarked that Du Cane Court, being but a single building, had little to offer the great reading public as a subject for a book: less, even, than one single entire street. But more people live in Du Cane Court than in many streets. It is a residential complex on a grand scale - built to last longer than many a detached home; in fact, for strength and durability, it is less like the cottages, and more like the palaces of old.

A Methodology Fit for the Challenge

I have named my book in such a way as to allow myself the freedom to include any curious details which lie at the fringes of my central themes. With regard to presentation, I have asked myself: Should I relate everything in chronological order, or let the subject matter dictate how the story is told? The natural method, in writing about an epoch or person of national importance, is to tell the story as it unfolded in life – where each circumstance leads on, seamlessly, to the next. One would not countenance a history of the Second World War which covers the Battle of Britain before Hitler's invasion of Poland; nor a biography that relates how the chief subject fell in love and married, before an account of the character-forming years of his youth.

Yet the history within these pages is less transparent. Within Du Cane Court, innumerable people live out their lives and countless events unfold, which are in no way interdependent beyond the fact that they are all tied to a single landmark. When a theme does recur - such as a controversy around applications for planning permission, or a negative attitude to children or pets, - it makes more sense to account for it at length in one place, rather than in the desultory fashion in which Father Time has bequeathed it to us. Yet there is more continuity in the chronological method, and perhaps more satisfaction for the reader. Therefore, as far as possible, I have made this my standard, but with the proviso that I may deviate from it when my subject assumes a life of its own, and appears almost to regulate itself.

The Employment of the Imagination

How does one integrate such a wide range of disparate facts as might be compiled for the local history of a residential block? My amusing friend, Alan, indicates the value of 'and' with a mischievous smile; as if this magical word were the verbal equivalent of the glue that bonds the parts of military aircraft together; but more than mere conjunctions are required. One must discover the story behind the facts, and be able to persuade the reader that it was there all along, as tangible as a fossil embedded in a rock, and yet as contemporary in its influence as the evolution of a species when it is written into the genes.

It is tempting to see the common bonds which exist between all people, and the special gift of empathy possessed by the writer, and then to maintain that every historian who earnestly seeks the truth behind the clues must find it. A traditionalist may say that the recorder of past events should not embellish them, either with imagination or with too much humanist detail; but set them down as they truly are, in all their naked glory. And yet the truer version of history is surely the one with a human story. For what is action without motive? To be overly punctilious is to eviscerate the past, to remove its beating, feeling heart, and the lungs by which it breathed; for surely a fossil during its lifetime was more than its bare bones?

Recording History as it Happens

Considerable attention has always been given to ancient history, although it is more recent history which has directly shaped our lives. It is also true that events and characters are most vividly recorded when they are contemporary at the time of writing. So it was that James Boswell was able to give us a most colourful and intimate portrait of his friend, Samuel Johnson; and so, also, Lockhart could render the same celebrity treatment to Sir Walter Scott.

These were mighty subjects to begin with, and Du Cane Court could well seem humble by comparison. Yet the hand of time will often glaze events and artifacts with a finesse (in the popular imagination) which maybe no one but a soothsayer could have foreseen at the outset. The style of art deco, in which Du Cane Court was fashioned, falls into this category; and, for its own merits, hopefully Du Cane Court does too.

Local versus Ancient History

Let us reflect, for a moment or two, on the relative merits or demerits of writing on the grandiose subjects of the distant past, compared to the humble subject matter of recent, local history.

There has to be a greater tolerance of falsehood and exaggeration in the area of ancient history, for we can speculate to our heart's content on the shape of a Palaeolithic tool, safe in the knowledge that no one can definitely confirm or deny what we say. But if we deal with an epoch which involves the living or the recently dead, we have a special duty to be accurate; and we need more tact and discretion than if our subject was ancient Rome. After all, what living relative of Caligula will defend his reputation against the charges of moral corruption and gross indecency?

Defamation

The historian, unlike the writer of fiction, does not have the luxury of hiding behind the familiar excuse: that any perceived resemblance between what has been described and real life persons or events, is purely coincidental.

Yet from the seed of a truism grow various concerns. For those mentioned in a work of local history are often ordinary people with little appetite for fame, and even less for lawsuits! The latter I have no appetite for myself, and so I have endeavoured at all times to be fair in my narrative. Furthermore, I have employed the artifice of the pseudonym, or of the third person, for the key players in certain outrageous episodes, so as not to give offence to private individuals. On occasion, I have even 'neutered' my subject, so to speak ... although more liberty is taken with those facts that have already entered the public arena, and I will not omit events of general significance simply to protect the sensibilities of personages with a delicate nature.

Generally, I am assuming that interviewees would like what they have told me to be written down, unless otherwise stated; and I pray that they will not be fazed by the mild publicity which stirs in my wake. I might add that I have mostly paraphrased the words of myself and others, whilst remaining true to the spirit of what was said, since to echo everything verbatim does neither the speaker nor the reader any favours.

On a final note, this work is intended for readers who not only have a serious interest in a facet of Balham's history, but who have a sense of humour as well. May I be lucky enough to find such people, and to bring them satisfaction in all of their various moods.

HISTORICAL BACKGROUND

*

Du Cane Court lies in one of the busiest districts of London, the borough of Wandsworth. In 1994, the population of this borough numbered about 266,700 [Encyc.Brit]. About one fifth belonged to ethnic minorities - primarily Afro-Caribbeans, South Asians and Africans – and the population of the block reflects this broad spectrum of humanity.

The River Wandle bisects the borough, and dozens of waterwheels once powered Wandsworth's mills. Indeed, water has played a key role in various ways, for nearby Norwood Grove was blessed with natural springs, hence the allure Streatham once held for the well-to-do – and for theatrical celebrities, before they moved to Balham, and ultimately to Du Cane Court.

Today, the Wandle is rarely seen, for it is concealed beneath centuries of man's development. Also hidden from view is the Falconbrook. Du Cane Court stands on the west side of Balham High Road, near a tributary of the River Falcon and close to subterranean pipes. Indeed, if you stand in a certain place on Boundaries Road you can hear the rippling murmur of the waters – and they are even observable under the manhole cover. During torrential rain the streams have swelled and caused flooding, with water being forced up through the pipes of the building. How unlike a nearby mansion, Helensburgh House, for which water was provided with such difficulty that the owner, a gentleman named Spurgen, instructed his workers to go on digging to the centre of the earth if necessary! Eventually, at 500 feet, they found a generous supply of water – and it was the purest in the region. How often have we wished our own water supply to be purer? But with our vast network of pipes gurgling away upon unmentionable solutions (that are occasionally blocked and misdirected), we must dream on!

On the bright side, Du Cane Court lies in a well-appointed area, amply served with shops and other small businesses. It is apt that perhaps the grandest building on the main road should be our own; for the antecedent of Balham High Road was Stane Street, a contrivance of the Romans, who were themselves such great builders.

The district of Balham was first mentioned (as 'Baelgenham') in a Saxon charter of 957 relating to the boundaries of Battersea. By 1340, some 200 acres of land were being cultivated in Balham. Some of this became known as 'Great Balams', an area today bounded by Chestnut Grove, Oldridge Road and Balham High Road. The plot was later owned by the family from whom our building derives its name.

The Huguenots

The Du Canes were actually French Protestants, or 'Huguenots', who had fled from their homeland to escape persecution [The Huguenot Soc].

Protestantism was introduced to France in the 1520s, and by 1560 there were more than 2000 Protestant churches in the country. Unfortunately, the new branch of Christianity was not well received.

Between 1562 and 1598 eight bitter wars were fought. The Edict of Nantes in 1598 gave almost complete religious freedom; but more strife followed, and the Edict was revoked in 1685. Clearly, old rivalries die hard, for more than a hundred years later, in the so-called 'Council of Blood' (1800), more than 10,000 Huguenots were executed.

Although a million or so Protestants remained in France, between 400,000 and a million people emigrated - to England, Germany, the Netherlands, Switzerland, Ireland and the English colonies in North America.

The Huguenots brought with them skills in banking and finance, and Wandsworth Museum itemizes a whole range of other trades which they practiced in the locality: dyeing, enamelling, making wigs and hats, and fashioning utensils out of brass and copper. Their descendants are now well integrated and, for the most part, know nothing of their ancestors. The Huguenot Society is trying to change all that. It is perhaps assisted by the fact that a number of characteristic surnames survive. These include Danvers, De La Rue, Denis, Du Quesne (later anglicised to Du Cane), Dumas, Grueber, Mercier, Perdu, Roquett and Viger.

The Du Canes as Landed Gentry

The Du Canes were originally from Flanders. They came to England in about 1570, first settling in Canterbury, then moving to London in around 1606. It may be that other members of the family followed later, since one authority states that members of the family emigrated from Normandy after 1685. The first refugee, John, died in approximately 1640; and by the 1660s the family owned a lot of property, but much of it was wiped out by the Great Fire. Nevertheless they recovered, and in the early 18th century they had the foremost rank amongst London merchants.

The estate of Great Balams was sold to Peter Du Cane in 1701[Gower]. He was already a major landowner in Steatham, and was keen to increase his investment in south London. The Du Canes kept at least 144 acres of this land until the early 19th century; and eventually, their farm house was replaced by a terrace of houses facing Balham High Road.

A wedding portrait displayed in the Tate Gallery [Barker] shows two of the richest banking families in the city of London in the 1730s - the Boehms and the Du Canes. It is by the Scottish artist, Gawen Hamilton, whom some contemporaries proclaimed a finer painter than William Hogarth. Two of the figures portrayed are Charles Boehm and Peter Du Cane, who were both governors of the bank of England, and among the financial survivors of the South Sea Bubble.

Conveyancing between the Great and the Good

The Du Canes have been involved in some notable transactions over the years [Lond.Met.Arch.]. In 1816, there was a resettlement of estates under the will of Bysshe Shelley, with Peter Du Cane and William Whitton acting as trustees. William Whitton was the plaintiff; and none other than Percy Bysshe Shelley was the defendant. It seems that the Shelleys had leased some land from the Du Canes, and that Percy would not agree to the condition that his family (and specifically his father, Sir Timothy Shelley) should make payments out of financial gains from the timber produced on this estate. Because of his stance, Percy and his heirs were excluded from any benefits.

We remember this eloquent poet as something of a rebel. He was, for instance, an apologist for atheism at a time when such a theological position would have been almost untenable, and it appears that his rebellious spirit had once again got the better of him.

Famous Du Canes

Many Du Canes have distinguished themselves. Indeed, the details of the family estate, which were transferred from Essex to the London Record Office at County Hall, Westminster Bridge, on 26th November, 1959, – numbered 40 pages!

From Burke's Landed Gentry, we learn that one Peter Du Quesne was elected Alderman in 1666; whilst Richard Du Cane was MP for Colchester from 1715 to 1722. He was also Director of the Bank of England, the Governor of Christ's Hospital, and a member of the Grand Committee of St Thomas's and Guy's Hospitals.

A certain Peter Du Cane of Braxted Park, Essex, was High Sheriff in 1745, and Director of the Bank of England and of the East India Company; as well as Vice-President of the London Infirmary. And another family member, also called Peter, was High Sheriff of Essex in 1826, and MP for Steyning in 1830.

Sir Edmund Frederick Du Cane (KCB, 1877), was Chevalier of the Imperial Order of the Rose of Brazil; and the Inspector-General of Military Prisons. In fact, he designed Wormwood Scrubs and generally reformed the prison system, assuring the public that those judicially confined would have 'Hard Labour, Hard Fare and Hard Board'. Then there was Sir John Du Cane, who was appointed Governor of Malta in 1927; and also Commander Peter Du Cane (C.B.E., 1964; O.B.E., 1942), who from 1931 was Managing Director of Vosper Ltd, the shipbuilders from Portsmouth responsible for the design of the *Bluebird*, with which Sir Malcolm Campbell achieved the world water speed record.

The Du Cane Estate in the Twentieth Century

On the threshold of the twentieth century, the family still owned huge tracts of land, including 5000 acres in Essex, and trustees were hired to apportion land to the descendents.

The family member who sold the parcel of land which was to accommodate Du Cane Court was Charles Henry Copley Du Cane (born on 25th May, 1864). He was Lord of the Manors of Great and Little

Braxted, and a member of the Coldstream Guards. The family also owned Streatham Common, which the Council felt should remain an open public space [Pub.Recs.Off.]. On 26th August, 1924, Frank Newman (acting for the Du Canes) wrote to London County Council to ask if it would 'pay my client a cash sum for the loss of the building values which such a condition would incur'.

Even as recently as the 3rd of July, 1950, the Du Cane estate in Balham encompassed Dendy Street, Chestnut Grove, Kate Street, Boundaries Road and St James's Road. In the 1930s, Messrs Newman and Son wanted the property in Chestnut Grove south of Kate Street to be included in a local business zone – and they requested that the population density allowed for Dendy Street and Kate Street be increased to that already existing! Evidently, the existing rules had not been followed.

A Lasting Legacy

I have heard that the last of the Du Canes to live in Balham resided in Elmfield Road – but the family have certainly left their mark, both in Balham and elsewhere. Apparently, a Post Office Directive of about a hundred years ago ordained that the names chosen for roads and buildings should have some connection with local history – and so, today, we have:

Du Cane Close, Shepherd's Bush, Hammersmith W12;
Du Cane Road, Shepherd's Bush, Hammersmith W12;
Du Cane Stores, Du Cane Road, Hammersmith W12;
Du Cane Housing Association, Hammersmith W12;
Du Cane Restaurant, Hammersmith Hospital W12;
Du Cane Arms Bar and Restaurant, Great Braxted, Essex;
Du Cane (Shoe Repairs etc.), Kew Road, Richmond, Surrey;
Du Cane Fruiterers, Balham High Road;
Du Cane Dry Cleaners, Balham High Road;
Du Cane Court, Balham High Road;
Du Cane Express Removals, Balham High Road;
(and there are even gas grills with the family name on them)

Of course, it is possible that the family made it a qualifying condition that major commercial developments on their land would bear their name.

Rapid Growth and Changing Identity

Until the late 18th century, the Balham economy was based on agriculture [Gower]. In a parish survey of 1803, its inhabitants numbered approximately 325. How different from the 1991 Census, in which the population was estimated to be around 11,000! But the regional boundaries have also changed. In the nineteenth century Balham had been part of Tooting, and only became a separate parish in 1855. Long ago, the fledgling area may still have been referred to as 'Upper Tooting', although in time Balham would become a desirable location in its own right. An Evening Standard report (from 1931) suggests that by the time Du Cane Court had entered the landscape, this had already happened. We learn that residents of both areas were anxiously contradicting any suggestion that they might live in Tooting; and on the Tooting side some people had even gone to the point of putting 'Balham' on their newspaper!

There was a time when Balham, and many other areas, were encompassed by Streatham. Later on, Streatham came under the borough of Wandsworth, and it is now part of Lambeth. Modern Wandsworth was established in 1965 by merging two thirds of its previous region with the metropolitan area of Battersea, while the remaining third went to Lambeth; and in the election which took Harold Wilson to power in the early 1970s, Du Cane Court was in Battersea South. But that is not all. The block was positioned in Wandsworth Central before it went to Battersea South – returning to Wandsworth later. Since its inception, it has also been moving amongst the smaller denominations, from Balham Ward to Bedford Ward to Nightingale Ward. By 1992, it had finally come to rest, like a wandering minstrel, under the wing of Tooting. One wonders what song it must sing for its supper simply to be left alone ... Clearly, the residents of 'the Court' could be forgiven if they occasionally suffer from an identity crisis.

Balham and the Railway

Brian Gostick (a former resident) once commented that the emergence of the railway 'both made and destroyed Balham'. It created a thriving portion of the metropolis in which many people wanted to live. Yet it ruined some picturesque countryside on the edge of town, and made a previously aristocratic area geographically and financially accessible to all.

By 1860 you could travel by train from Balham or Streatham to Victoria – and by 1865, the railway even connected Balham to the south coast and to the west end of London. The extension of the London Underground in the 1920s was the initiative of Frank Pick [Jones.&.Woodward]. In 1923, Pick and Holden, the architect, started a long collaboration, extending what is now known as the Northern Line up to Edgware; and then down to Clapham South, Balham and Trinity Rd (later Tooting Bec), with all of the stations following a similar design.

The opening of Balham Underground Station – on 6th December 1926 – was the catalyst which led many enterprising individuals who worked in the city to move south and settle in Du Cane Court.

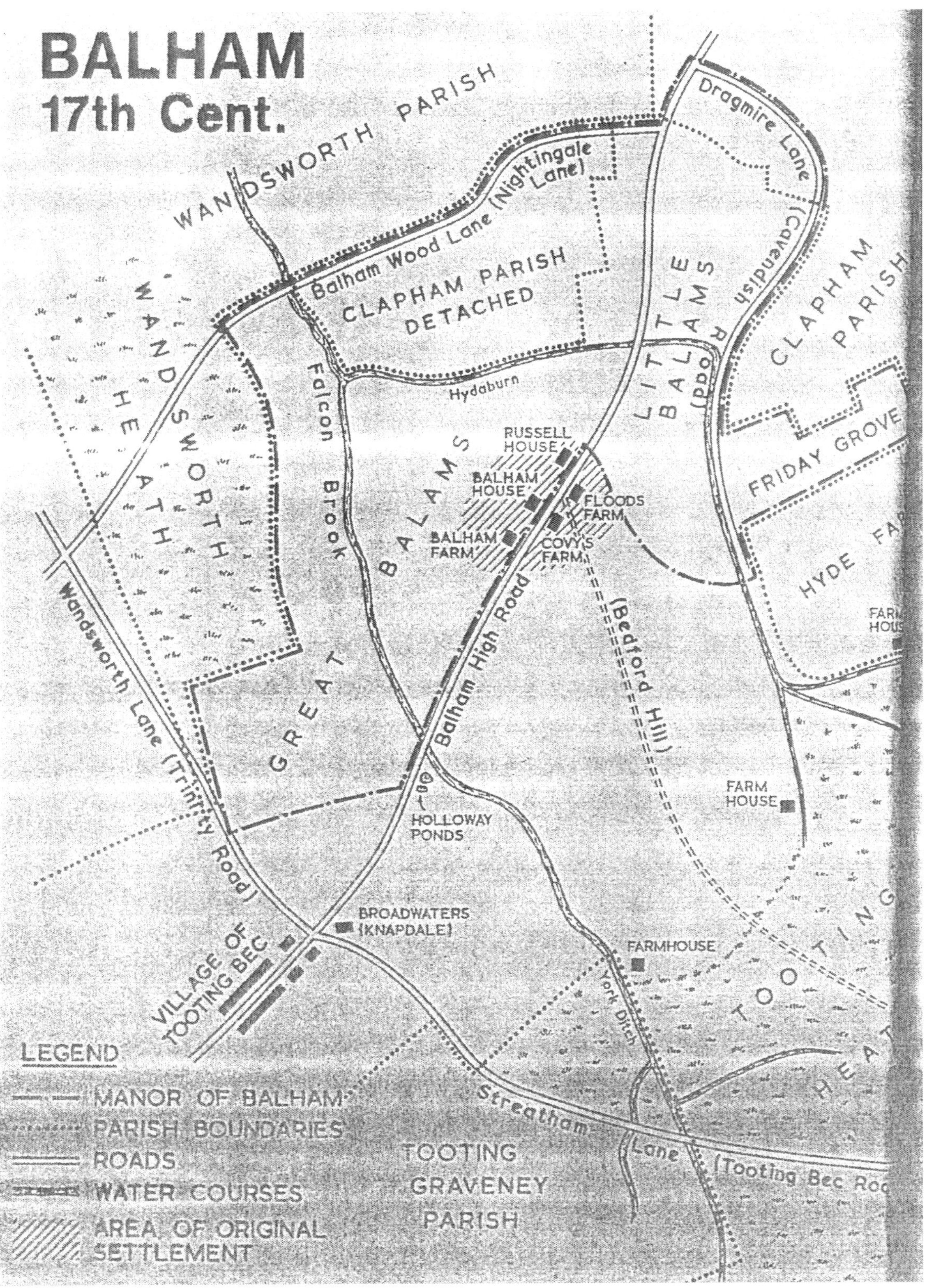

In the 17th century Balham was still very rural, and remained so until the mid-19th century, after which it became subject to rapid development. By the outbreak of the First World War, it was much as we know it today. (Courtesy of Graham Gower – who actually drew it.)

Note: It has been suggested that the area above which is designated as 'Wandsworth Parish', may actually have been 'Battersea Parish'.

Dear Mr Vincent,

Thank you for your letter of 17th July, addressed to my husband, Charles Edward Byron Du Cane. Unfortunately he died in November 1996, so he cannot answer your letter himself. I am, however, sending a copy to my son, Leslie Du Cane, who lives in London and knows quite a lot about the family history, and also to my nephew, Charles Du Cane, son of my husband's elder brother, Commander Peter Du Cane. He, too, I believe should be able to give you some information.

The property at Balham, when the Du Canes bought it, comprised a farm and its surrounding land. Charles Henry Copley Du Cane, who sold the land, was my father-in-law, and Ella and Florence were two of his sisters. Ella was an accomplished water-colourist and illustrated a number of travel books, *The Italian Lakes, The Banks of the Nile, The Canary Islands, The Flowers and Gardens of Madeira,* as well as *The Flowers and Gardens of Japan.* In the case of the last three titles, the text was written by her sister, Florence. Charles Henry Copley died in France. He was given the name Copley, because his mother, Georgiana Susan Copley, was descended from the American artist, John Singleton Copley.

The Du Cane family were originally Huguenots. They were expelled first from France and then from the Low Countries by the Duke of Alva and arrived in England at the end of the 16th century. They became merchants in London, and bought land in Essex, at Braxted near Witham, where the family resided until the estate was sold by Charles Henry Copley.

My son tells me that there are a lot of papers relevant to the history of Du Cane Court in the archives of the Duke of Portland. I have located a catalogue of these in the University of Nottingham Library through the internet, entitled 'University of Nottingham Library, Manuscript and Special Collections, Portland (London) Collection, Catalogue of Deeds. Documents from the Surrey Estate of the Duke of Portland 1829-c.1860. The web site is mss.library.nottingham.ac.uk/cats/port_londonple surrey.html. If you look at this, you will find references to the name Du Cane.

In the meantime, I wish you every success in your research.

Yours sincerely,

Rosamund Du Cane

ROSAMUND DU CANE

A letter the author received from Rosamund Du Cane.

Dear Mr Vincent

With reference to your recent telephone call, I have been looking back at our previous correspondence of 2003 and I find that I passed your enquiry on to both my son, Leslie, and to my husband's nephew, Charles Du Cane. As I wrote in my letter of 21st July 2003, Leslie said that there are papers relevant to the Du Cane property in Balham in the University of Nottingham Library. The relevant catalogue can now be viewed on line, under the heading **Portland (London) Collection: Catalogue of Deeds and Documents from the Estates of the Dukes of Portland, 1304-1933.** The sub-heading reads 'Catalogue of Deeds and Documents from the Surrey Estate of the Dukes of Portland, 1829-c.1860 – The material relates entirely to Grove House at Norwood, Surrey, whose lease was bought by the 4th Duke of Portland in 1839 and surrendered by his successor in 1860. The freehold belonged to the Du Cane family, a city family who had migrated to Essex and who remained prominent landowners on the southern fringes of London. Their name is commemorated in Du Cane Court, Balham.'

The first reference in 1829 is to Phoebe Du Cane, who died in 1831 and was the widow of Peter Du Cane of Braxted Lodge, Essex and the last reference in 1860 is to Charles Du Cane of Braxted Hall, Essex. All this can be found online at 'Nottingham.ac.uk/mss/online/online-mss-catalogues/cats/port-londonple-surre..' If Google doesn't like such a long address, try 'Duke of Portland's Estate' and then enter 'Du Cane'.

My husband's nephew, Charles Du Cane, told me that the Du Cane Family's association with the Manor of Balham goes back as far as 1710 and that his father, Commander Peter Du Cane, sold the last pieces of the land after World War II. Commander Du Cane, in about 1940, put on loan with the Essex County Record Office many papers concerning the Surrey property. Essex subsequently passed them to London and they are available for the public to view. I am not sure where these would be now; perhaps the Guildhall Library could help. This was all the information that Charles was able to provide.

I believe you know more about the history of this property during the first half of the twentieth century than we do. Since none of the family was living in that part of London in the 1930's, I do not suppose there was much opposition to the building of Du Cane Court. I was

A sample from another letter received from Rosamund Du Cane.

A GRAND ESTATE

*

The Influence of Landowners on Architecture

Rarely, if ever, 'has a great landlord assumed a dominant, creative role in the development of his land' (John Summerson tells us in an essay of his). Apparently, he 'has lavished immense care on his country seat and the landscape round it, but [his] London land has been a matter purely of business'. This principle very much holds true for the various property barons who have owned Du Cane Court, with the proviso that they would sometimes creatively 'develop' the original structure in order to increase their income.

These days, however, the tide of legislation is running against the great landlord, and much of the power he once had is in the hands of the local authority. Perhaps the Du Canes sold their investment in Balham because they saw how the old order of things would change.

A House on the Land

According to a period map, it would appear that at least five main buildings once occupied what is now the estate of Du Cane Court. The largest of these was owned (presumably under a lease) by a doctor and his wife. I was fortunate one day to meet his grandson, Robert Addington, at his pleasant waterside home behind Angel Station. The venue for our dialogue was an alluring garden, with a patio that faced a lush array of green foliage leading down to the edge of the peaceful Regency Canal; an apt setting, indeed, given the splendour of an even more special home - and the bygone way of life he would describe to me ...

'My maternal grandfather and his wife actually married in the grounds of their great mansion, which they referred to as Brookfield House. He was Scottish, and probably came to the house in the 1890s - or maybe 1889; and he sold up around 1923 or 1924, at a time when Balham was very prosperous.'

Robert was candid with his information, and so affable as to put me completely at ease. He was keen to tell his story, and I was eager to hear it. It was as if the ghosts of 'Brookfield' had waited patiently for their moment, and now – like our surroundings – they could blossom in a perfect meeting of minds. I saw from a photograph that the front of the house was very similar to 222 Balham High Road, which has since been converted into flats; yet when Robert showed me photographs of the garden, it was truly a glimpse into another world.

'There's so much space,' I said. My host enlarged upon this theme ...

'Well, the land at the back of the property was actually on three levels, and my mother told me that, because of the mist on her wedding day, she could not see to the bottom of the garden! And the house was no less incredible. It had a self-contained pharmacy, and was home to four children and eight staff: including the gardeners, three maids, a cook and a coachman named Mr Faithful. I used to astound people by saying that I never saw my mother wash a cup and saucer in her entire life! Nor did I ever see her do any cooking. But she *was* keen on needlework. As for gardening, or cultivating plants in the greenhouse, she would not have been allowed to get involved - although she did become enthusiastic about horticulture later on, when she had a property of her own.

The doctor, himself, was very handsome and rather vain. He would laugh at his own jokes – but he had an excellent bedside manner, and his patients (especially the old ladies) loved and respected him. He knew how to live well, for there was a coach house on the grounds with a horse and carriage, as well as a car and a chauffeur. Doctor William Taylor, however, chose to go everywhere in his horse-drawn carriage, and he must have looked very impressive in his top hat, accompanied by a footman wearing a cockade. He was a pillar of the community, and he really played his role to perfection. Unfortunately, his wife led a terrible existence, and the doctor's dedication to his work was maybe why his family life failed.' His wife also appears to have had a timid disposition.

'She was very afraid of thunderstorms,' Robert told me, 'and several people known to the family had been victims of lightning. On her wedding day an electric storm raged which was so fierce that she hid in the cupboard, and had to be coaxed out of there in order to complete the day's proceedings!' (I think she would have liked Du Cane Court, as it was fitted with a lightning conductor from the outset.)

'And how did the doctor feel about his magnificent dwelling? He must have been sorry to leave,' I suggested, but Robert told me otherwise.

'When the high road was widened to accommodate trams, Doctor Taylor was compensated for the loss of part of his gravel pathway at the front; and after he moved, he never looked back. He had no regrets about the estate, although it was undeniably beautiful. Nevertheless, the place left a deep impression on my mother, for, upon passing Du Cane Court, she would exclaim with pride: "That's where our house used to be!"

When my grandfather died, he left everything to three people: my mother, Aunt Jane, and his much-loved governess, Miss Bromley, who had joined the family after they left Brookfield. My father was furious at being overlooked in this way. He had worked all his life, whereas his wife hadn't worked at all, - and much of her money she had got from him anyway. So he went to court over the inheritance, and secured the lion's share.'

Identifying Truth and Myth

Myths and rumours abound regarding Du Cane Court. A former resident, Jessie Boran, was once on holiday in Paris. Upon ordering an attractive glass, and giving her postal address at Du Cane Court for the item to be sent on to, she was told that Monsieur Du Cane used to reside in one of the buildings which were removed to make way for the new block, and that he sold up to a Chinese person. Another fanciful notion was that Du Cane Court was originally designed with tennis courts. Yet within a delicate shell of truth may be the germ of an idea from which a fiction grows ... for the mysterious East does play a part in this little history. The grounds of our building were designed by a Japanese landscape gardener (and, curiously, the elegant reception lounge in another building by our Scottish architect, Nell Gwynn House, was furnished in the Chinese style). But what about the tennis courts? Well, Robert Addington was able to shed light upon this: for the land behind the doctor's house contained a croquet lawn, access to a bowling green ... and tennis courts.

There was an indenture in June, 1903, between the lessor, William Taylor of Brookfield High Road, Upper Tooting, - and a butcher, a builder and a Balham 'gentleman' of 14 years, allowing right of way over a path which would be maintained by the lessees. Initially, the cost was £30 per annum. The lessees were not given access on Sundays or after 11pm, although an exception was made on Sundays for any committee member of the bowling club at number 47a, Boundaries Road.

On 26th April, 1921, another contract was finalized. This allocated a portion of the grounds (containing three tennis courts and a pavilion) for use by the Herondale Lawn Tennis Club at a rate of £50 per annum, and for a period of five years commencing on the 25th of March, 1922.

I remarked upon what wonderful facilities these are to have in your own back garden, but by 1921 the children had flown the nest, and so the venerable doctor presumably felt that he would have no further use for them, except as a source of income.

Brookfield House was a residence on a grand scale, and the life within its walls calls to mind that compelling television series from the 1970s, 'Upstairs, Downstairs'. Mr Addington felt that it could not have been more than 50 yrs old when it was demolished. Since the land was not sold for development until 11 or 12 years after the doctor had left, one wonders what happened in the mean time. Was the property poorly maintained, thence giving rise to the condition of 'planning blight', whereby official permission would have been given to destroy it? Perhaps Mr Pobjoy, a taxi-driver from Du Cane Court, can enlighten us. He claims that there were two famous murders in Balham in the Victorian era. One of these is well documented. It (coincidentally) implicated a doctor, and occurred in 'The Priory' by Tooting Bec Common. The other allegedly took place in one of the buildings which Du Cane Court superseded. Because of the murder, nobody wanted to buy the house. Eventually the purchase became untenable, and so the place was razed to the ground. So far, I have been unable to verify the second tale, but it makes for a good story!

A New Way of Life

Robert Addington said that the value of property dropped throughout his lifetime until the 1970s; and I wonder if the subsequent sharp rise in prices at Du Cane Court was a reaction to all the years of inertia? At any rate, apartment block living was the protocol for the future, and by the 1920s and '30s big country houses were becoming less fashionable. In a world where human labour was increasingly expensive, the prospect of employing a large number of staff had begun to seem less attractive; and could be happily contrasted with a scenario where you still have the staff, while someone else worries about recruitment and wages. One author, Jonathan Glancey, asks us to imagine (in the stately homes which were replaced) the damp, the mice, the noisy plumbing, unpredictable electrics and general sense of decay, and 'we can see why these efficiently-run new blocks took over the skyline'.

Nevertheless, the remnants of the former lifestyle lingered. In Eresby Court, Knightsbridge, a whole top floor was given over to servants; whilst at Du Cane Court a new standard was being set, with the staff living amongst the residents.

Mr Glancey also draws attention to how every block was a 'Court', as if inheriting a country tradition. Ah! But if only the *raison d'être* was to always please the residents!

The front of Doctor Taylor's house. It would later be razed to the ground to make way for Du Cane Court. (Courtesy of Robert Addington.)

A view of the grounds. (Courtesy of Robert Addington.)

Two views of the grounds at the back of Doctor Taylor's house. (Courtesy of Robert Addington.)

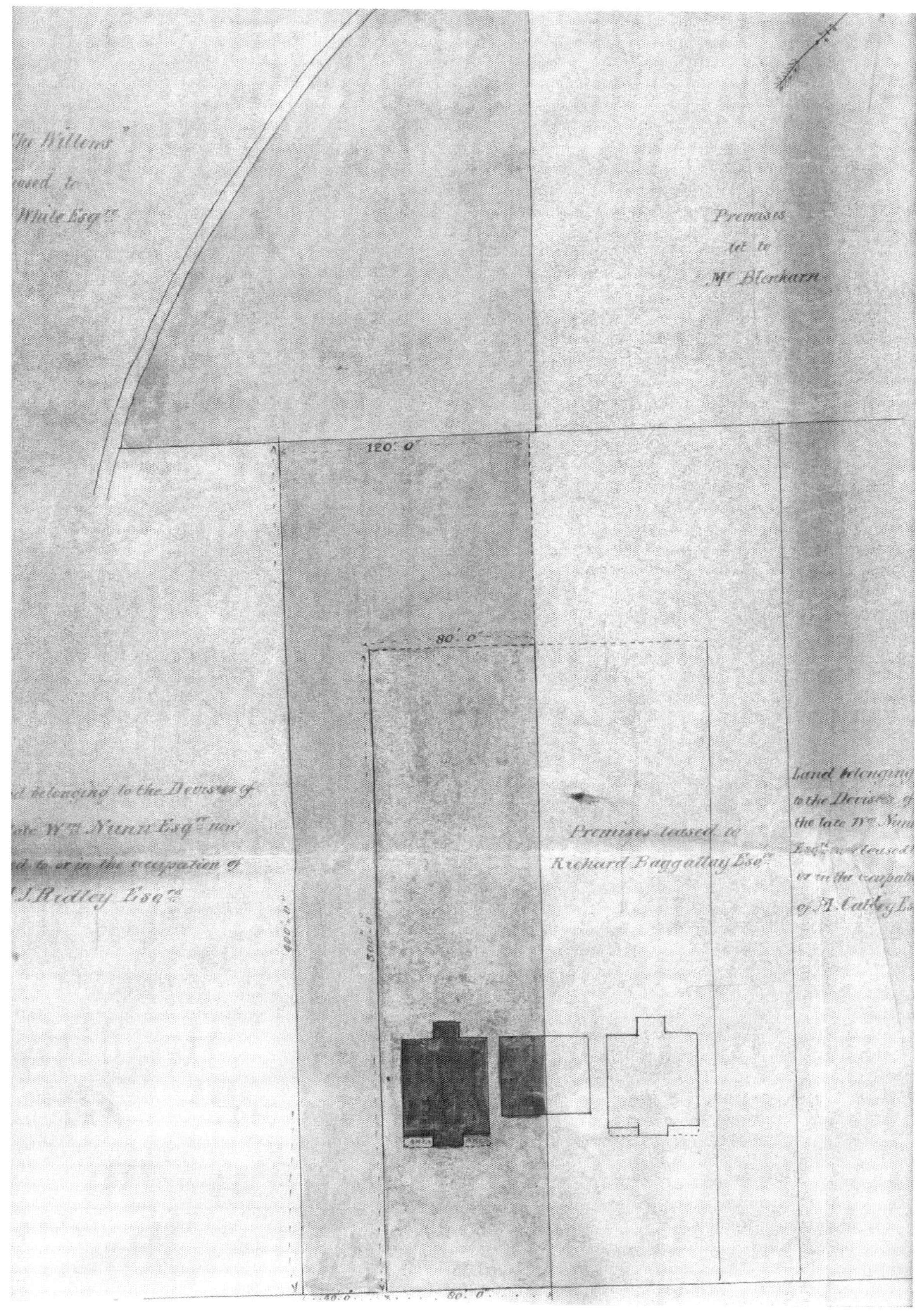

A diagram of Dr Taylor's house, outbuildings and land. (Courtesy of Robert Addington.)

dated this

twenty sixth day of April 1921

between Dr. William Taylor of "Brookfield", Upper Tooting, S.W.17., his heirs, executors or assigns (hereinafter called "the Landlord") of the first part and the Herondale Lawn Tennis Club (hereinafter called "the Tenants") of the second part.

Whereas in consideration of the Tenants paying to the Landlord the sum of £50. per annum payable half yearly on the 24th day of June and the 25th day of December the Landlord hereby agrees to let a portion of his garden to the Tenants to be used by them as three tennis courts and Pavilion for a period of five years commencing on the 25th day of March 1922.

It is hereby agreed that the Landlord shall be liable for the repairs and up-keep of the Pavilion, and the Tenants shall be liable for the repairs and up-keep of the Tennis Courts and for the payment of rates.

Signed by the said William Taylor in the presence of } William Taylor

E. E. Bromley
226 Balham High Rd
S.W.17

Signed on behalf of the Herondale Lawn Tennis Club in the presence of

58 Dafforne Rd. S.W.17

Vice President

45 Tierney Rd
Upper Tooting S.W.17.

Captain

52a Carnmead Rd

The doctor presumably had a lease on his property. Above is an agreement in which some of the land is subleased to the Herondale Lawn Tennis Club. (Courtesy of Robert Addington.)

Several photos of the venerable doctor and his wife – and a photograph which may have been taken inside his house. (Courtesy of Robert Addington.)

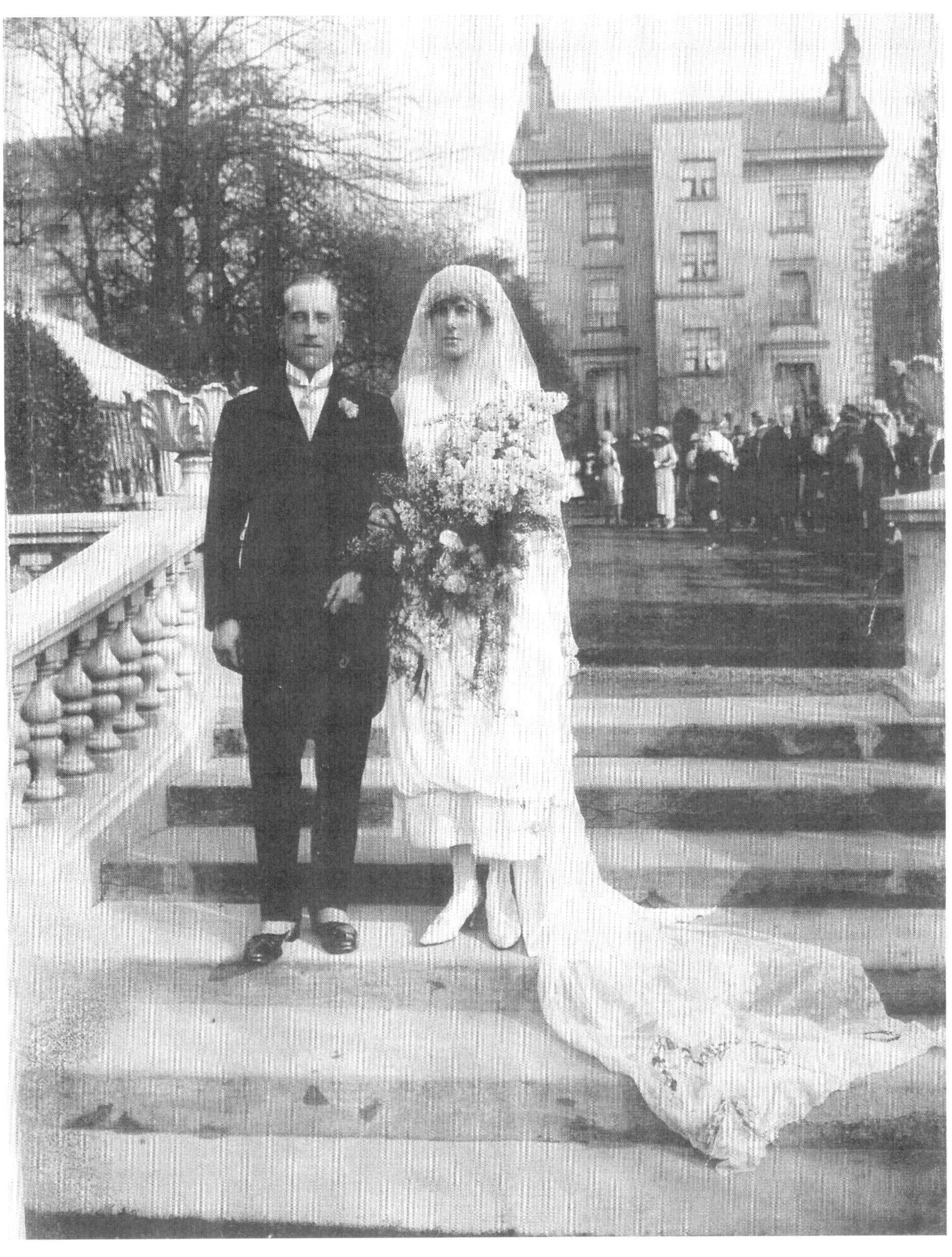

The doctor's daughter on her wedding day. (Courtesy of Robert Addington.)

The doctor's daughter, with her two sons. The youngster on the left would one day supply me with useful pictures and information. (Courtesy of Robert Addington.)

THE NEW TRUST AND ITS ARCHITECT

*

The company responsible for the creation of Du Cane Court was 'The Central London Property Trust'. It was a private enterprise with the mission 'to purchase, take a lease, exchange, or build, or otherwise acquire land or buildings ...'

The 'Trust' was incorporated under the Companies Act on 2nd February, 1932, with a nominal capital of £10,000 - divided into 200,000 shares of one shilling each. Its net profits increased rapidly, as in an Extraordinary General Meeting of 28th March, 1935, the capital of the company increased to £120,000 – divided into 200,000 shares. An extraordinary meeting indeed!

When it was first formed, the company purchased a block of flats known as Bernard Mansions in Herbrand Street, Russell Square, London. It subsequently sold to Bernard Mansions Ltd, in which the Trust held substantial shares. The same pattern was followed for other blocks, including Du Cane Court, whereby a company was created, and shares issued as a means of raising capital. Indeed, the allottees of the Trust, and of its various offshoots, included quite an assortment of people. Among them were a physician, a butcher, a police constable, a civil servant, a cotton operative, a clerk, a shopkeeper, a widow, a professor and a methodist minister.

Du Cane Court Ltd was founded on 8th February, 1935, with a nominal capital of £20,000 in shares. The records show that originally a charge not exceeding £36,000 was created on the building, in which apparently 758 flats were to be let at rentals from £55 to £175 per year. Another, more reliable, estimate puts the number of flats at 632, with the figure rising to about 676 due to various alterations. However, one thing we can be sure of is that the expectations were as high as the block itself, for the advertising literature of the day claimed that the flats in Du Cane Court were 'undoubtedly the best value for money in London'.

The Central London Property Trust was also responsible for Sloane Avenue Mansions and for Nell Gwynn House - both in Chelsea, – the latter being erected on a freehold site exceeding three quarters of an acre. George Kay Green was the architect of all three apartment blocks, and probably of other buildings which the Trust created. These included Bishopric Court and Shelley House in Sussex; and Osborne Court on the Isle of Wight.

The company also took possession of Hightrees House, designed by R.W.H. Jones and located on Clapham Common West Side. It was a fine addition to the portfolio, consisting of 150 flats, and a visually striking exterior with lines of red and white bricks, known in professional parlance as a *streaky bacon* effect.

In the early 1940s, the Trust held mortgages with Pall Mall Building Society; and, furthermore, a document produced by Waterlow & Sons shows that for the period from 20th September, 1943, to 19th March, 1944, around 150 mortgages were lodged with the Royal Mutual Benefit

Building Society (although it is likely that most of these were not for large blocks of flats).

Du Cane Court was almost certainly the biggest undertaking of George Kay Green, and he had wonderful plans for it which were not all realized. With its various facilities, Nell Gwynn House makes for an interesting comparison. It stands on Draycott Avenue and was completed in 1936, with 436 flats and a series of conservatories, as well as its own Health and Leisure Club with pool spa, saunas, gymnasium and beauty salon. It also had a restaurant and a cards room; and a billiards and games room. In 1948, it even had a music club with Sir Adrian Boult as president. One might say that the name of Nell Gwynn bestows a romantic air upon the site, for she was the lover of King Charles 11, who had a hospital put up in her name. By the end of this narrative, the reader will have formed his own opinion as to whether our architect was, himself, a romantic at heart.

Out of Green's portfolio, the property which bears Nell's name would be the jewel in the crown - but for the limited gardens, plus the fact that nearly all of the units contained are studio flats, with only 15% of them being owner-occupied.

Sloane Avenue Mansions has 197 flats, none of them with more than a single bedroom, and lies on one third of an acre of land. It is seen as the 'poor relation' of Nell Gwynn House: a rather harsh judgement of what is still an attractive building. There is a humorous theory that it was constructed out of the leftovers from its sister block - but since the date I have for it is 1934, two years before the completion of Nell Gwynn House, it would appear that another myth has been mortally wounded!

The inhabitants of Du Cane Court have far more public space than those who live in either of these other residences - although Nell Gwynn House does contain a sumptuous foyer.

Conveyancing of the Land and Building

On the 14th of January, 1935, the Central London Property Trust purchased their Balham estate from Charles Henry Copley Du Cane, of Le Lohier Dinan in the Republic of France, with Sir John Philip Du Cane and Frank Newman acting as trustees from the county of London.

The land was purchased for £28,800; and, once completed, Du Cane Court was sold for £96,000. This presumably gave a handsome profit, even allowing for the costs of construction, and was far in excess of the estimated fee of £36,000 (see above). Work on the building must have proceeded apace, for, according to the Land Registry, most of it came into the hands of the Royal Liver Friendly Society as early as the 29th of September, 1936; with the remainder being acquired by the society on 27th January, 1938. This twofold conveyancing process concurs with the prevailing belief: that construction was undertaken over two stages - the front of the block being completed first, and then the back.

The society retained its interest until 1972, when it sold to Nessdale Ltd - at least according to Companies House. Yet I have it on good authority that First National Bank purchased the building in 1967 for £1 million pounds. I rang the Royal Liver Society for clarification and was thus informed:

'The Society had no interest in the building beyond the collection of ground rent.'

'But my understanding is that you were the owners,' I said.

'No. The Society did not own it. That would have been the management company, which collected the monthly rent from the residents, and then the service charges after the flats were sold. The Royal Liver owned many ground rents in London until the early 1970s, when they sold them all. It holds no ground rents in London now.'

'Was there a reason for such a sea-change in policy in this particular period?' I probed, hoping my blunt poker might kindle some fire before the embers of the conversation went cold, but silence was the only wisdom I received. 'Can we discuss the records relating to such a long involvement ...?'

'Unfortunately, we have no more information.'

Yet on one level they *did* own the building. I spoke to Lynn Barclay of Belgrave Properties. She explained that, presumably, the management company held the Head Lease, and, through it, purchased the greater financial interest in the building. However, at the end of the tenure, full ownership would have reverted back to the freeholder. This makes sense, as Du Cane Court Ltd purchased a lease on the building for a term of 99 years from 29th September, 1936, at a yearly rent of £4000, – while the freehold was acquired by the Royal Liver Friendly Society. Imagine my surprise, therefore, when I discovered that Lieutenant Commander Peter Du Cane was the owner of 'the Du Cane Balham estate' in 1938! Later, it emerged that this referred to other property in Balham. But I must say that, with so much obfuscation surrounding a subject which is only 70 years old, I am amazed at how we can be sure of anything when we contemplate the edifices of the ancient world!

Central London Property Trust vs High Trees House Ltd

It is interesting to record how the same Trust which created Du Cane Court was also involved in a landmark case in the history of property law [Cont.Law.Inf.Net.]. The year was 1946. The company had gone bust and was attempting to reprise lost monies. Lord Denning presided over the case, and it helped to launch his illustrious career.

In 1937, the defendants had taken out a 99-year lease on Hightrees House. With the exodus from London early in the war, it was clear that they could not pay the ground rent, and so a 50% reduction from the commencement of the lease was agreed. After the war, the Trust argued that the reduction was only a temporary measure, and so it attempted to collect *all* of its money - including arrears. But the court ruled that once a promise was acted upon, it was binding in law. And so the modern principle of 'promissory estoppel' was established.

Bryan Gould, a Labour MP from New Zealand, used to lecture about the case, and, incidentally, he lived in Hightrees House for a while.

Winding up the Central London Property Trust

One forms the impression that the Trust did very little after the war – although, incredibly, it was not until 19th April, 1966, that Michael Lionel Philips was appointed a liquidator; and, according to Companies House, the Trust was not finally dissolved until August, 1986.

Architecture as a Profession in the 1930s

The 1930s was an ambivalent age for architecture. On the one hand, a series of imposing and memorable structures were erected, many of them blocks of flats, and all with the hallmarks of a new style. Indeed, an article in 'The Builder' on July 30th, 1937, remarks that the importance of architects in salaried positions has recently grown in relation to the volume of work conducted by government and large business concerns, even though the salaries do not seem to have increased in proportion.

On the other hand, in another of the architectural journals of the day [JRIBA.20/3/39], E.J. Carter records some sardonic responses to his article, 'The Case for a Learned Society'. One elderly member of the Royal Institute of British Architects said: 'If you know of a learned society for architects, tell me, I'd like to join'; while another remarked that he knew of one good case for a learned society - a coffin! The problem was how to define a field which encompasses science, the arts and the law. Mr Carter makes the intelligent point that a bad building may become as unhealthy for its occupants as an inappropriate medical prescription, and it is therefore very important to get it right. One senses a new discipline struggling to find its way, with contradictory opinions about whether local authorities make good patrons. One voice complained that there was no steady supply of work, whilst another declared that such patrons as local authorities make it easier for architects and engineers to plan ahead.

Our own architect made his name working through a private enterprise, and he may have struggled to find work in his younger days, but became marvellously productive in the 1930s - with his all-embracing career interfering with his private life in much the same way as Doctor Taylor's had; and, curiously, both of these men were from Scotland. Perhaps the work ethic north of the border is especially strong.

The Un-Decorated Architect

George Kay Green had almost reached his journey's end when he created Du Cane Court and Nell Gwynn House. Perhaps he felt frustrated, having attained success so late in life (although, as we shall see, his first love may have been art rather than architecture). He could well have reflected upon the ground-breaking lives of others who went before him. James Burton, christened 'Haliburton' and also a Scotsman, was already an important speculative builder when, in his late twenties, he proposed to work on the Foundling Estate - and by his early forties Mr Burton had built almost 600 houses there; and Thomas Cubitt was famous in the building world by the age of 32 for his novel approach, employing all of the requisite tradesmen on a permanent basis.

Discovering anything about our own architect was a challenging task. He is not mentioned in the Times Obituaries up to October, 1939. He was not a Fellow of the Royal Institute of British Architects, nor did he have any letters after his name. Surely the creator of such a colossal work as Du Cane Court could not have been a mere amateur, an upstart? Charles Jones, an architect who lives in 'the Court', says that he was just another employee, and that the Central London Property Trust could equally well have chosen someone else for the job. Perhaps, as he was not decorated, his fee was less, and so he represented value for money to his employer. Yet as recently as 1938, no formal qualifications were required for a man to call himself an architect. Even the Architects Registration Council was not created until 1931; and we know that Green applied for membership in 1932 and was admitted in 1933 - remaining a member until his death in 1939 ... although I understand that anyone who had been a practising architect for a couple of years or so could easily be registered.

It is all so different today. However, it would not be long before the tide of opinion found a new direction; and there was some prestige attached to the occupation by the time Winston Churchill was refashioning his beloved Chartwell – and struggling to get formal recognition for his skills.

Fortunately, Mr Green achieved at least one public distinction by the end of his life, for on 24th September, 1938, he is recorded as the Superintendent Architect for London County Council.

An Intimate Portrait

It has, no doubt, often been observed by the chronicler of human life, that it takes but a few moments of magic for a character to evolve, from a faceless name, into what feels like a living, breathing acquaintance; and I had many such moments when I spoke to Charles Kay Green, who, drawing largely upon the reminiscences of his mother, was able to supply the ingredients for an intimate portrait of his father. At the time Charles was living in a modest house in Maidenhead, with his amiable wife and a lodger who had a keen interest in greyhounds. He was the last remaining son of the architect, and was only two or three years old when he lost his father to cancer.

George Kay Green was born in 1877. He was well-connected, being the son of Mr William Green, the founder of William Green and Sons, Law Publishers, which became the most reputable firm of its kind in Scotland. The middle name, *Kay*, was probably introduced by George's mother, because it carried upper class connotations. Sometimes, in correspondence, the council addressed him as Mr 'Kay-Green', although the hyphen is actually a mistake; and the man himself occasionally signed his letters, 'Geo. Kay Green' – 'Geo.' being a popular Scottish abbreviation for 'George'.

Testimonials and Early Career

He was educated at George Watson's College, Edinburgh. From 1892 to 1896, he served as an apprentice under the architect, Mr Thomas Leadbetter. Then he spent two years studying at the University of Edinburgh and the Edinburgh School of Art. In 1899, he commenced practice as an architect, and continued until 1903, when he again studied painting at the Royal School of Art.

Some of his works of art were exhibited by the Royal Scottish Academy. In 1905 a studio was opened in Edinburgh, where he was appointed manager. Then on the 12th of March, 1908, he applied for the post of Director and Curator of the Aberdeen Art Gallery and Industrial Museum. His referees noted that he was dependable and well-mannered; and they referred to his ability as a writer and lecturer, to his general intelligence, and to his artistic ability. (Apparently, he secured all of the first prizes in the drawing classes at George Watson's College.) The references came from persons of high rank, including the Chief Educational Editor of Thomas Nelson and Sons, the Deputy Lieutenant of the City of Edinburgh, and the Director of Drawing and Painting in George Watson's College.

In his application, Mr Green mentioned that his mother was a daughter of the late Captain Edward Howling, commander of the ship, 'The Duke of Sutherland', which was apparently shipwrecked in Aberdeen Harbour in 1853. This is a quaint detail to include, for it has no relevance to the job at hand - but perhaps with his father's daunting reputation, he felt that he should balance the scales by noting some accolade on his mother's side of the family. Even stranger is the absence of these facts from any official records – although there have been other vessels of the same name.

A Religious Background

It seems likely that George Kay Green had a traditional upbringing, and one little book written by his sister-in-law, Margaret, would strongly suggest that his family and their associates were God-fearing people. The title of her extraordinary production was 'The Abrahamic Covenant or Birthright of Israel in its National and Temporal Aspect' - a Jewish subject, although she had a Christian burial. It was expensively bound with a suede cover, and dates from 1913 when she had 50 copies printed privately.

Margaret claimed that the Jewish people are entitled to the land of Israel as an everlasting birthright from Abraham. By not accepting Christ as the Messiah, Israel (in her opinion) must have delayed the fulfilment, but the promise was unconditional - and would be fulfilled through the assistance of a Christian nation, Great Britain, whose heraldic image points to Britain's appropriateness in this venture. It contains the harp, which is Israel's national musical instrument; and also a shield, which is supported on one side by a unicorn - calling to mind the prophet, Moses, when he likened his powers of conquest to the horn of the wild ox. And so George's sister foretold of the Balfour Treaty, and the creation of the modern state of Israel.

In these days of devolution, it is interesting to come across a Scottish family which was patriotically British, but we should not be too surprised. After all, the massive buildings which Green has left to posterity were all south of the border; and, given the religiosity of his family, they might be seen as modern temples dedicated to the art of good living.

His Private Life

Charles says that each enquiry into his family opens a can of worms - or (as an historian would prefer to put it) a heaven of possibilities. The architect and his wife, Edna, made an unusual match for each other. George Green was a disciplinarian, but Edna was also a strong character, and she wanted to rule the roost. They married in 1933. She was some 25 years younger than him; and the difference was further accentuated by the fact that George was grey and had lost most of his hair by his early fifties. In photographs, he bears a remarkable resemblance to Alastair Sim.

Charles had some kind of medical condition whereby his hands would shake involuntarily, and he wondered whether he might have inherited this from his father. His mother would joke that there was a metal tray around George's chair, no doubt to catch the crumbs as they fell from his plate; but George would have enjoyed his meals, as Edna was virtually a cordon bleu cook.

The sharpest contrast between the husband and his wife lay in their comparative wealth, for Green was a rich man who became poor, whereas Edna (from Hounslow) was the lower middle class girl who would become rich. The architect had to show that he married Edna because of his feelings for her, and not purely because of her dedication to him; whilst it was for her to prove that she had not married him just for status. And in the end perhaps their bond *was* about love, for when George died, his wife respected his memory and was proud of his achievements, and also proud of him as a man. 'In fact,' said Charles, 'she was practically obsessed with him.'

'He was an excellent dancer', she would proclaim. And it was probably at a dance that they both met.

A barrister of some repute was attracted to Edna, but having missed his chance he was moved to account for his feelings by writing a poem. He must have penned it quickly, for it is not well-crafted; yet it is a curious piece, crossed with a mixture of humour and angst, and embellished with comical sketches in the margins! It speaks of feminine fraud and asks (somewhat pathetically): what penniless lawyer can compete with the wealth from a block of flats? Considering it also refers to the 'The Mansion of Balham', we are left in no doubt that the author felt Du Cane Court would make his rival in love a very rich man.

Apparently, Edna was a bit of a flirt, for she played the barrister and her eventual husband off against each other. The poem was written at a dinner they all went to, probably at the Savoy, and Edna, ever the social climber, later took great pleasure in telling everyone that her son, Charles, was conceived at the Savoy Hotel.

Edna's sisters married well - as did her friend, Hilda, - and she was determined to follow suite. An architect of monumental properties must have seemed like a good catch for her. She and her husband would live in luxury and dine with the Lord Provost of Edinburgh. An enviable life, indeed!

'Once she had stuck her talons into him, she wouldn't let go,' Charles told me, 'but since the two of them hailed from different worlds, their respective families refused to speak to each other.'

And there were other problems. George Kay Green was often away on business. As the first anniversary of their wedding approached, he wrote to say that he couldn't get back from some work in north-west Wales in time to celebrate the special day. His wife was so incensed that she threw her wedding dress into the fire! Later on, she would relate the story for its entertainment value, but it was no joke at the time. Charles said that his father did a lot of work in Wales - and that he had some professional involvement with a Canadian. Apparently, the associate had a marvelous plan which George was privy to, and for which the architect did all of the design. But then this stranger departed from the scene, leaving Green unrewarded for his efforts. Edna would always say, 'George is a wonderful architect, but not a very practical businessman.'

When he died, Edna certainly did not inherit a fortune, and was left with two young boys to bring up on her own. Life became something of a struggle for her – which is a great irony when you consider how many people of unexceptional talent (like so many ticks upon a fine complexion) have made a good living out of her husband's buildings since his death. It was only natural that she would pursue a rich relative for financial assistance ...

'I remember on one occasion receiving a stiff reception at Margaret's fabulous house,' Charles told me. 'I had just consumed the most delicious peach imaginable, which my aunt had grown in her garden.

"Would Charles like another peach?" she asked me.

"Yes, please," was my eager reply. Unfortunately, I was expected to say, "No, thank you" - and I never lived it down!'

Edna also petitioned the Architect's Benevolent Fund for help, but her situation was not completely desperate. She had been left two houses in south London, which may have been 233 and 235 Upper (or Lower) Richmond Road. One of these was a guesthouse, and the other was rented out to Americans seconded into the US Air Force. As for her sons, they later inherited from their Aunt Margaret.

Building Materials in Short Supply

So what did this mysterious gentleman from Canada have to offer? Perhaps the answer lies in the issues faced by the building trade between the wars. There were many cheap sites around London after the First World War (JRIBA 27/6/1938), but by the autumn of 1920, wholesale prices of required materials were three times the 1913 level. The author of a 1920 book about East Ham recorded the erection of a number of cinemas, and remarks that 'where the material comes from is a mystery'; and a report in The Builder in the 1930s highlighted the difficulty of obtaining sufficient supplies of steel. Until 1929, the scrap derived primarily from home sources, and afterwards mainly from America; but in a 1938 article we are told that 'American supplies have now diminished'. Perhaps Green's colleague was reassuring him that Canada could fill the gap in the market, and that this golden age for building had not come to an end.

Green's Residences

Various addresses were given for George Kay Green at different times. When he was at work on Sloane Avenue Mansions, he was stationed at 7 Pall Mall East, London SW1. The same address was given for the Central London Property Trust Ltd, Gwynn House Ltd, and also Du Cane Court Ltd. On a technical drawing for Du Cane Court, dated 6th February, 1935, there is another address - '172 Buckingham Palace Road'. This property lay above Victoria Coach Station, officially opened in 1932, on one of the three floors let as office space and collectively known as 'Coastal Chambers', because of the coach service from the station to the seaside. G. Kay Green is mentioned among the tenants in a 'Birthday Souvenir' of March 10th, 1938, celebrating six years of service. Equipped with a restaurant that had seating for about 350 people, and a full license for music and dancing, I wonder if the place would have fed his imagination?

Later, as the Superintendent Architect for London County Council, he occupied County Hall at Westminster Bridge.

But these were all business addresses. His home, which he rented from 1936-37, was 1 Walpole Street, Chelsea SW3, and this is where Charles was born. He also lived in Wye Court, Surrey, where he had a Japanese Garden with a pond and three bridges athwart it – which perhaps ties in with the inspiration to have Japanese gardens at Du Cane Court. Finally, he moved to (or near) the vicinity of Richmond.

So much for Mr Green and his career. Soon the edifices which he left behind would have to survive a great war. Yet no danger was apparent in an almost surreal holiday card, received at 1 Walpole Street from Edna's sister-in-law who was on vacation in Volksgenosse, Germany. She praises the beauty around her and innocently declares, 'This is the most wonderful place we have ever been to'.

A peace march in Balham, in 1919. Marion Hopkins, shown on the left, was an elderly lady when I interviewed her. The photograph is symbolic of the hopeful optimism of people after World War 1, and the determination to build a brighter future. Part of that future, both for Balham and for Marion, was Du Cane Court. (Photograph is reproduced here, courtesy of Marion Hopkins.)

Charles Henry Copley Du Cane, the man who sold a plot of land - which had been leased to Doctor Taylor - to the Central London Property Trust. The Trust then built Du Cane Court. (This photograph is courtesy of Rosamund Du Cane, and was actually taken by Robert Du Cane in Dinard, France, in about 1936, the year after the land was sold.)

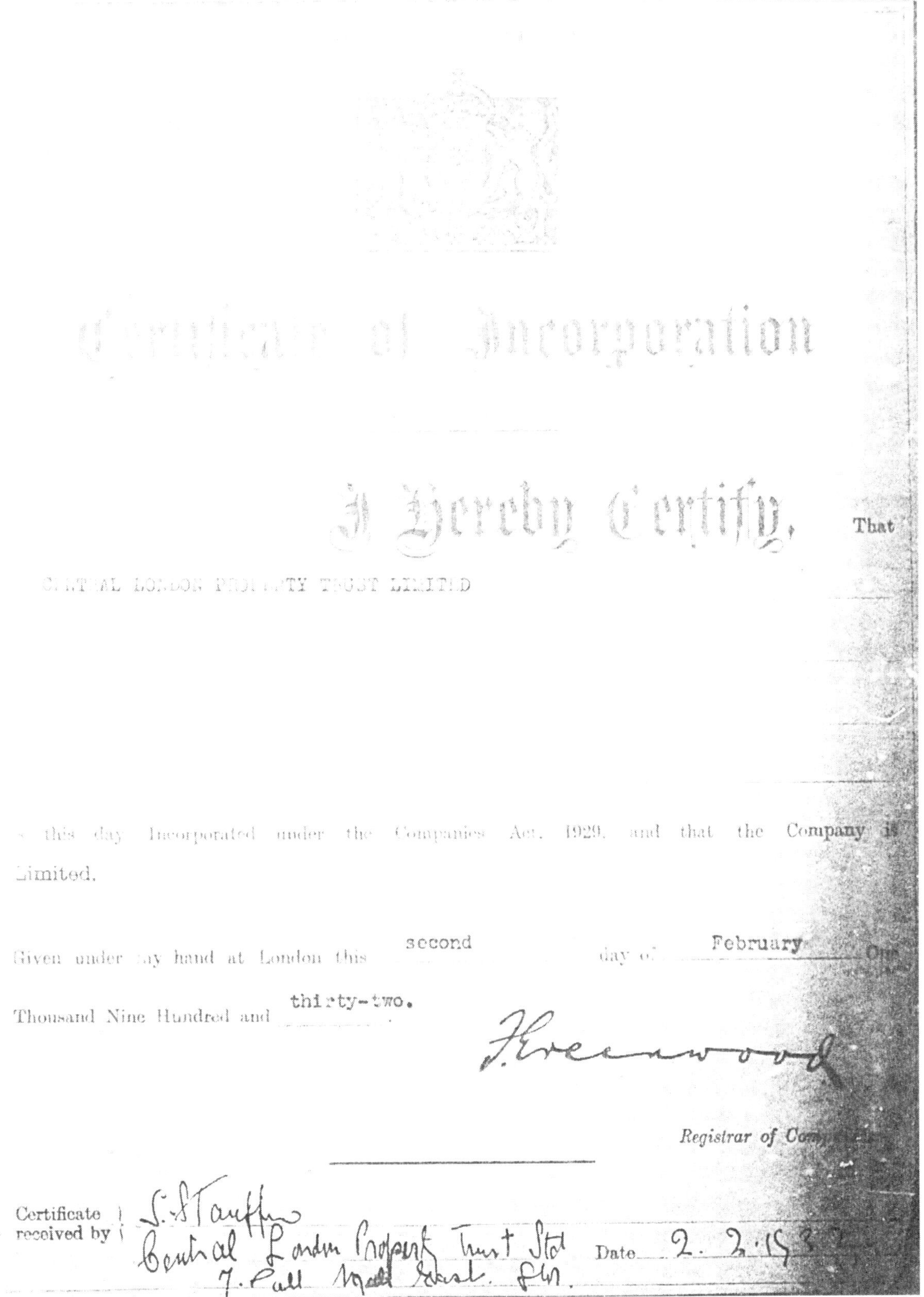

Certificate of Incorporation

I Hereby Certify, That

CENTRAL LONDON PROPERTY TRUST LIMITED

is this day Incorporated under the Companies Act, 1929, and that the Company is Limited.

Given under my hand at London this second day of February One Thousand Nine Hundred and thirty-two.

F. Greenwood

Registrar of Companies.

Certificate received by S. S. Tauffer
Central London Property Trust Ltd
7. Pall Mall East. SW.
Date 2. 2. 193[illegible]

The document which registered the creation of the Central London Property Trust. The Trust would later build Du Cane Court. (Courtesy of Companies House.)

262368/3

THE COMPANIES ACT, 1929.

COMPANY LIMITED BY SHARES.

Memorandum of Association

OF

Central London Property Trust Limited

1. The Name of the Company is "CENTRAL LONDON PROPERTY TRUST LIMITED."

2. The Registered Office of the Company will be situate in England.

REGISTERED 2 FEB 1932

3. The Objects for which the Company is established are—

(1) To purchase, take on lease or in exchange, to build or otherwise acquire any lands and buildings and any estate or interest in and any rights connected with any such lands and buildings.

(2) To sell, lease, exchange, mortgage, or dispose of for such consideration (pecuniary or otherwise) as may be thought fit, and to develop and turn to account any land or other property acquired by the Company or in which the Company is or may be interested, and in particular by laying out and preparing the same for building purposes with roads, open spaces, recreation grounds, and any other conveniences, constructing, altering, pulling down, decorating, maintaining, furnishing, fitting up, and improving dwelling houses, flats, offices, factories, warehouses, shops, wharves, aerodromes, works, and any other buildings, and by planting, paving, draining, sewering, farming, cultivating, mining, quarrying, letting on building lease or building agreement, and by advancing money to and entering into contracts and arrangements of all kinds with builders, tenants, and others.

(3) To deal in any land or real estate or any other property, whether freehold, leasehold, copyhold, or customary copyhold, and estate and interest therein ; to create, buy,

The Central London Property Trust here laid out its mission statement. (Courtesy of Companies House.)

Central London Property Trust Limited.

262231 / 17 *Incorporated under the Companies Act, 1929.*

SHARE CAPITAL - £120,000

DIVIDED INTO

200,000 Six per cent Preference Shares of Ten Shillings each and
400,000 Ordinary Shares of One Shilling each

ISSUE AT PAR OF

200,000 Six per cent. Preference Shares of 10/- each

200,000 Ordinary Shares of 1/- each

AND

£100,000 Five per cent. Mortgage Debentures

in Denominations of £10, £50, £100 and £500,

Payable as follows:—

	PREFERENCE SHARES.	DEBENTURES.	ORDINARY SHARES.
On Application	2s. 6d. per share	10 per cent.	In Full on Application.
On Allotment	2s. 6d.	40	
On 1st June 19..	5s. 0d.	50	
	10s. 0d. per share	100 per cent	

The subscribers for Preference Shares and Debentures have the right to subscribe for Ordinary Shares at the rate of one Ordinary Share for every two Preference Shares subscribed, and one Ordinary Share for each £1 in value of Debentures subscribed.

The security for the Debentures will be a floating charge on the undertaking of the Company and all its assets subject to certain specific charges on certain of the Company's properties as hereinafter mentioned and to the Company's right to create specific charges on properties which the Company may acquire in the future for the provision of the purchase price or cost of erection of buildings or improvements.

Interest on the Debentures will be paid on the 15th October and the 15th April—the first payment, calculated on the amounts paid up from time to time, being made on the 15th October, 1935.

The Debentures will be transferable by duly registered transfer in common form.

The Debentures will be redeemed by annual drawings at 105 per cent. commencing on the 1st January, 1937, by setting aside in each year a fixed sum for the service of the Debenture interest and redemption sufficient to redeem the whole of the issue on or before the 1st January, 1977. The Company reserves the right to pay off the whole of the Debentures at 105 per cent. at any time subject to giving the holders thereof six months' notice of such intention.

REGIS... 1 APR 193

Directors.

THE RIGHT HON. LORD TEYNHAM, Well House, Sandgate, Kent.
(Director, Fanti Consolidated Investment Company Limited).
C. W. NEVILLE, Esq., Holmbush Manor, Slinfold, Sussex.
(Director, Bernard Mansions Limited).
COMMANDER H. O. JOYCE R.N. (Retd.), Thurlow House, Bouverie Road West, Folkestone, Kent.

Solicitors.

MESSRS. LEACH, SIMS & CO., 10, Bedford Square, London, W.C. 1

Auditors.

MESSRS. GALLEWAY & CLARKE, *Incorporated Accountants*, 70, Finsbury Pavement, London, E.C. 2.

Secretary and Registered Office.

R. B. DAND, A.C.I.S., 7, Pall Mall East, London, S.W. 1.

THE CENTRAL LONDON PROPERTY TRUST LIMITED was incorporated in February, 1932, as a Private Company with a nominal Capital of £10,000 divided into 200,000 Shares of One Shilling each for the objects specified in its Memorandum of Association and particularly to acquire Properties and Freehold sites in the area of Greater London with the object of building thereon, selling the same to others for building purpose or otherwise turning the same to account and also carries on the business of estate owners and managers. The Capital of the Company has recently been increased to £120,000 by the creation of 200,000 further Ordinary Shares of One Shilling each and 200,000 Six per cent. Preference Shares of Ten Shillings each.

The Company when first formed purchased a block of flats known as Bernard Mansions in Herbrand Street, Russell Square, W.C., which was subsequently sold to Bernard Mansions Limited, in which the Company has a substantial holding of shares. Such shares are yearly increasing in value owing to the policy adopted by Bernard Mansions Limited of applying the profits in redeeming debentures.

The Company afterwards acquired a site in Chelsea which it disposed of to Sloane Avenue Mansions Limited (a Company formed for such purpose) and contracted to erect thereon a modern building consisting of 195 flats which were

Notice of 400,000 shares issued by the Trust. (Courtesy of Companies House.)

)RESSES, AND DESCRIPTIONS OF THE ALLOTTEES. Form No. 45a.

This margin is reserved for binding, and should not be written across.

\ddress	Description	Number of Shares allotted: Preference	Ordinary	Other kir
		18868	6729	
Pontardulais Swansea	Cashier	100	25	
Avenue Bromley Kent		250	187	
…rondon Derbyshire	Technical Chemist	100	25	
…ucklebury Reading	Spinster	20	5	
…tona Tyrone, Northern Ireland	Teacher	20	5	
…t Inverness	Clerkess	250	62	
Avenue Thornton Heath	Engineer	300	75	
…d E. Dulwich SE 22	Clerk	100	25	
…l Rd. Swindon	Clerk	20	10	
…te Glasgow	Cashier	10	2	
…nkfoot, Perthshire	Retired	300	124	
…t Dunfermline Fife.	Police Constable	50	22	
…ncis Avenue Walsall		20	5	
, Biggar, Lanarkshire	Butcher	250	62	
…n Road Wednesbury	Housewife	250	62	
…uxton, Cambs.	Spinster	100	75	
…se Eastgate Street Lewes	Surveyor	10	2	
…d Av. Monkseaton		250	62	
Rd. Southport		400	100	
. Melton Rd. Willerby E.Y.	Nurse	20	5	
Rd. Perth	Ret ed Nurse	200	150	
Crescent St. Helier Jersey	Methodist Minister	40	10	
…ingham, Whitehaven	Clerk	20	5	
Seabank Rd. Nairn	Solicitor	200	50	
		22148	7884	

(Signature)

(State whether Director or Manager or Secretary)

Some of the allottees of the Trust, who were a motley crowd. (Courtesy of Companies House.)

~ 18

THE COMPANIES ACT, 1929.

[No Registration Fee payable.]

Receiver or Manager's Abstract of Receipts and Payments.

Pursuant to section 310.

[Name] of Company CENTRAL LONDON PROPERTY TRUST Limited.

[Name] and Address of [Recei]ver or Manager. James Laughland Alderman's House, Bishopsgate, London E. C. 2.

[Date] and description [of sec]urity containing powers under [whic]h Receiver or [Man]ager is appointed: Charged by the mortgages hereinafter mentioned under the powers contained in 152 instruments of mortgage, viz:- As to 101 dated 8th day of April 1939 and made between Central London Property Trust Ltd of the one part and Land Charges Ltd of the other part, as to 27 dated 31st May 1939 and made between the same parties, as to 6 dated 15th June 1939 and made between the same parties, as to 13 dated 11th November 1936 made between Central London Property Trust Ltd of the one part and Sophie Augustine Stauffer of the other part, which 147 mortgages are now vested in Royal Mutual Benefit Building Society, and as to 3 dated 8th July 1939 made between Central London Property Trust Ltd of the one part and Royal Mutual Benefit Building Society of the other part, and as to 2 dated 30th September 1937, being charges under the Land Registration Act 1925 of land comprised in Title Nos 148783 and LN 24875 of which Central London Property Trust Ltd are the registered proprietors and Royal Mutual Benefit Building Society are the registered chargees.

[Perio]d covered by the [Abs]tract. From 20th September 1943 To 19th March 1944

PUBLISHED AND SOLD BY

[W]ATERLOW & SONS LIMITED,

LAW AND COMPANIES' STATIONERS AND REGISTRATION AGENTS,

London Wall, London, E.C.2, Parliament Street, London, S.W.1,

8, Newhall Street, Birmingham, 3.

COMPAN[IES] 27 MAR 1944 REGISTRATI[ON]

Presented by Jas. Laughland Aldermans House, Bishopsgate, London E. C. 2.

21.

[continued over.

At one point, the Central London Property Trust had around 150 mortgages with the Royal Mutual Benefit Building Society. (Courtesy of Companies House.)

been reproduced, while others were exhibited in the Royal Scottish Academy.

In 1905, Messrs. Percy Bacon & Bros., of "The Studio," Newman Street, London, opened a studio in Edinburgh, and I secured the appointment of manager. During the two years this exhibition was open, I acquired valuable organising and artistic experience which, coupled with my previous training and experience in artistic and architectural matters, I respectfully submit would enable me to fill the post in question to the satisfaction of all concerned.

As regards Lecturing, I have already had experience of this work, as my testimonials will show, and I would respectfully point out that my practical experience and training enable me to treat the subject from a technical as well as from a theoretical standpoint. While calling upon the Members of the Committee, I was impressed with the feeling that an intimate knowledge, both of our National Art Galleries and the Continental Galleries, is imperative for the proper fulfilment of the duties of this post, and although I am acquainted with the Galleries in London, Liverpool, Glasgow, and elsewhere, I would, in the event of the Committee appointing me to the Directorship, make a fresh tour not only of these Exhibitions, but also of the Continental Art Galleries. I should thus be able to acquaint myself with the management of each exhibition, which in itself would prove of great value, and at the same time such a course would afford the opportunity of collecting matter for a series of lectures that would give the necessary initial stimulus to any course of action which might be ultimately adopted in the interest of the Art Galleries.

I trust my application may receive your favourable consideration, and have the honour to be,

Your obedient Servant,

GEORGE KAY GREEN.

A fragment of the application submitted by George Kay Green, later to become the architect of Du Cane Court, for the post of Director and Curator of the Aberdeen Art Gallery and Industrial Museum, in 1908. (Courtesy of Charles Kay Green.)

From JOHN GUNN, Esq., M.A., D.Sc.,
Chief Educational Editor, *Thomas Nelson & Sons, Edinburgh.*

62 BLACKET PLACE,
EDINBURGH, *7th March*, 1908.

HAVING learned that Mr. GEORGE GREEN is a candidate for the post of Director of the Art Galleries, Aberdeen, I consider it a duty, as it is a pleasure, to grant him this testimonial, in the hope that, as an expression of opinion founded on personal knowledge, it may carry some small degree of weight with the members of the Committee.

My acquaintance with Mr. GREEN began many years ago, when called on to preside over a young men's meeting connected with our church, and I soon learned to esteem him as a useful and active member, of fine character and disposition, and much intelligence and thoughtfulness.

As a trained architect, Mr. GREEN has a professional knowledge of one fundamental form of Art, and his tastes and his practical experience have led him to a wide acquaintance with other forms. I have heard him lecture, with much success, on his own subject, and I should judge him capable of good work in this line.

Mr. GREEN has many qualifications which seem to me important for such a post, such as a business experience and capacity which are not always found in men of artistic tastes and artistic occupations, and I am sure that he would combine with these such a high ideal of service and such a personal influence as would do much to ensure success in his work.

JOHN GUNN.

A reference countenancing Green's application for the post in Aberdeen. The references which Green received tell us something about his personality, his talents and his professional conduct. The mention of the church is notable, as this – as well as a little book written by his sister-in-law - would suggest that he moved in religious circles. (Courtesy of Charles Kay Green.)

From HIPPOLYTE J. BLANC, Esq., R.S.A., F.R.I.B.A., *Hon. Treasurer and Member of Council of the Royal Scottish Academy; President of the Edinburgh Architectural Association, &c., &c.*

25 RUTLAND SQUARE,
EDINBURGH, 12*th March*, 1908.

GENTLEMEN,

I understand that Mr. GEORGE K. GREEN, of this City, is an applicant for the post of Director and Curator of the Aberdeen Art Gallery and Industrial Museum.

I have known the family, of which Mr. GREEN is a member, for many years, and latterly have come to have an intimate acquaintance with the applicant.

He has had a very superior training in painting, and specially as an architect.

During the period when engaged in these occupations, he has made himself specially informed and equipped by the study of drawing and painting, and by attendance at the University Art Class in this city, and in addition, has acquired a considerable knowledge of business methods from appointments he has successfully occupied.

Mr. GREEN is a young man with much more experience of Art matters than is generally looked for in a man of his years. He is very intelligent, energetic, and a facile writer. With all, he possesses a gentlemanly personality, an invaluable quality, in my opinion, for dealing with men and affairs, such as he would be called upon to deal with in the important appointment he seeks.

His qualifications, in my opinion, would make Mr. GREEN an acquisition, as Director and Curator.

Yours faithfully,

HIPPOLYTE J. BLANC, R.S.A.

Another reference supporting Green's application for the post in Aberdeen. (Courtesy of Charles Kay Green.)

Two other works of George Kay Green, architect of Du Cane Court: Sloane Avenue Mansions and Nell Gwynn House, both also in London. (Photographs taken by the author.)

Besides his apartment blocks, Green also worked on the Tudor Close Hotel, in Sussex. (Photographs taken by the author.)

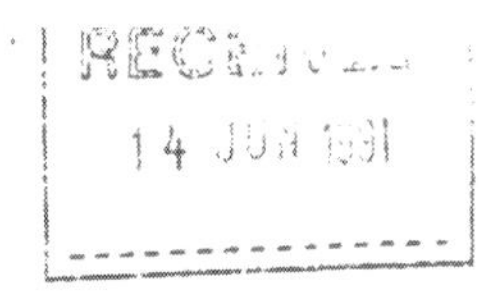

Architects Registration Council of the United Kingdom
ESTABLISHED UNDER THE ARCHITECTS (REGISTRATION) ACTS 1931 TO 1938
73 Hallam Street London W1N 6EE Tel: 071 - 580 5861 Fax: 071 - 436 5269
Registrar: David W. Smart B.A. F.M.S.

LM/SN

12 June 1991

Charles Jones
Nightingale Centre
8 Balham Hill
London
SW12 9EA

Dear Sir

G KAY-GREEN

I acknowledge receipt of your letter dated 6 June 1991, enquiring about the above named.

Mr Kay-Green was admitted to the Register of Architects in 1933 and remained so until his death in 1939.

Unfortunatly there is very little information on the file I now have. However I can tell you that between 1900 and 1932 he was the `responsible architect` for:

Tudor Close Hotel, Rottingdean nr Brighton.
Hotel Peacehaven, Telscomb Cliffs nr Newhaven.
John Henry Lee Ltd, (alterations) for Selfridges & Co, London,
Sloane Avenue Mansions, Chelsea.

At the time of his application in 1932, Mr Kay-Green held the position of 'Superintending Architect` with Central London Property Trust, 7 Pall Mall East, SW1 and Saltdean Estates Co Ltd, Saltdean, Brighton.

Unfortunatly, I cannot be more specific regarding dates.

I do hope this information will be of some use to you.

Yours faithfully

Linda Moir
Assistant Registrar

Green became a registered architect in 1933, although he was not a member of The Royal Institute of British Architects. (Courtesy of the Tenants' Association.)

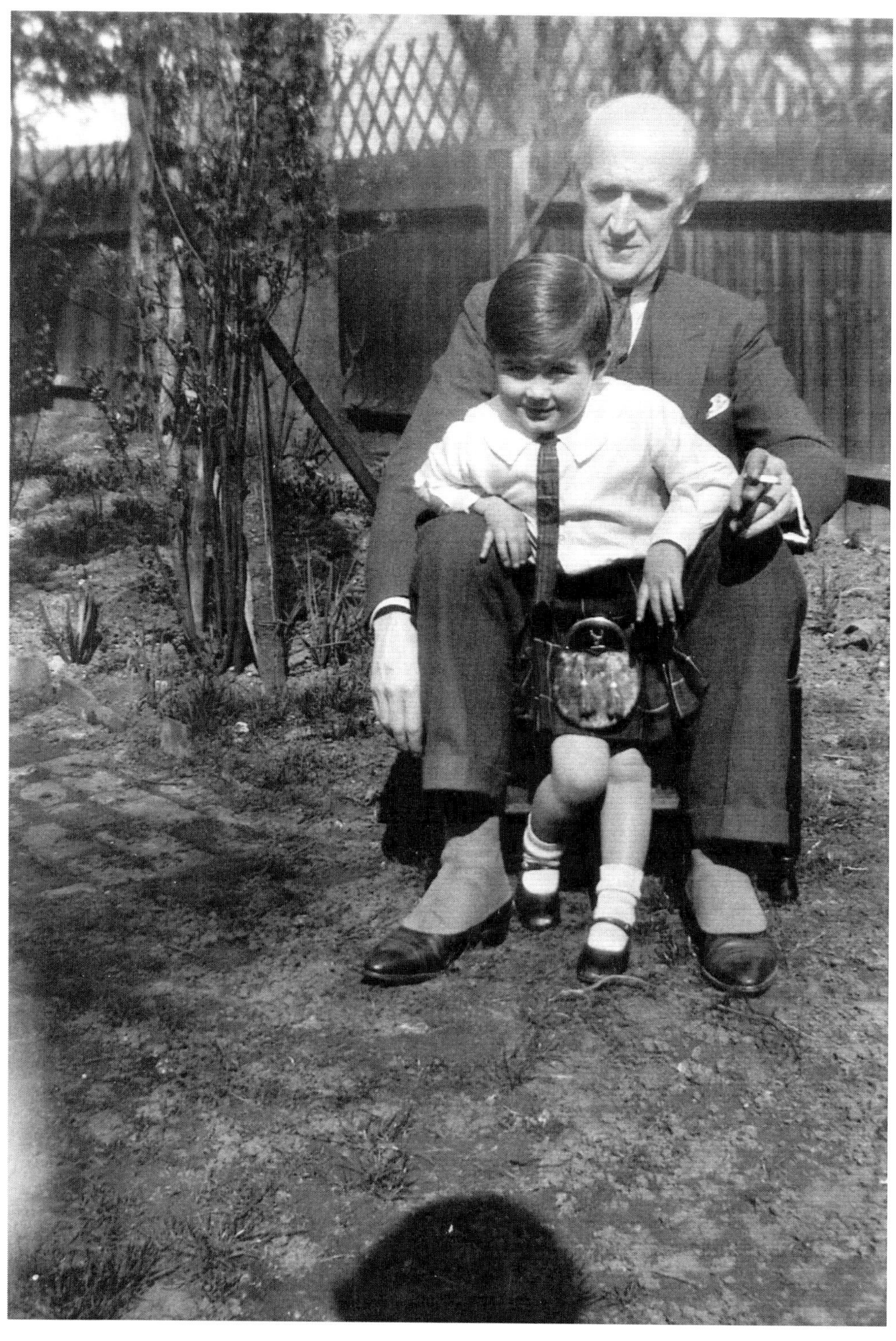

George Kay Green with his son, John. (Courtesy of Charles Kay Green.)

George Kay Green with family or friends. The lower left picture shows him (presumably) on his wedding day.

The Triumph of Virtue (?)
or
How She was saved from a terrible Fate!

(Illustrations by Edwardo Botticelli:
Doggerel by Ward Dorane.)

I met her at dinner,
The dinner was good,
But not so the lady,
Who said that she would
Succumb to temptation,
And week-end with me
In my Dover Street Chambers,
Suspending with glee
Her vows to poor Green, who
Quite soon became Blue,
When he heard what his volatile
Consort would do.

× × × × × ×

At the close of the evening
She sat by the side
Of the Dover Street Tempter,
But she studied with pride
The noble façade of
Her architect lord,
Whilst she listened to ME
(i.e. Myself), & felt bored.

A poem (with illustrations) written by a jealous barrister, who had his eye on the lady whom George Kay Green won in marriage. The modest piece indicates that she had her own eye on the fortune which she believed would come from a building in Balham, and that she would be prepared to fall from grace in order to share in that fortune! (Courtesy of Charles Kay Green.)

‘All women are cats’ – according to Green’s rival in love.
(Courtesy of Charles Kay Green.)

The rest of the curious poem. The woman in the architect's life apparently dreamed of having a new car, whilst the 'penniless' barrister drowned his sorrows. However, it may all have been harmless banter. (Courtesy of Charles Kay Green.)

A NEW KIND OF ARCHITECTURE

*

The Housing Crisis After World War 1

In the (London) Evening News of 1920, there was a photograph of a woman patrolling the pavements of Oxford Street with the message on her back: 'House Wanted. If you know of one, please stop me.' Unfortunately, in the 1920s and '30s most private buildings were accessible only to the middle classes and the highest paid manual workers. Nevertheless, with a housing crisis on its hands, places like Du Cane Court would surely have been popular with local government - representing an economical use of land and materials in relation to the number of homes provided.

The Growth in Rented Apartments

The first block of flats designed for the middle classes was built in 1853 as part of a redevelopment of Victoria street, Westminster Hamnett.&.Randolphe. From the late 1870s the number of flats multiplied rapidly. Between the wars, more than 1300 new blocks were erected in London, containing over 56,000 flats. Among them were Northgate (1936), Viceroy Court (1937), Stockleigh Hall (1937), and the following buildings which, like Du Cane Court, were notable for their size:

Latymer Court in Hammersmith, with 360 flats;
Russell Court in Woburn Place, with 500 flats;
Park West in Edgware Road, with 550 flats;
the White House, opposite Great Portland Street Tube Station (by Regent's Park), with 800 flats; and
Dolphin Square, on the riverside in Chelsea, with 1250 flats.

But unlike at Du Cane Court, it was sometimes a case of 'one size suits all', for the White House and Russell Court were both largely comprised of one-room service flats.

At the other end of the extreme, one commentator at the Ideal Home Exhibition in 1938 found the *house* designs so varied as to 'destroy any coherence of architectural thought'. Blocks of flats are generally very different in this regard – and maybe the public, or at least the planning regulators, would have appreciated the consistency of their design.

Different Methods of Construction

In the 1930s, the concrete-clad steel structure employed at Du Cane Court was still something of a novelty. Steel frames came into vogue in the early twentieth century, and Charles Green understood our building to be the first in Europe to employ such a frame in combination with pre-stressed, reinforced concrete. (At any rate, our building was certainly state-of-the-art, because Freyssinet had only perfected his methods of pre-stressing concrete a few years earlier.) But responding to necessity is just as important as making history, and, in a letter dating from the 1930s, George Kay Green expressed a preference for structural steelwork and (reinforced) concrete over reinforced concrete alone, because construction is cheaper and faster.

In the USA, the 'Hydraulic Jack' method was used, allowing the top floor to be fabricated on the ground, before being lifted up to its appointed place with the help of huge cranes. This method was only used with steel-framed structures, and never caught on here.

In chronological order, the building industry has introduced: bricks and mortar, bolting, riveting, welding, and finally rods wired together. But all of the phases have overlapped. The beauty of bolts is that they are easily screwed into place and can be carried in the pocket. They are desirable in the event of an earthquake or subsidence, because they are more flexible than rivets, which, in turn, are more flexible than welding. Rods tied together with wire are also extremely flexible, and may be thinner than a steel frame, – but they could pose real danger when the building comes to be destroyed.

With welding, the end result is one continuous plate. The Japanese ship builders were the first to weld plates together, and in doing so they superseded British industrial practice. Steel structures are nowadays welded or bolted together, whereas in those days they were generally riveted. Rivets are steel beams with knobs and holes, allowing them to be easily slotted into place. They were produced in a cauldron or brazier of 'coke', which was scorching hot coal that had already been used to make gas. There would be someone on the ground responsible for the forging of the rivets; and the shout would come down to him that, say, eight were required. In response, he would use his tongs to select one at a time and throw it up to the worker above, who caught it in a shovel or a kind of leather pouch. The recipient offered it to a couple of colleagues, who fixed the protrusions into the holes of the existing frame. While the rivet was still soft, the two labourers would then hammer - one at each end – in perfect unison, and so bring the plates together.

Johnny Morris (who later entertained us with his charming television series, 'Animal Magic') was involved in the process as a young man, and once described it in a radio programme. He said that it involved considerable skill and timing, and could potentially result in diabolical injuries - especially as no protective clothing was worn. It was, however, much faster than using nuts and bolts.

Once, in a close examination of Du Cane Court, a nut or bolt was found, implying an unusual mode of construction for the time. Whether rivets were used as well, who can say? Indeed, in the light of funding difficulties, maybe the process changed as the building developed?

General Trends across the sea - and one Superior Paradigm

In the last 120 years, three imposing types of structure have been employed in New York City [Robertson]. The first was the cast-iron building of the 1880s and 1890s. The second 'generation' included the Empire

State Building (1931), which had a steel skeleton encased in stone – and so broadly followed the same protocol as Du Cane Court. The World Trade Centre was part of a new trend. It was a throw-back to the first generation, with the interior columns eliminated to create more floor space for the tenants; but unlike Du Cane Court and other buildings which utilized concrete, or masonry, for reinforcement and fire containment, it had only plasterboard, or 'sheetrock' as it is sometimes known, with spray-on fire protection. So when tragedy struck in 2001, the whole thing was doomed. Yet the 767 aircraft which delivered the *coup de grâce* were only about 20% heavier than a certain 707 (B-25 bomber) which lost its way in the fog one day in 1945, and crashed into the Empire State Building. It is surely a tribute to the design that someone looking at this landmark today would never guess what had happened.

Companies employed in the Creation of Du Cane Court

An article in The Builder introduced Du Cane Court to the architectural world at large, on the 29th of October, 1937. It had involved the work of 36 enterprises, 30 of which were limited companies. Out of those for which records are still kept, nine have changed their name over the years, and I found (circa 2000) only seven of the original 30 to be still trading.

Some of these companies may be seen through their individual fortes to be part of architectural history. For instance, by the 1930s many kinds of protective coating could be applied to steel - the most effective being that of glass fused onto the surface at a temperature of 700 to 900 degrees centigrade. (Somewhat curiously, stainless steel without the coating was more costly.) The composite is called 'glascrete', and it was employed at Du Cane Court by J A King and Company Ltd.

At the time, asbestos cement was used to encase electric cables and steelwork [JRIBA.6/3/39]; and there was even an asbestos felt strip available for wrapping pipes – which, unlike hair felt, does not harbour vermin. No doubt the vermin would have had difficulty breathing! The glorious advantage of the material lies in its fire-resistant properties, but prolonged exposure to it destroys the lungs. At Du Cane Court asbestos was employed (by Stonart Asbestos Flooring Co Ltd) for jointless flooring; but before any of the local literati are tempted to reach for their fountain pens and their poisonous inkwells, we should remember that the floors at Du Cane Court are carpeted, and that asbestos is really only a problem when it is broken up. Realistically, a scurrying mouse or beetle may crumble a little of it by nibbling, but one assumes that even the most eccentric resident would not follow its example!

An elderly person once said to me that when Du Cane Court was built, it was 'a good year for bricks'. And there must have been some lively debate at the time as to what would make the best building blocks. One 1930s advertisement draws attention to the remarkable strength of 'stock bricks'. We are told that their special acoustic properties make them ideal for cinemas and theatres, and that they are the only bricks which are improved by the weather. Stock bricks are basically customized bricks, and it would be inspiring to learn that they were used at Du Cane Court, but, even without this reassurance, the briefest of ambles around the building will reveal what fine condition much of the brickwork is still in. We have three companies to thank for our brickwork, and one of them, The Accrington Brick and Tile Company, was advertising a special sandfaced brick in the 1930s which would have been very durable [JRIBA.8/5/39]. I am not sure whether it was ever employed here, but 'air bricks' *certainly* were. These were darker than usual and were manufactured with holes, to allow air to circulate more freely through the kitchens.

An advert for radiators in 1937 speaks of the scientific spacing of the columns rendering an effective distribution of warmth; and the example shown looks very much like the radiators that were fitted at Du Cane Court, most of which were made from cast-iron and will never wear out. Another late 1930s advert praised lead pipes [JRIBA.8/5/39], claiming that they will easily outlast the building in which they are installed. And no doubt if they supply drinking water, they will outlast the residents, too, who will be dispatched by lead poisoning. Thankfully, our own supplying pipes are iron and not lead – although some of the drainage may be via lead pipes.

The partitions here were installed by ICI Ltd, and I am told that all of the bathroom and kitchen windows at Du Cane Court were fitted with obscured glass, although subsequently some residents have changed the panes of glass in their kitchens. However, the windows in the principle rooms cannot be changed (except by management), being an integral part of the overall plan; and there is some history attached to them, for they were the answer to a technical problem. Basically, the floors inside the flats here are largely wooden, but there are six inches of concrete in the kitchen and bathroom floors, which apparently limits the height that the ceiling may safely be raised to. Enter a new player upon the stage – Crittall Manufacturing Co Ltd – replacing the favoured tall wooden sash window with a new standard, the metal frame, which allowed the window to be broader (about eight feet wide in the case of our own building), and so admit plenty of light and make a room of moderate size seem quite voluminous. Walter Crittall was apparently influenced by the Dutch style, and his company dates from the nineteenth century. The manufacturing process behind these windows involved the complete immersion of the frame into molton zinc, for a long period of protection against corrosion. Our own windows follow his standard, and were the responsibility of W.H. Henley and Co.

The window frames at Du Cane Court are painted white, but it is likely that they were originally dark green, like those at Westbury Court over Clapham South Station. There, the proliferation of moss seems to match the windows rather well, and renders a degree of faded elegance to the design – although it is presumably a blemish emerging not out of human improvisation but neglect.

More than one commentator has suggested that there used to be gates at the front of Du Cane Court, which would have made for a grand entrance. In fact, a venture named Haskins Ltd *were* responsible for *collapsible* gates; but the story goes that these imposing features were soon removed, so that the iron out of which they were made could be put aside for the war effort. Certainly, they do not figure in an early (circa 1938) photograph which I have of the building; and Sylvia Say, who arrived with her parents here in 1939 (before being evacuated), has no memory of them.

The elevators at 'the Court', installed by Benny Lifts Ltd, were old-fashioned, with a grating in front of the door that had to be pulled shut before the passenger could be on his way; while T. Clark and Co. Ltd was responsible for the Electrical installation. This company still exists, and in 2000 Robin Wyborn, the Commercial Director, kindly replied to a letter of mine. He wrote that the electrical services in a residential block like Du Cane Court would typically have been carried out using a metal conduit, buried within the fabric of the building, into which rubber insulated copper conductors were drawn. These days, the cables are fixed into the ceiling and partitions, and the insulation (involving plastic) is faster to install and more economic.

Make Way for 'the Court'

Patrick Loobey told me that tall trees had to be cleared for the construction of Du Cane Court. They may have been almond trees, as these were a regular sight at that time; but quite apart from falling prey to the tree surgeon's saw, such flora may not have endured the ravages of time and pollution anyway. These days, plane trees are more common, and have the advantage that they can absorb pollution through their bark – and then shed their bark when they need to.

The large lawn in the southern courtyard at the front of the building is quite uneven, and one resident feels that the excess rubble from construction may have been put into the soil, and grass shoots planted above. Anyhow, the whole venture was a great undertaking, and a builder who visited our grounds once exclaimed: 'The place looks so solid that the foundations must be as deep as they are high!' However, a more conservative opinion from another professional was that they are probably only three yards deep.

Issues with Planning Regulations

While creating iconic buildings like Du Cane Court, George Kay Green had the occasional brush with authority. Once he was required to put a notice in The Times newspaper. On 13th March, 1933, he replied that 'if work has to be held up for [a notice] to appear in the Times, I feel it is going to materially affect the expedition of the contract'. Yet on another occasion, he seemed to say that he, himself, wanted the notice. Maybe he thought the publicity would prove useful.

In the 1930s eleven inch cavity walls were recommended, although at Du Cane Court the outer walls are less than 10 inches. So did our architect take shortcuts in order to get the job done? To be fair, work on the building was begun just prior to the introduction of effective planning controls. Nevertheless, in June 1935, E.P. Wheeler from the London County Council insisted the framework should safely support a load of 100lbs per square foot, and that the minimum thickness for panel walls was 8 ½ Inches. He also writes (and I paraphrase) that 'the preliminary plans submitted by Mr Green showed a certain violation of the rules, but in an interview of 13th March, 1935, Mr Green stated verbally that he intended to comply with the provisions' [Pub.Rec.Off.]. And the height of Du Cane Court was another bone of contention, and also, perhaps, the density of tenants per acre.

I am not sure which of Green's works Mr Wheeler was referring to in his correspondence, but interactions of this kind reveal something of the relationship between architect and council. They show, for instance, that G.K. Green was a man who would push the boundaries, although he seems to have retained a polite relationship with the town planners; and, apparently, in 1932 the London County Council had given consent for the erection of a block of flats of a greater height than that prescribed by the appropriate act. One of my interviewees felt that a relaxation of the rules was not surprising, given how much more council tax could be levied from this new block of apartments, than from the handful of private dwellings which it replaced.

In 1937, further controversy was caused by a sign which Claude-General Neon Lights Ltd wanted to display on the roof of Du Cane Court [W.Council]. It was to be about 70 feet long with letters three feet high; and was, unfortunately, scheduled to overlook Balham Park Road which is residential, rather than Balham High Road, which is predominantly commercial. However, the disapproval must eventually have been revoked, for my local hairdressers tell me that a sign for Du Cane Court *was*, in fact, displayed when they came to Balham in the 1950s or 1960s. It was in red neon lights, and stood above 'F' block facing Balham Park Road.

Cashflow and other Problems

An early advertisement declared that Du Cane Court would be ready for occupation in April, 1936. Yet in the October, 1937, issue of 'The Builder', there is a photograph of 'the Court' which would seem to indicate that the back of the building was still under construction, and Mrs Beerman – who moved here on February 19th, 1940 – feels that the back was possibly not completed until 1938. Furthermore, the District Surveyors' Returns may indicate that the entire project was not officially 'signed off' until 1939 or 1940; but, even if this is so, it is not unusual to have a long hiatus between the literal completion of a building, and the rounding off of records appertaining to it.

There is a theory that after the front of Du Cane Court was finished, the whole venture began to run short of money. Indeed, the flats at the front had their own waste disposal facility, larger radiators, and both gas and electricity - whereas other flats had only electricity (although this is a dubious advantage in a block where, in recent decades, there have been numerous old people slowly losing their minds, with the attendant risks of a gas explosion!) It is also noticeable that the floorboards creak more in some corridors than in others; and, true to form, a high-quality finish was employed in the corridors at the front of the building (with, perhaps, oak for the doorsteps and elm for the side-panels), while those at the rear would at best be only cork-oak, or some kind of composite. And there are subtler observations to be made. Inside the flats, some doorknobs are brass, whereas others are made out of a less expensive material - probably bakelite.

A letter from the London County Council on July 29th, 1937, gave permission for 33 garages, two squash courts and a cycle store; as well as a playground and crèche, with accommodation for perambulators. And yet one or two of my interviewees told me that children were not allowed at Du Cane Court! Perhaps the original expectation was that the place would be occupied by families – but, in the fullness of time, so many single people arrived that they became overwhelmingly the majority.

There is presumably a 'petrol interceptor' under the garages, for this is always present where water runs on a forecourt; and it might once have carried petrol away, although probably not in the last 50 years or so.

A letter from the superintending architect on 20th April, 1938, puts things into perspective. It states that neither the squash courts, nor the lavatories and covered play area, had been erected, although a playground had been penned off 'at the extreme end'. In fact, it seems that the 'less is more' tenet was prevailing, for, by September 16th, 1938, the proposed cycle store was being used as a further garage. Not only that, my interviewees do not remember roof gardens at the end of the East and West wings, although they were part of the original plan.

Emerging from the fog of financial difficulty was the usual recipe of verity and rumour. One person I spoke to wondered, given the proximity of the building to Wandsworth Prison, whether convicts worked on the construction! But even disregarding such a whimsical idea, it seems that there were health and safety issues. Several workmen may have been killed in the construction of Du Cane Court; and the architect, Charles Jones, cites an astonishing study from the mid-1970s, which confirmed that the construction sector still had a dreadful record for fatalities even then, with just over one per day. My friend and fellow resident, Pat Grimshaw, gave me one graphic example. Her elderly mother received 'care in the community' in the mid-1990s, and a woman sent to attend to her from the organization, 'Crossroads', said that she had always been curious about Du Cane Court. Apparently her grandfather had worked on the building, and come to a most unfortunate end. One day, he fell from the scaffolding into a cement pit. Whether he fell from a great height and was killed on impact, or died from suffocation, I cannot say; but, as far as I know, his body was retrieved for burial.

The Finished Product

Quite apart from any failure to meet the original plans, Du Cane Court, upon completion, was a magnificent building. It had a reception area as grandiose as the foyers of many cinemas and fine hotels – and with a compass of 84 feet, it exceeded the length of a tennis court. Luring the adventurous visitor to the upper floors was a generously proportioned staircase with a golden handrail. There were about 1200 habitable rooms nestled in a gross floor space of 428,400 square feet, while balconies at the front overlooked a busy thoroughfare. Two courtyards faced the high road, each about 115 feet by 130 feet; and to the rear were two enclosed courtyards, each approximately 115 feet square. Ponds decorated the gardens, which were made faintly exotic by the imagination of a famous Japanese landscape gardener, Seyemon Kusumoto.

Du Cane Court was reckoned to be the largest private block of flats under one roof in Europe. What this means is that – with the exception of residences on the ground floor, and a few in J block with their own staircase and external entrance, - every flat is accessible from every other, making it possible to stay in touch with a whole network of friends without even having to go outside: a delightful prospect, indeed, for an elderly person with a penchant for sociability on a cold winter's day.

But the immediate environs offered far more than simply this. There was a fine restaurant and ballroom on the seventh floor, and areas where you could play cards or table-tennis. And to lubricate a party atmosphere, the Du Cane Court Wine Company Ltd had a range of alcoholic beverages on the premises for sale under an off licence. Finally, on the ground floor there was an Express Diary, a porters' desk, and an office with a manager who would attempt to regulate the whole of this remarkable, self-contained world to the satisfaction of landlords and tenants alike.

The block also had a quaint postal facility (courtesy of Lamson Engineering Company Ltd) with letter chutes on every floor, connecting with a post box in the reception area between the two lifts. Two collections occurred most days, with one on Sunday, and there was a solid brass strip running from the seventh floor to the ground. Hilda Middleton, who came to live here in the late 1950s, remembers the glass-fronted post box and says that you could see if any letters had got stuck! Eventually, like a sluggish intestine, the system began to have processing difficulties, and was discontinued when the original lifts were restored to their former glory in the early 1970s. Nevertheless, it was an unusual piece of history, and calls to mind the 'pneumatic tube' between Euston and (near) St Paul's, through which postal bags were pulled by the force of suction from source to destination; or the ingenious facility in some hospitals whereby blood samples are sucked from one department to another - although on our own esteemed premises, the only force operating was that of gravity.

There were also telephone kiosks on every floor, which would have been used by anyone who did not have a telephone in his flat (although there is some doubt as to whether *every* kiosk had a telephone installed). And a visitor wishing to stay the night could sleep in one of the designated 'guest rooms', if his host was unable to put him up, although in recent times these rooms have been sold off as composite units, which are even tinier than studios.

At the back of the building was an outhouse referred to as 'The Lodge', which has been a storage place for the equipment of painters and builders, and (after the war) was the home of the Head Porter.

Advertising the new Block

The documentation tells us: 'Every consideration has been given to the planning of Du Cane Court in order to ensure that all flats have the utmost light and air'. There were a number of layouts for the apartments at Du Cane Court, although the sizes of 'habitable' rooms varied little. Generally they were about 15 feet by 11 feet, or 14 feet by 10. This constancy meant that it was arbitrary which room inside a property would serve as the lounge, and which as the bedroom – or the dining room; and such flexibility suits most people very well. It can, however, be frustrating for someone living alone (or, in other words, with no partner to 'escape' from) who would welcome one really big living area for entertaining family and friends.

Installed as one unit, and built into the wall of each living room, was a clock and a radio with two stations. This would have been quite a novelty at the time, as was the central heating system, which was thermostatically controlled according to the outside temperature. And if that was not enough, one might have recourse to an electric fire (thanks to Electroway Heaters Ltd). We are also told the 'Permutit system for rendering water soft has been installed at great expense' .

A couple of other integral features would have made a flat here attractive from the outset. One was the generous amount of inbuilt cupboard space (and there was the potential for further storage in the basement); another was the décor. Kitchens had a white glazed porcelain sink, complete with teak draining board and a 'hopper', which conveyed any refuse to a container in the basement. Both kitchens and bathrooms were tiled; while the bathrooms were also fitted with a white enamelled medicine cabinet, and a chromium-plated, heated towel airer.

The restaurant had a low tariff, and à la carte cooked meals could be obtained up to 10.30 in the evening [Wands.Soc.]. There were afternoon teas and a lounge bar where tenants were able to obtain light meals. The licensed club came with a membership fee of five shillings per annum; and the rentals were reasonable too. A 5-room maisonette would have made a magnificent home for anyone, but even the unfurnished studios, priced from £70 per annum, were ideal as *pied-à-terres* for those whose main dwellings were outside London.

The adult working population of Balham *in toto* was reckoned to have been predominantly clerks, whereas the brochure for Du Cane Court boldly proclaims: 'We have extremely interesting people in residence who have come from India, Canada, China, South Africa ...' and many would have held posts in the city. One person I spoke to even thought the flats were first occupied by French refugees, but it seems likely that this was simply a misconstruction of the Huguenot story.

The advertisers were also very keen to exploit the excellent public transport links for their own benefit: boasting 495 Southern Railway trains daily between Balham and Victoria, which was touted as a nine minute journey! Are these the natural effusions of an ebullient vendor, or has transport technology since gone into reverse gear? Anyhow, Du Cane Court soon became fashionable, and brought a degree of prestige to Balham [Gower]. There was a system for the easy collection and delivery of laundry; and maids were available, as was a ladies' hairdressing establishment for those who would look their best for their menfolk.

The Impact of Du Cane Court on the Community

So what was the opinion of the local populace? Did the building seem incongruous to them? We must remember that this was barely a generation after sheep were still allowed to graze on common land. One observer noted in 1928:

'All along Tooting's high road stand old houses, strange cottages, and queer yards, which are sandwiched, as it were, between blocks of modern shops' [St.News.4/5/28]. And in 'Wandsworth Notes', there is the following entry from 1930:

'It is difficult to remember what Balham looked like 50 years ago. Balham Hill and the high street were lined with houses of well-to-do folk', and waters overflowed a lake and passed through a meadow down to the high street, which was 'bordered by stately elms'. The author, J.H. Bloom, also paints an idyllic rural picture of the vicinity as it had formerly been, noting amongst its wildlife a great proliferation of birds. But they were reminiscing – and a general dislike of urban development may, by the 1930s, have been somewhat *passé*. Of course, there could have been other grounds for objection. After all, large blocks of flats have often been depicted as breeding grounds for crime and squalor. The Rookeries in Clerkenwell was full of criminals; and the Peabody Trust and Guinness Trust were both unsanitary places. On the other hand, a 1930s council block, Alton Hall, actually won an award.

In all my interviews, I could discover no record of anyone casting aspersions on Du Cane Court. Is cynicism about contemporary architecture a recent phenomenon? I suppose it was all so long ago, that even the oldest of my interviewees would have viewed any alteration from the familiar through the fresh and less judgemental eyes of youth. For them, excitement and curiosity were the order of the day. One resident, Marion Hopkins, who was living in Balham even in those far-off days, remembered the place being built.

'My father would take me round to the site when the construction was no more than scaffolding ... and as for my great grandfather, he came over with the Huguenots,' she added, fortifying her connection with local history.

Another interested party, born in 1929, was living in Chestnut Grove when 'the Court' was built.

'My first recollection of the building was when I accompanied my mother there,' he told me. 'I remember a huge crane on the site and flagpoles on the roof.' All of this must have been a source of great wonder for the boy.

The maisonettes at the front of Du Cane Court were still a fairly new concept, although they had been mentioned in advertisements for other buildings as early as 1902, when the common term for them was 'half-houses'. Also new were electric labour-saving devices, which would presumably have been installed as standard. How different it all was from the hovels where some poor souls lived, especially in the north of England. George Orwell vividly described the slums of Wigan and Sheffield, built before the corporation houses, where there could have been many occupants to a single room. Generally they had no bath, and were beset by a lack of hygiene and by windows that would not close. Then, to add insult to injury, there might have been a 150-200 yard walk to the lavatory, which maybe 36 people shared.

The Period Style

Over the years, many people ambling down Balham High Road must have paused as they passed Du Cane Court, mesmerized by its iconic architecture. It belongs to the age of *art deco*, a period commemorated for its florid style. Initially in this era, no expense was spared [V&A.Mus.], but the Wall Street Crash (1929) and ensuing depression replaced the penchant in America for luxurious items with a demand for less expensive goods, such as chromed steel, coloured glass and bakelite.

The genre is also characterized by imaginative lighting and revolving doors – with the reception areas of the Strand Palace Hotel and Du Cane Court being fine (and rather similar) examples of this.

Du Cane Court, although built during 'The Depression', is redolent of the first, lavish period of the predominant style. Some of the floor had the marbled finish of green terrazzo, which was laid like concrete. This can still be seen by the lifts, but is rather cracked now, and being expensive to maintain has been partially concealed beneath a carpet. According to May Arkell, the floor of the foyer was originally white marble decorated with a black Italian design – and it was not covered for many years. Finally, a ruby-red carpet was laid there in the 1970s, and then a green carpet in the 1980s, before blue became the primary colour in recent years. As for the other attributes which imbue the foyer with character ... Hilda Middleton told me that in the 1950s, the pillars which dominate the area seemed to be composed of black marble, while the lifts were lined with satin or quilting.

Beyond the sumptuous details, the style of art deco was characterized by striking colours and geometric forms: witness the proportioned courtyards and the hundreds of identical and perfectly aligned windows at Du Cane Court. Curiously, it was a style without a name for many years, until the term we now apply became popular in the 1960s.

The art deco movement began with the Paris *Exposition Internationale des Arts Décoratifs et Industriels Modernes* of 1925, and more or less ended with the New York World Fair of 1939 [Peel.et.al.]. There is some confusion between *art deco* and *art moderne* - although perhaps the latter was largely the commercial application of artistic movements like Cubism and Expressionism, whereas art deco draws from many sources, even ancient Egypt.

One feature of the age was a fondness for building on a grand scale. The dimensions of Du Cane Court have already been noted. But what about the Chrysler Building (1928-30); the Empire State Building (1930-31); and the Rockefeller Center (1931-39)? Indeed, Manhatten Island was well able to support such ambitious projects, for 'the southern tip and centre of the island are virtually solid granite'. The foundation of other cities was maybe less secure – but this did not deter anyone. Even Hitler was excited by the magnificence of what could be achieved, and he commissioned Albert Speer to construct edifices which would stand 'for a thousand years'. To this end, Speer utilized giant blocks of stone like the ancient Romans. Everything he built was on a massive scale, and the Deutches Stadium was planned to hold 405,000 people.

An Age of Decadence and Excess

Art deco has always had its fair share of detractors. Purists dismissed it as gaudy and vulgar. However, some intellectuals will maintain that architecture is a barometer of a nation and its priorities – and by this reckoning, the productions of every age have their own significance. A few years after World War 1, those who were well off had begun to enjoy life again, and revel in their self-expression [Renshaw]. So art deco reflected a pioneer spirit ... an era of prohibition and speakeasies ... a time of hedonism. In America, gigolos and wife swapping were 'all the rage'; and judging from the stories I have heard, the populace of Du Cane Court conformed to the wild new lifestyle.

An era excited by the life of the senses would naturally have a predilection for curvature in its architecture - and this is clearly evinced in photographs from the key journals of the day. Also recognized was the importance of space around large buildings, allowing their beauty to be properly appreciated. Du Cane Court certainly conforms to such patterns.

A former lecturer on architecture at the University of London, a lady named Ms Valls, has seen parallels between Du Cane Court and three buildings of Le Corbusier - in particular the impressive Unit d'Habitation (with 15 floors), erected in Marseilles after the Second World War. Furthermore, Corbusier already had designs for a block with four courtyards some years before, and maybe our own apartment block was based loosely upon them. At any rate, the style of art deco is now a valuable part of our heritage, and there was no other movement to compare with it in the post-war years.

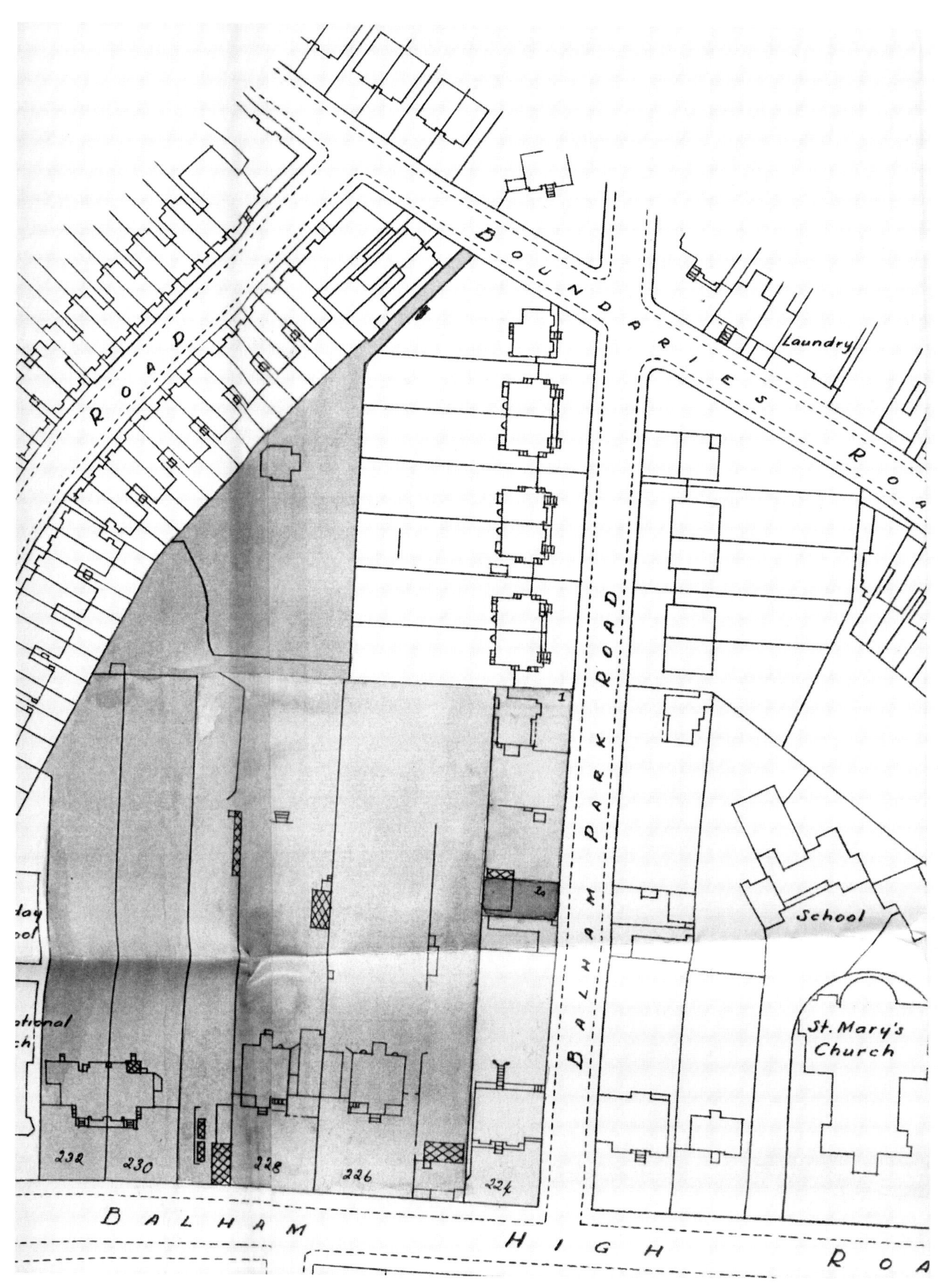

This map shows that plots 224-232 occupied the land which would later accommodate Du Cane Court. (Courtesy of Wandsworth Borough Council.)

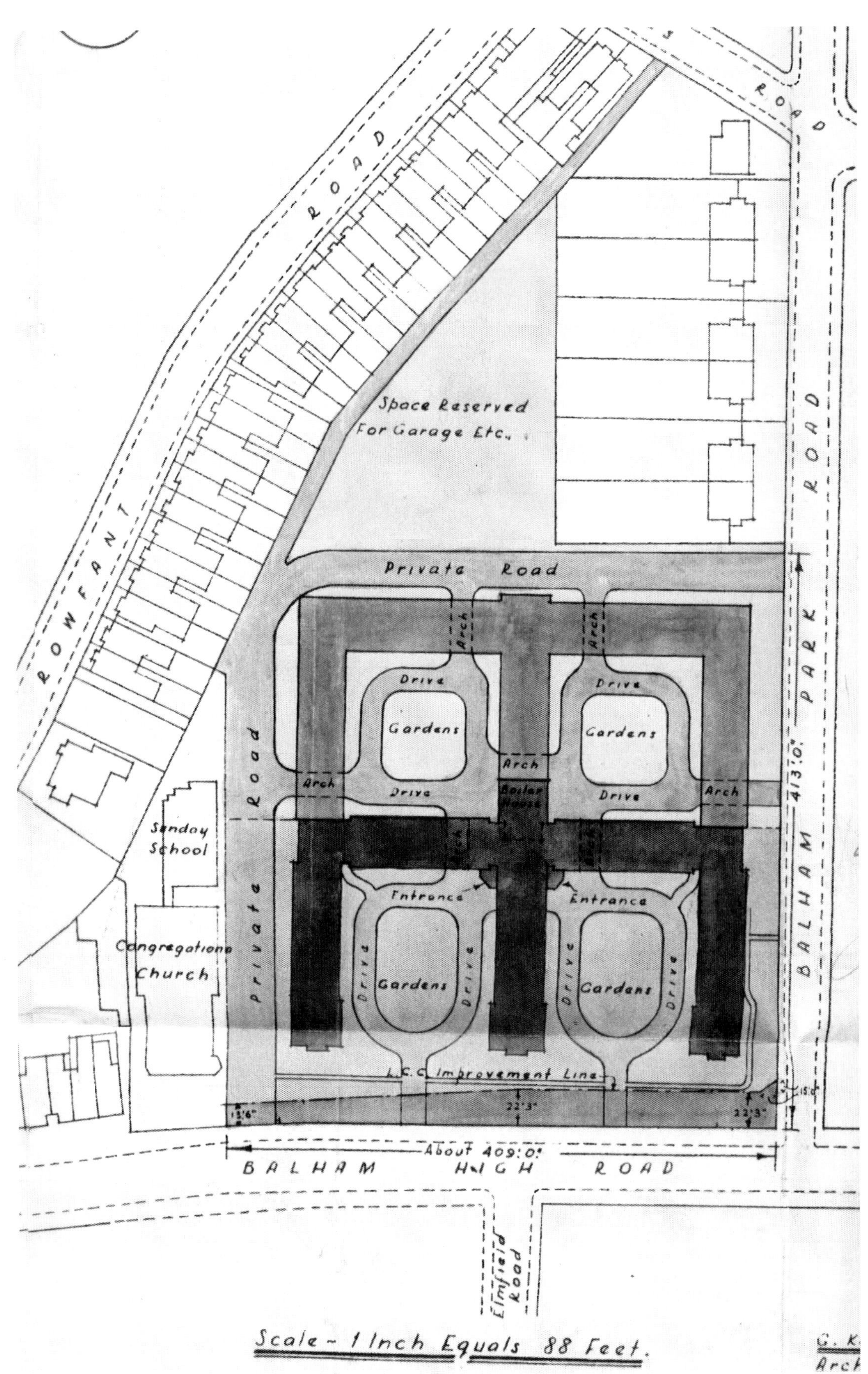

Above is shown the location of the new building. (Courtesy of Wandsworth Council.)

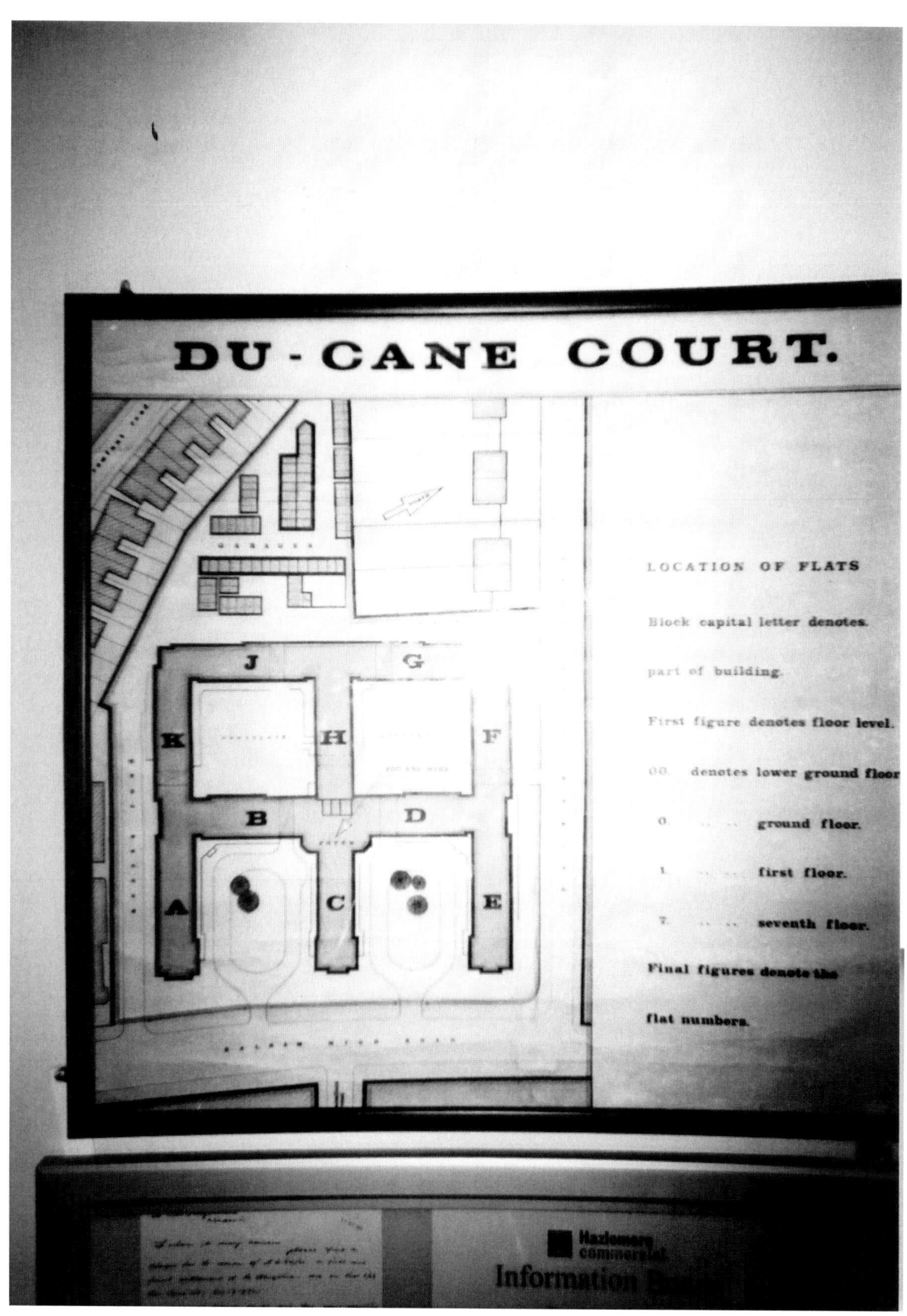

A plaque on the wall in the building's reception area.
It indicates the location of so-called 'blocks', A to K. Note the absence of a block I.
(Courtesy of Estate Office.)

Du Cane Court in construction. Photograph presumably taken in 1935, or early 1936. (Courtesy of Estate Office, Du Cane Court.)

Dear Mr. Vincent,

Thank you for your letter concerning the history of Du Cane Court. Unfortunately we no longer manufacture Bulldog floor clips. These clips were to fasten wood batten to concrete floors. The legs of the clips were pressed into the green concrete, and once the concrete was set, the arms of the legs were opened and the floor battens were nailed into position with special friction tight nails. Various wood structures were put on top of the battens.

I will try to look out the records, but do not recall any mention of the contract or Mr. Kay Green.

Yours sincerely,

David Kahn
Chairman

Above is a letter which I received from The Altro Group plc, which was called The Adamite Company Ltd in the 1930s. It contributed ‘Bulldog floor clips’ to the construction of Du Cane Court.

xxxviii JOURNAL OF THE ROYAL INSTITUTE OF BRITISH ARCHITECTS 8 *May* 1939

The "Nori" Quintet . . . .
I'm "Nori" the Sand Faced,
—Good Looking at that.
I'm "soft" in appearance
and tend towards matt.
I'm "Nori" the Sand Faced,
High-class and well made,
In usual sizes and varying
shade.
From a short distance the face of this Sand-faced Wire Cut Brick has an almost velvety appearance—eminently suitable for high-class buildings where it is desired to depart from the ordinary. It can be supplied in variations of one colour, or to give full multi-colour effects.

ACCRINGTON BRICK & TILE COMPANY . ACCRINGTON

Telephone: 2684 *Accrington* *Telegrams:* "*KILN,*" *Accrington*

London Representative: ERNEST HOLLIDAY, Nori House, Holmwood Road, Cheam, Surrey.

Accrington "Nori" Bricks

Accrington Brick & Tile Company contributed to the construction of Du Cane Court, although sand-faced bricks were not, as far as I know, employed at Du Cane Court. (Source could not be traced, as the company is no longer trading.)

T. Clarke plc

REGISTERED AND HEAD OFFICE
STANHOPE HOUSE
116/118 WALWORTH ROAD
LONDON SE17 1JY
TELEPHONE: 020 7252 7676
FAX: 020 7701 6265

BRANCH OFFICES: BRISTOL. NEWCASTLE. PETERBOROUGH. BOURNEMOUTH.

Your ref   Our ref RHW/SM   Date 13th March 2000

Du Cane Court,
Balham High Road,
London SW17 7JS

Dear Mr. Vincent,

I am in receipt of your letter of 3rd March 2000 regarding Du Cane Court and although this building is known to us, we do not have any surviving records for that period.

T. Clarke being a firm of electrical contractors would have carried out the installation of the electrical services, and being one of the largest and longest established such Company then, as now, would have been able and well suited to provide the necessary resources for such a large complex.

The construction of a similar size project today would probably, but not necessarily, use different techniques that would influence the type of installation material used for the electrical services.

Typically, the electrical services in a residential block similar to Du Cane Court built in the 1930's, would have been carried out using metal conduit (pipework) buried within the fabric of the building, into which rubber insulated copper conductors would be drawn. Today, the installation would be carried out using PVC/LSF (plastic) insulated and sheathed cables fixed within the ceiling voids and drylined partitions, providing a faster and more economic installation.

One of the other major differences, today, would be the greater level of provisions and services to cater for the ever growing reliance on electrical appliances, equipment and lighting, not to mention control systems, door entry, CCTV, telephones, internet facilities etc.

I am sorry that we are not able to give a more detailed account of our work at Du Cane Court, but I trust that this will be of some use.

For your interest, I also enclose a copy of our Brochure which features some of the jobs that T. Clarke have carried out over the last two centuries.

Yours sincerely,

Robin Wyborn
Commercial Director
T. Clarke Plc

A Public Limited Company and Member of the T. Clarke Group

Companies within the T. Clarke Group: All Registered in England

T. Clarke Public Limited Company.	No.	119351
T. Clarke Electrical Contractors Limited.	No.	1581523
T. Clarke (Midlands) Limited.	No.	189434
Veale-Nixon Limited (Newcastle)	No.	385769
Meggitt Marsh & Co. Limited.	No.	439738
Weylex Properties Limited.	No.	865008

National Inspection Council for Electrical Installation Contracting
NICEIC
APPROVED CONTRACTOR
Certificate No 84

T.Clarke was the company responsible for the installation of electrical services at Du Cane Court.

The first photograph above was taken shortly after the completion of the building. (courtesy of Estate Office, Du Cane Court); and the second, about 1960 (courtesy of Patrick Loobey).

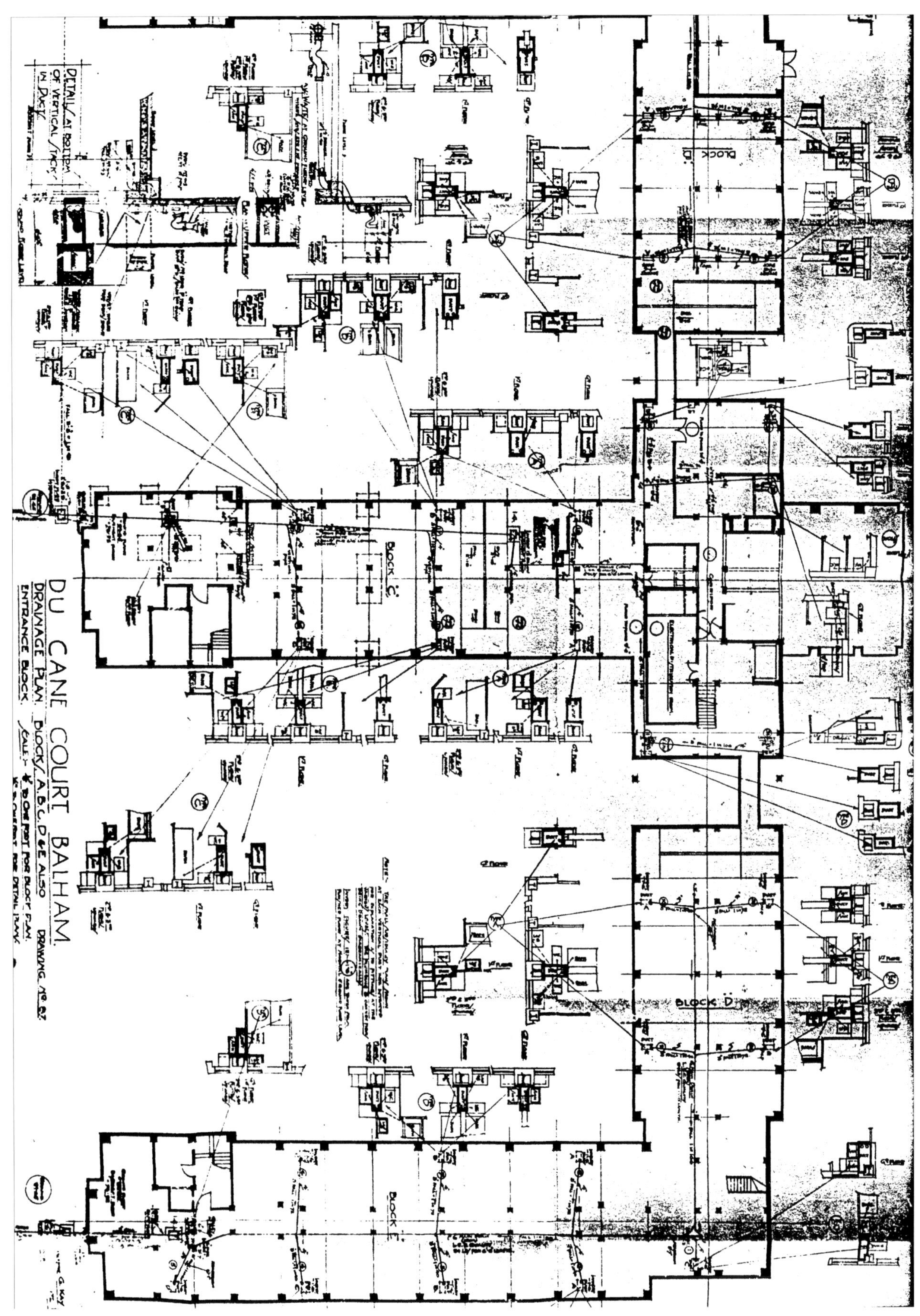

The original drainage plan for Du Cane Court. (Courtesy of Charles Kay Green.)

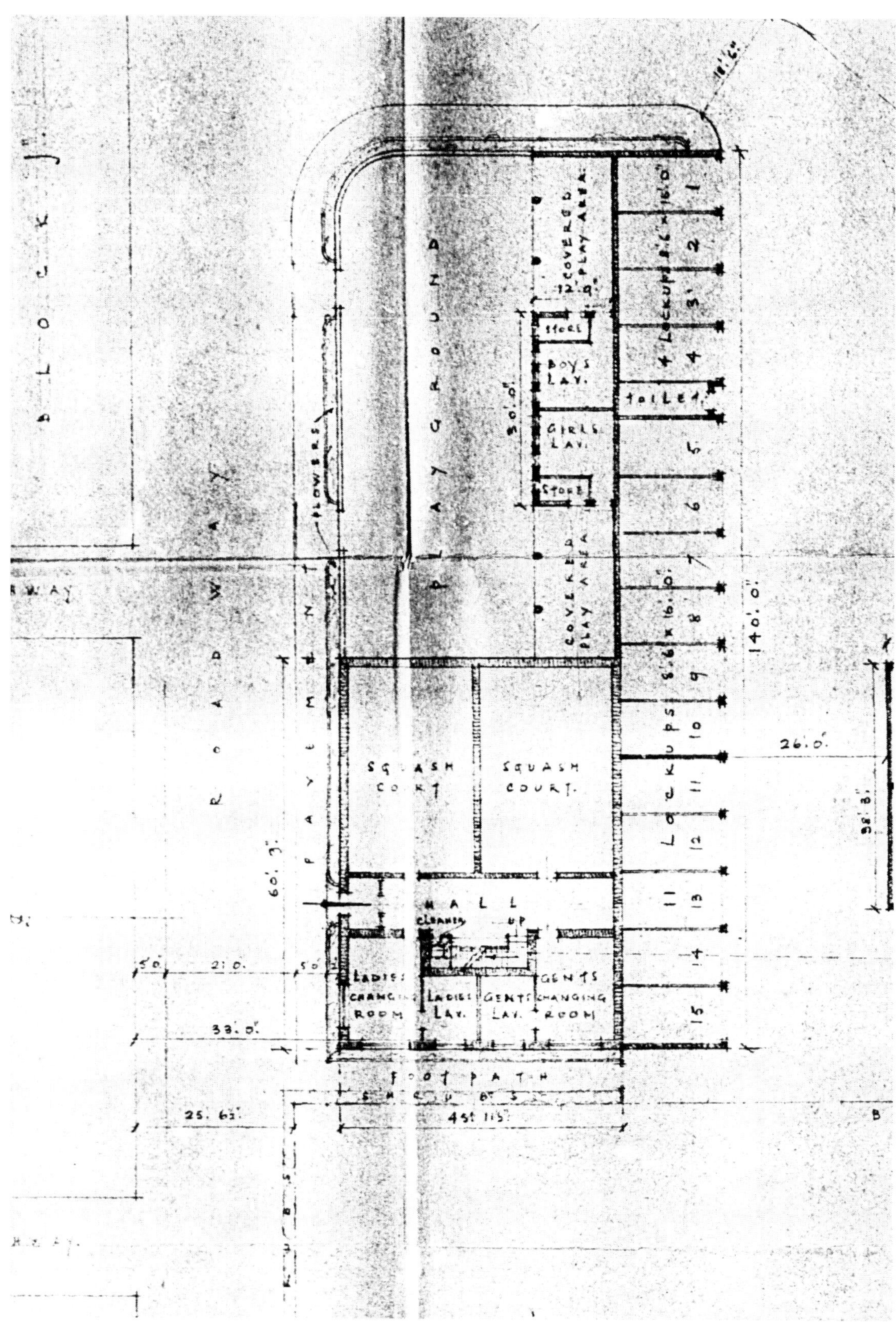

Changing rooms, squash courts and a playground can be seen in this plan. In another plan, dating from 24th May, 1938, a crèche is shown where the hall is indicated above; as well as a covered way (which presumably contained the squash courts). It is likely that, by this time, the block itself was more or less complete, and that the architect was just adding the finishing touches. (Courtesy of Charles Kay Green.)

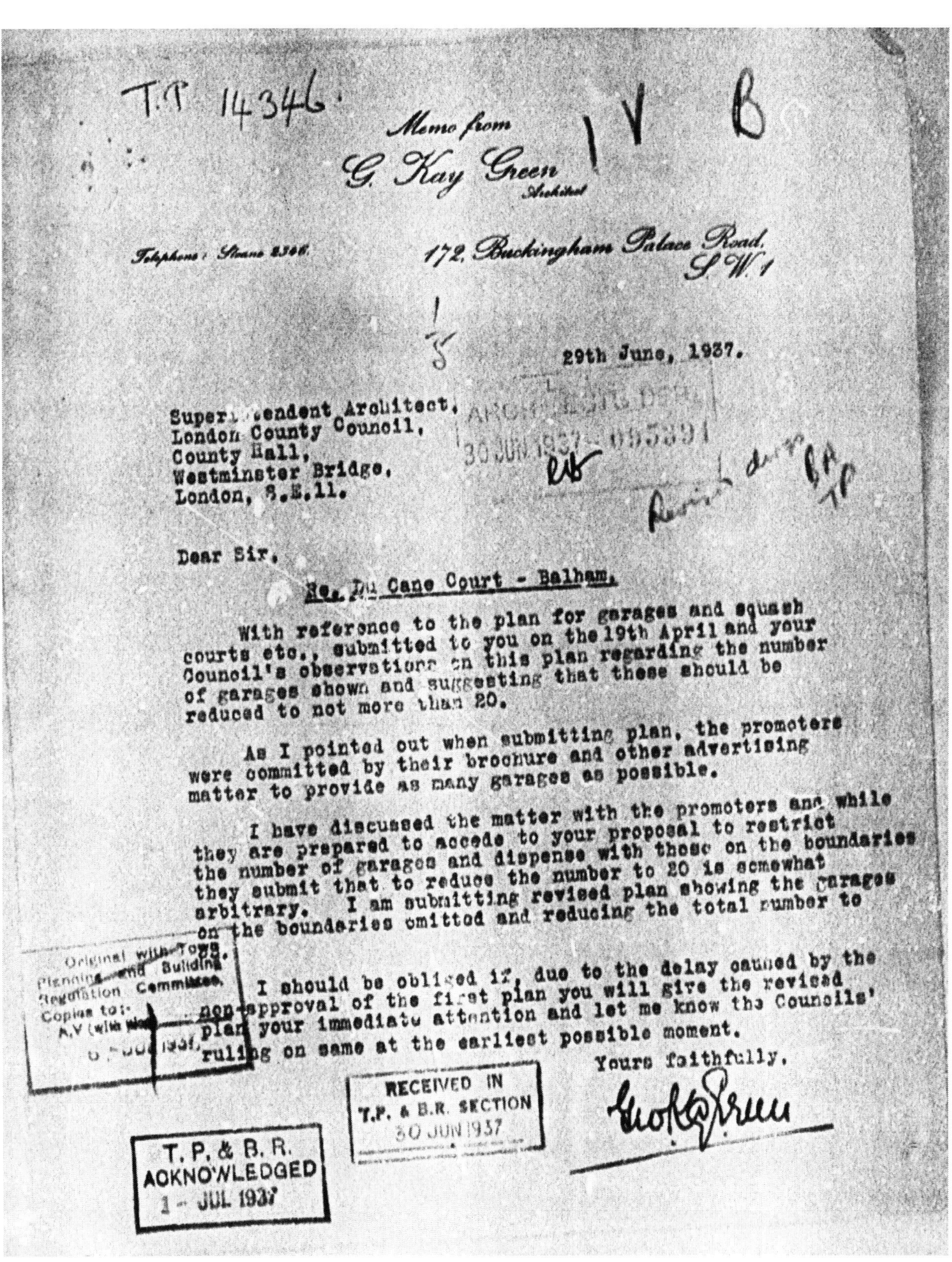
T.P. 14346.

Memo from
G. Kay Green
Architect

Telephone: Sloane 2346.

172, Buckingham Palace Road,
S.W.1

29th June, 1937.

Superintendent Architect,
London County Council,
County Hall,
Westminster Bridge,
London, S.E.11.

Dear Sir,

Re. Du Cane Court - Balham.

With reference to the plan for garages and squash courts etc., submitted to you on the 19th April and your Council's observations on this plan regarding the number of garages shown and suggesting that these should be reduced to not more than 20.

As I pointed out when submitting plan, the promoters were committed by their brochure and other advertising matter to provide as many garages as possible.

I have discussed the matter with the promoters and while they are prepared to accede to your proposal to restrict the number of garages and dispense with those on the boundaries they submit that to reduce the number to 20 is somewhat arbitrary. I am submitting revised plan showing the garages on the boundaries omitted and reducing the total number to 28.

I should be obliged if, due to the delay caused by the non-approval of the first plan you will give the revised plan your immediate attention and let me know the Councils' ruling on same at the earliest possible moment.

Yours faithfully,

G. Kay Green

Although the original plans included squash courts as well as garages - in the end, it was the garages that took precedence. (Courtesy of Wandsworth Borough Council.)

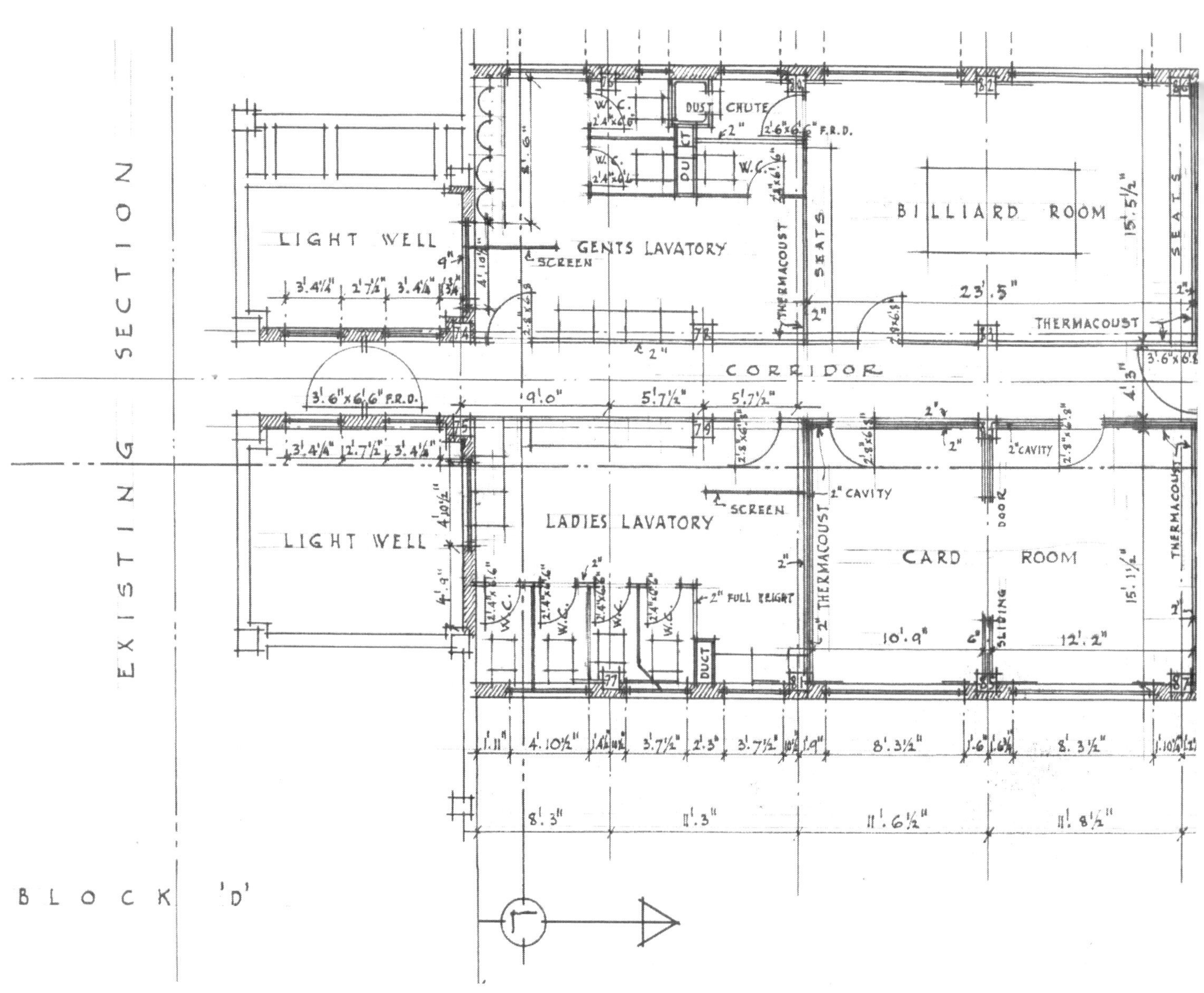

On this page and the next, we see the layout of the social facilities on the seventh floor of H block. The billiards room, alone, is just over 23 feet wide. (Courtesy of Charles Kay Green.)

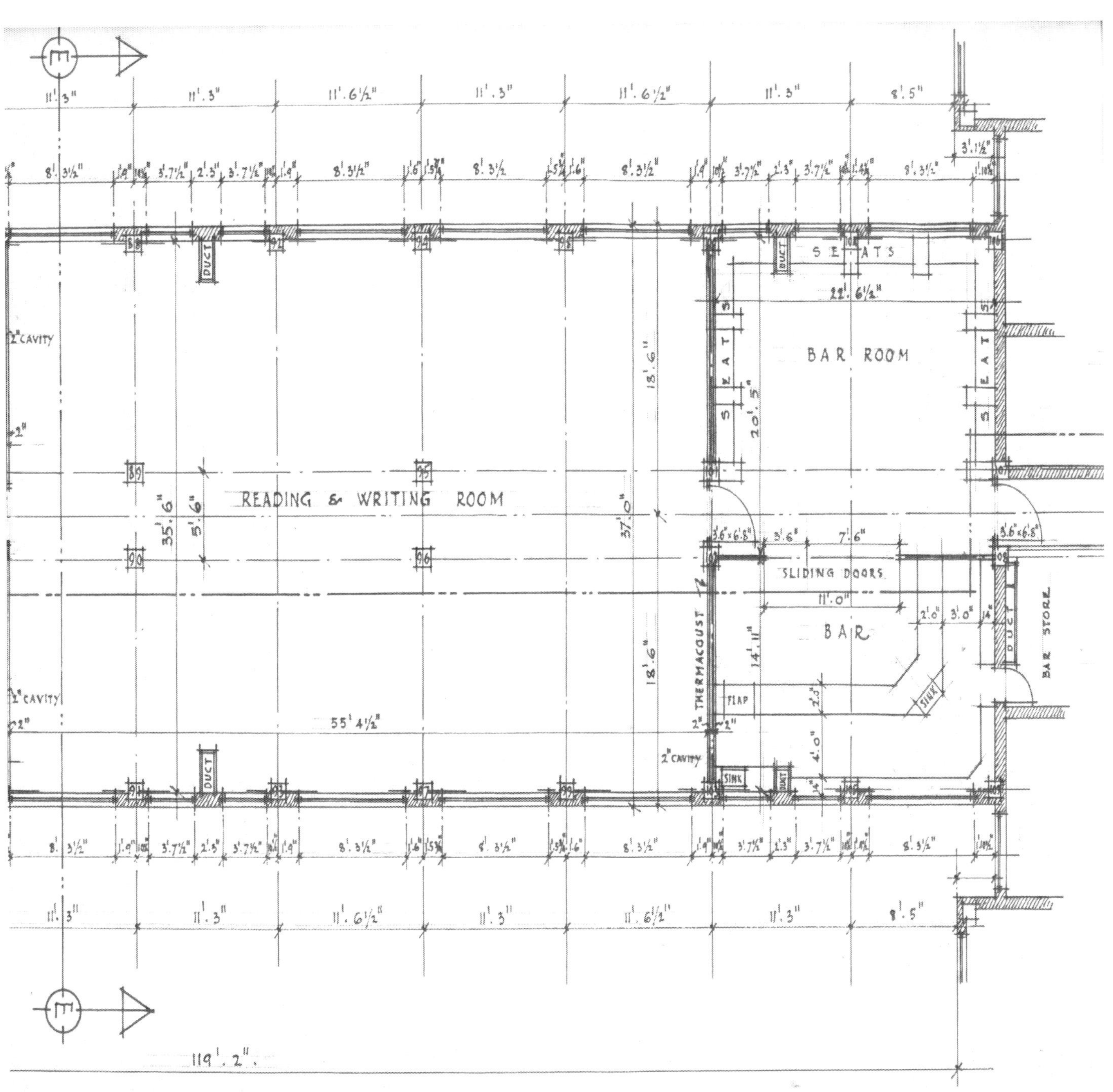

The social facilities on the seventh floor of H block–continued from the previous page. (Courtesy of Charles Kay Green.)

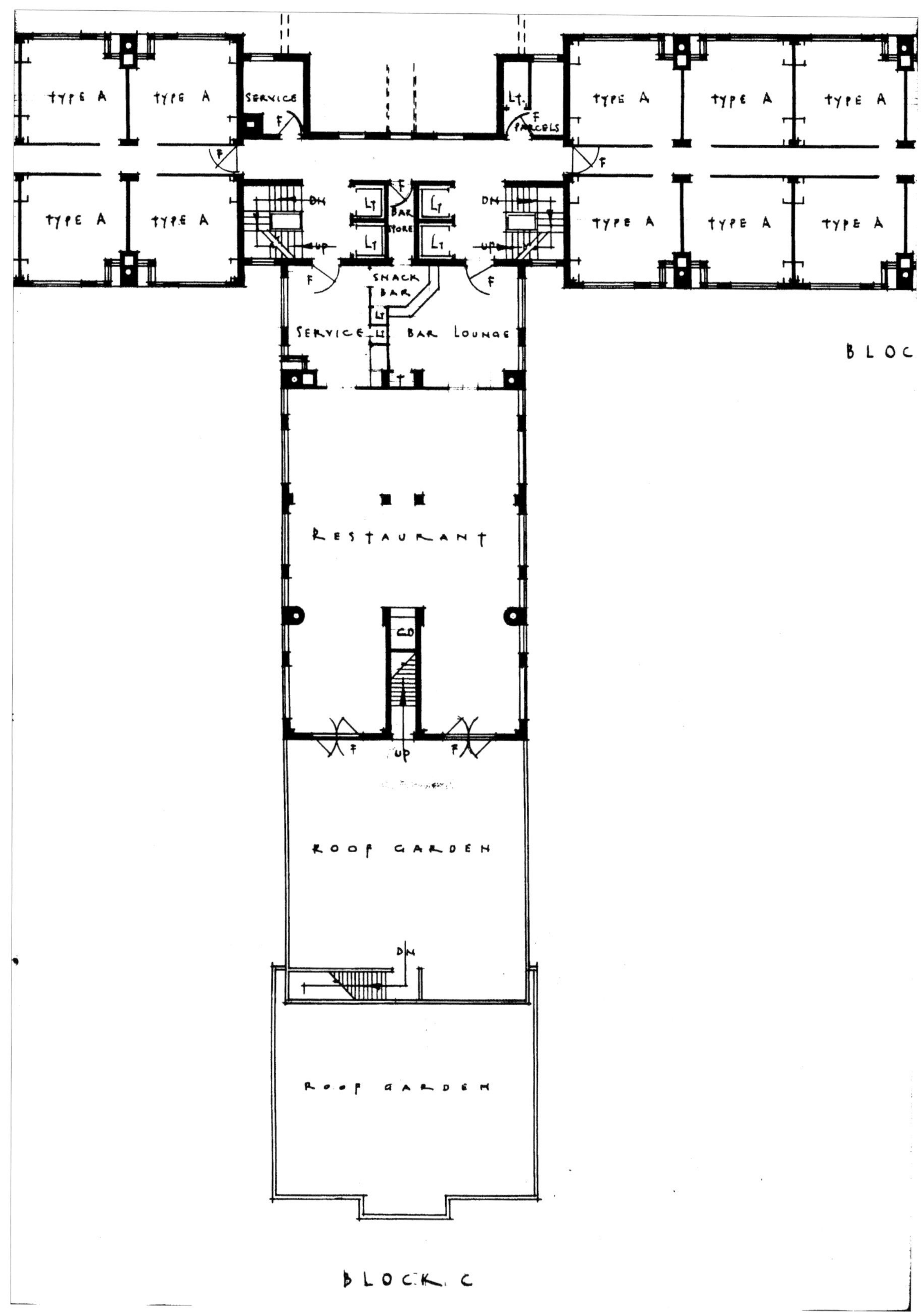

Part of the plan for the seventh floor of block C. There are a number of flats, as well as the famous restaurant, which has two roof gardens in front of it. Blocks A and E (which cannot be seen here) protrude either side of block C, and were designed with a few flats of the same type as those shown. Like block C, both A and E had two roof gardens. (Courtesy of Charles Kay Green.)

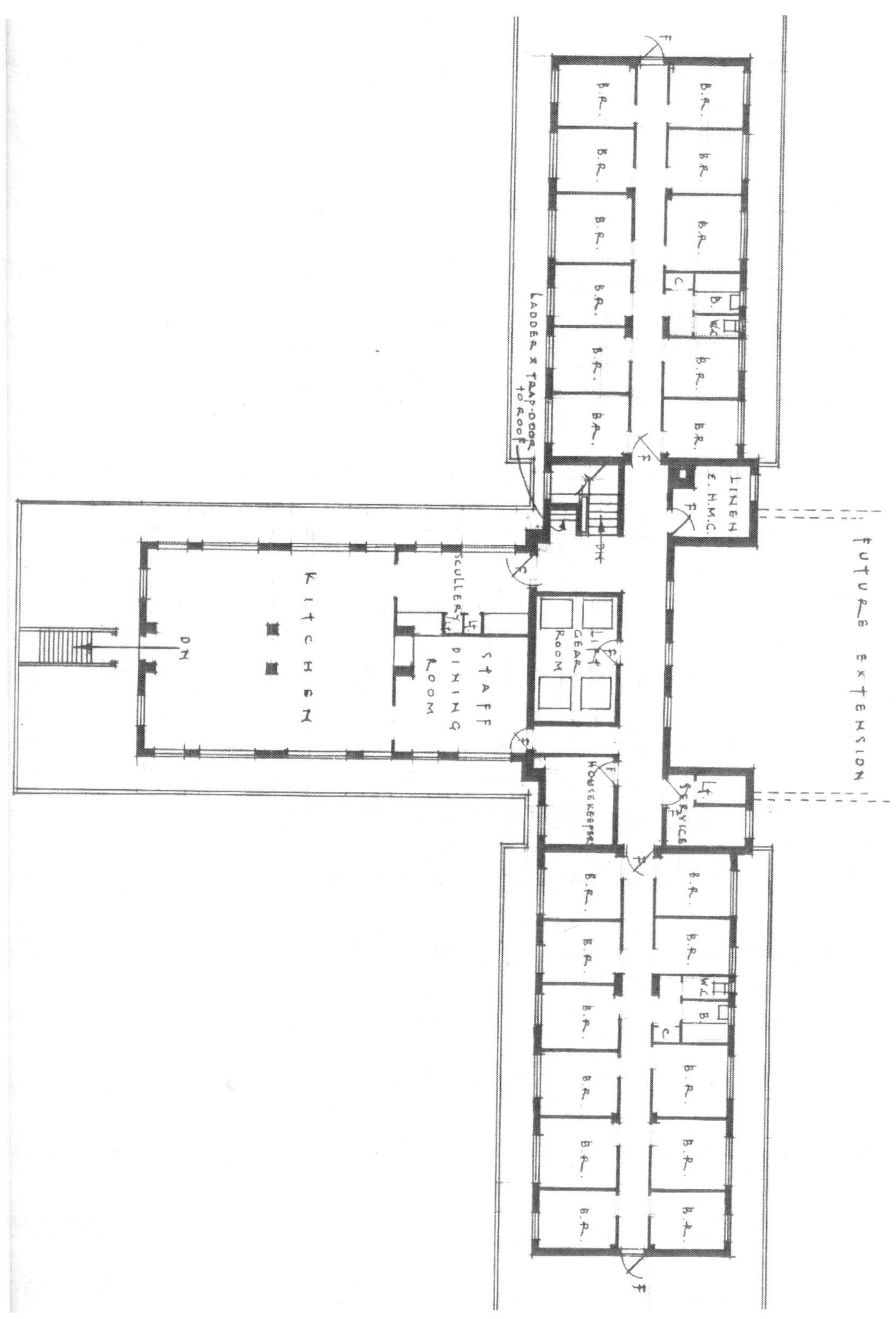

A staff dining room, scullery, kitchen and bedrooms in the eighth floor plan.
Key: BR = bedroom; B = bathroom; HMC = housemaids' closet.
(Courtesy of Charles Kay Green.)
Note: Other 'special' facilities included a manager's flat on the ground floor – and a tiny (staff) bedroom and bathroom unit elsewhere.

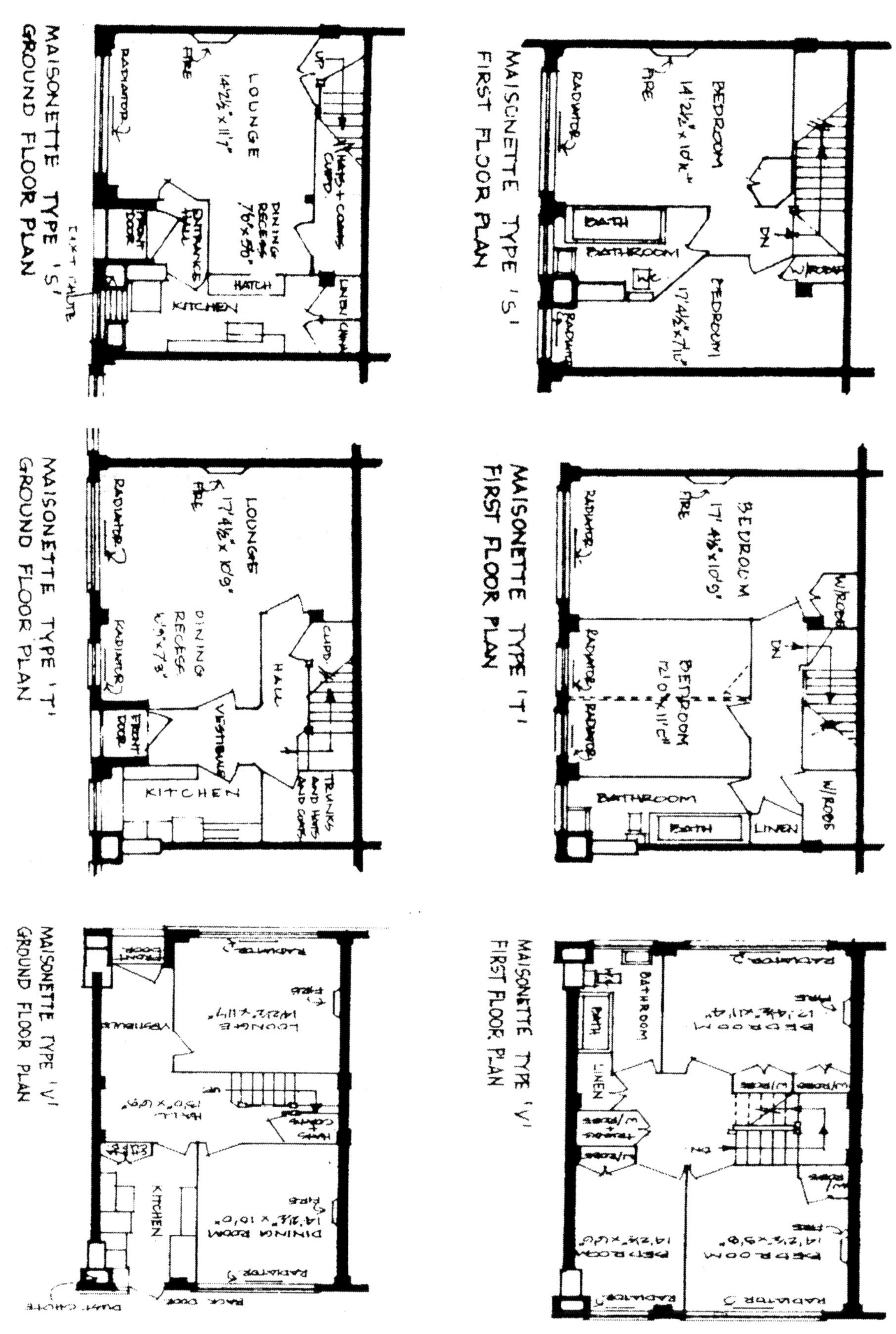

Plans for different types of maisonettes. (Courtesy of Charles Kay Green.)

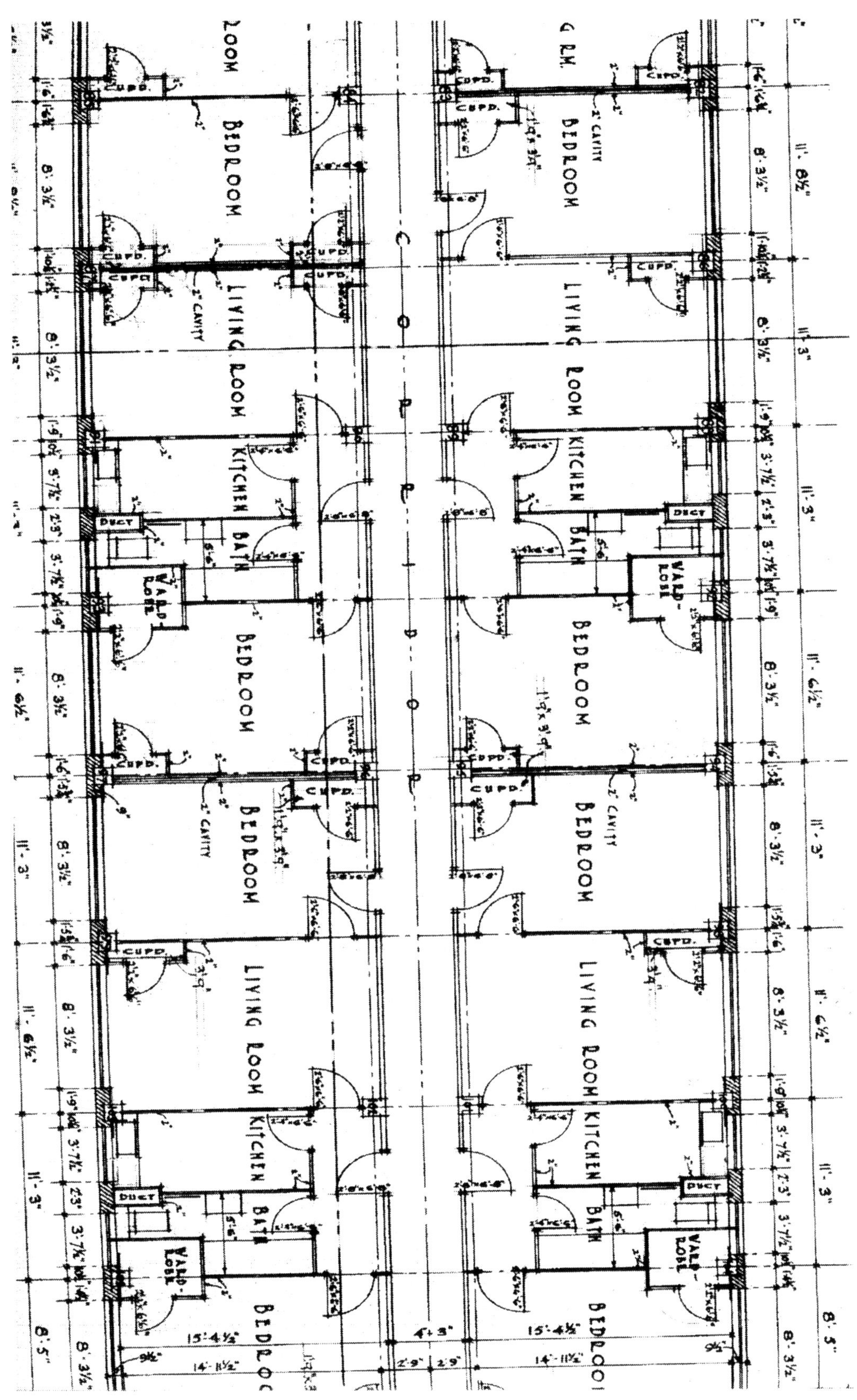

Here is the plan for H block, floors 1, 2, 3 and 6. It shows the layouts for one and two-bedroom flats. (Courtesy of Charles Kay Green.)

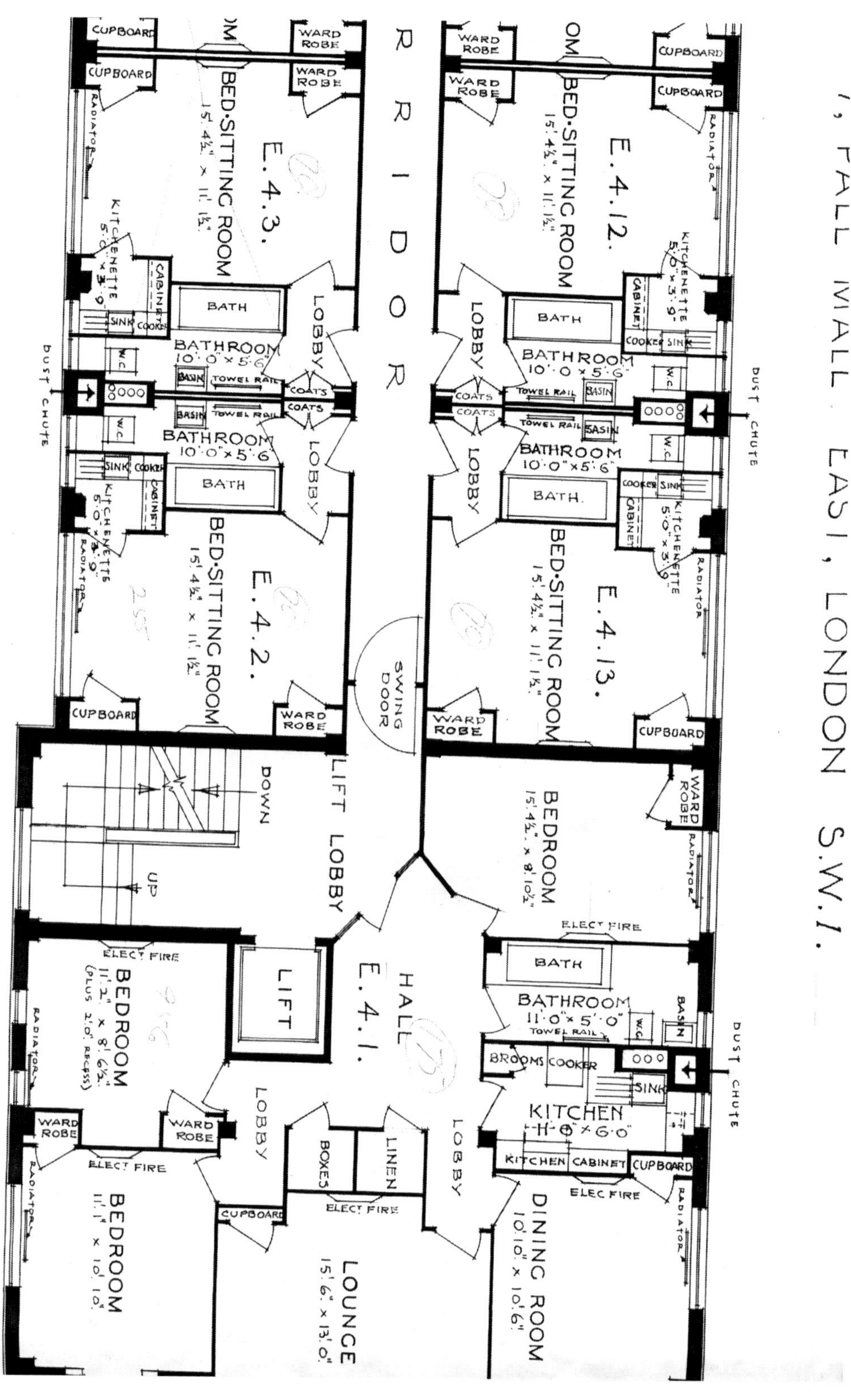

The plan for some studios on the fourth floor of E block; and for an apartment at the end of the corridor, with three bedrooms, a lounge and a dining room. The writing on the diagram was there when I acquired it. The figure '70' is mysterious, although '255' is probably the area of a studio flat in square feet. (Courtesy of Charles Kay Green.)

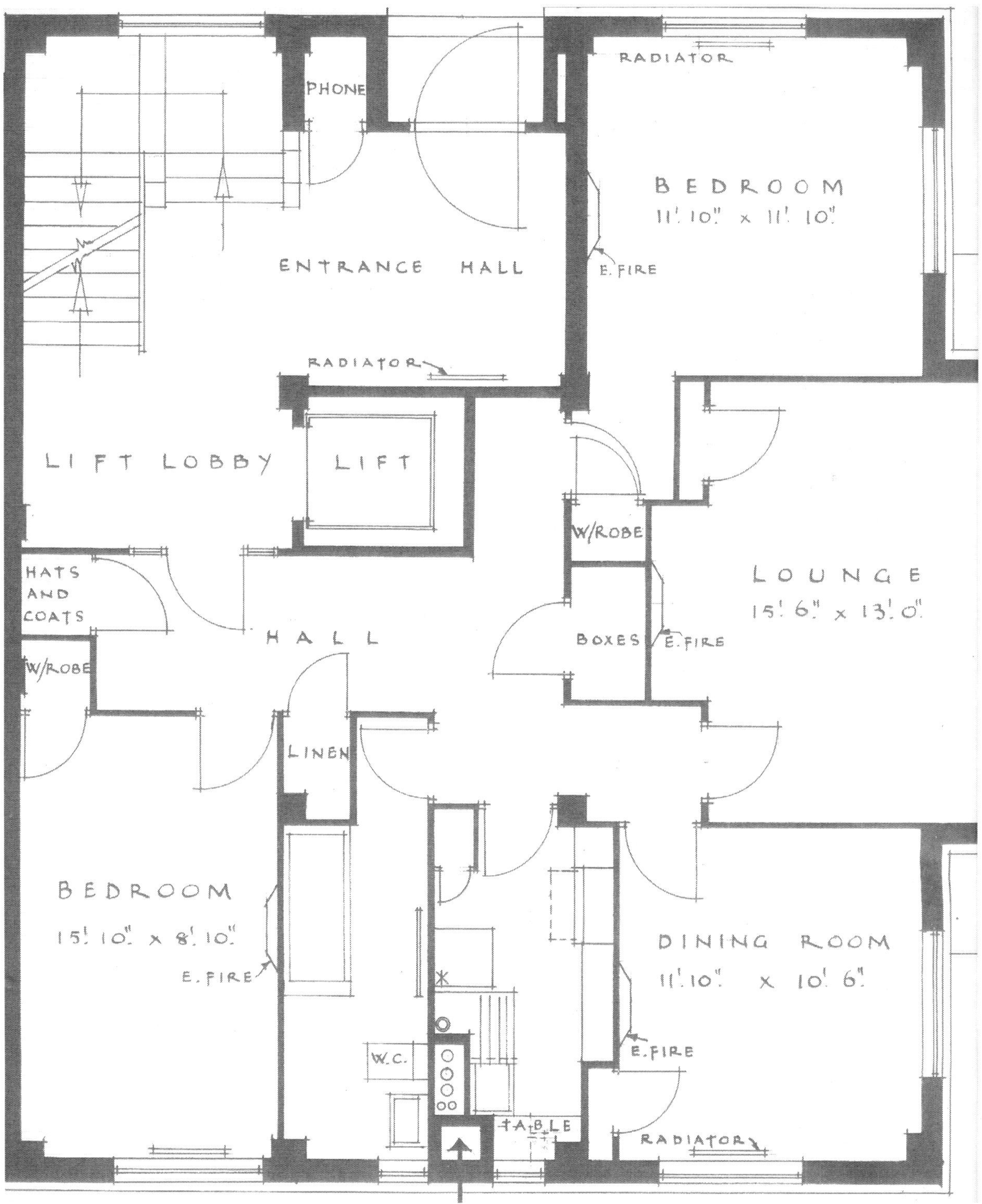

The layout of a large flat in C block. (Courtesy of Charles Kay Green.)

ENTRANCE HALL.

A view of the spacious Central Entrance Hall, showing the double main staircase, lifts, post box, and Hall Porter's kiosk.

SOUTHERN RAILWAY FARES, BALHAM to VICTORIA.				
Season Tickets.				
	1st Class.		3rd Class.	
Weekly	£0 7 0	... ...	£0 4 9	
Monthly	£1 4 9	... ...	£0 16 6	
Quarterly...	£3 7 0	... ...	£2 5 0	

CHEAP DAY TICKETS.
Are issued every week-day by all trains after 9.30 a.m. Sundays by all trains. Return by any train on the day of issue. Return Fare 1st Class -/11d., 3rd Class -/7d.

Scale of INCLUSIV

UNFURNISHED FLATS

at DU CANE

ACCORDING TO POS

FLATS		Per Annum £	s.	d.	Per Week
One roomed Flats, each with Bathroom and Kitchenette, from		70	0	0	26/11
Two roomed Flats	,,	90	0	0	34/8
Three roomed Flats	,,	130	0	0	50/-
Four roomed Flats	,,	170	0	0	65/5
Five roomed Flats	,,	190	0	0	73/1
One roomed Shared Bathroom Flats, each with separate Kitchenette		60	0	0	23/1

THE DELIGHTFUL COMMONS OF WANDSWORTH, CLAPHAM, TOOTIN

An excerpt from the 1930s brochure for the building, showing the costs for renting different flats – none were for sale in those days, – and an artist's impression of the reception area. (Courtesy of May Arkell, who lent to me her copy of the brochure.)

RESTAURANT.

This illustration shows the Restaurant, which is situated on the top floor, with the roof garden directly connecting, at the far end. In warm weather, meals will be served in the garden.

E RENTALS for

AND MAISONETTES

, COURT

ITION AND SIZE

UNDERGROUND RAILWAY FARES.				
		Season Tickets.		
From Balham.	Ordinary.	Weekly.	Monthly.	Quarterly.
Trafalgar Square ...	4d.	4/-	16/6	45/-
Piccadilly Circus ...	5d.	4/6	18/6	50/-

BUS FARES FROM BALHAM UNDERGROUND STATION.
To Trafalgar Sq. and Piccadilly Circus ... Single 5d. Return 8d.

CHEAP MID-DAY BUS FARE.
To Trafalgar Square and Piccadilly Circus. 3d. (Approximately 10 a.m. to 4 p.m. Monday to Friday only.)

MAISONETTES		Per Annum £	s.	d.	Per Week
Three roomed Maisonettes	from	130	0	0	50/-
Four roomed Maisonettes	,,	170	0	0	65/5
Five roomed Maisonettes	,,	195	0	0	75/-

THESE FLATS AND MAISONETTES REPRESENT THE BEST VALUE BEING OFFERED IN MODERN HOMES AT ECONOMICAL RENTALS IN LONDON TO-DAY

G BEC, STREATHAM AND MITCHAM ARE ALL WITHIN EASY REACH

Another excerpt from the brochure, showing the costs of renting a maisonette, and an artist's impression of the restaurant. (Courtesy of May Arkell.)

FISH.

Haddock and Poached Egg.... 1/-
Kippers (2)........................ 8d
Fillet of Plaice or Sole......... 10d
Fillet of Plaice with Chips...... 1/-
Fillet of Cod........................ 1/-
Sole Mornay (15 minutes)...... 1/6
Crab Mayonnaise.................. 1/3
Lobster Mayonnaise.............. 1/6
Salmon Mayonnaise.............. 1/3
Prawn Mayonnaise................ 1/3

ALSO SEE OTHER MENU.

SALADS.

Green (French or American dressing).......... .... 4d
French Salad........................ 5d
Egg and Salad Mayonnaise...... 9d
Tomato or Potato Salad......... 5d
Prawn, Tomato and Green Salad....... .... 1/3
Vegetable Salad.................. 1/-

VEGETABLES.

Potatoes.............................. 3d
Potatoes Mashed (large portion) 5d
Cabbage.............................. 3d
Spinach 4d
Spinach with Cream (large portion)........................... 6d
Celery................................. 5d
Carrots................................ 4d
Tomatoes............................. 4d
Asparagus (with dressing or Melted Butter).................. 9d
Mushrooms Grilled or Fried ... 1/-
Cepes Bordelaise.................. 1/6
Spanish Pimientos................ 1/-
Macaroni au Gratin.............. 9d

VARIOUS.

Butter (per portion).............. 1d
Roll.................................... 1d
Bread (2 slices).................... 1d
Cream................ .... 2d
Jam..................................... 3d
Honey.................................. 3d
Red Currant Jam (per portion) 2d
Pickles, Chutney, Horseradish (per portion).................... 2d
Mayonnaise (per portion)....... 3d
Extra Mayonnaise................. 2d
Savora 3d
Fruit Juice (Pineapple or Orange) 4d

SWEETS.

Stewed Prunes or Figs........... 4d
Stewed Apricots, Gooseberries, Peaches, Pears, Pineapple, Raspberries or Strawberries
(with Custard).................. 5d
(with Cream).................... 6d
Fruit Salad.................. .... 6d
Sweet of Menu (per portion)... 4d
Fruit Jelly.......................... 4d
Sago Pudding (20 minutes)..... 6d
Ice Cream. 6d
Banana à la Royale.............. 1/-
Pear Bordelaise (portion for 2)............................. 1/6

SANDWICHES.

Ham, Beef, Lamb, Cheese, Egg and Cress, Tomato............. 6d
Crab................................ 10d
Chicken 1/-

Du Cane Court
Balham
MENU
We cater for small and large parties in Restaurant or Private Room. All English or Continental Dishes as desired. Special Menus or the usual. See Manageress or Ring Battersea 3228.

The original menu for the restaurant, which was situated on the seventh floor of C Block. The images on this page and the page which follows have been electronically lengthened, in order to make them more readable. (Courtesy of May Arkell.)

BREAKFAST.

ENGLISH.

Tea or Coffee.
Kippers or Haddock.
Toast and Butter.
Marmalade or Jam.

1/3

Tea or Coffee.
Bacon and Egg.
Toast and Butter.
Marmalade or Jam.

1/3

Tea or Coffee.
Sausages and Tomato.
Toast and Butter.
Marmalade or Jam.

1/5

Tea or Coffee.
Bacon and 2 Eggs.
Toast and Butter.
Marmalade or Jam.

1/6

AMERICAN.

Fresh Grape Fruit.
or
Orange Juice.
Choice of Cereals or Sweet Corn.
Coffee.
Toast and Butter.
Honey or Marmalade.

1/-

Stewed Prunes
or
Fresh Grape Fruit or
Orange Juice.
Coffee or Tea.
Toast and Butter.
Honey or Marmalade.

1/-

CONTINENTAL.

Pot of Coffee or Tea.
Toast and Butter.
Marmalade or Jam.

8d

Orange Juice.
Pot of Coffee or Tea.
Toasted, Buttered French Bun.

8d

LUNCH. Our Daily Menus from :

1/3 Fish or Meat (2 veg.) Coffee or Sweet.
1/6 Soup. Fish or Meat (2 veg.) Coffee or Sweet.
2/- Soup. Fish. Meat (2 veg.) Coffee or Sweet.

OTHERWISE SEE LA CARTE.

Don't forget our Sunday Chicken Lunch.

DINNER.

Table d'Hote 1/6

Choice of Soup, Fish or Joint and 2 Vegetables,
Sweet or Coffee.

À LA CARTE.

Pot of Tea (per person)	3d
Pot of Coffee (per person)	5d
Cup of Coffee	3d
SPECIAL Coffee (black)	5d
English or French Chocolate	4d
Horlicks	5d
Bovril (small)	4d
Bovril (large)	6d
Stewed Prunes	4d
Portion of	
Bread and Butter	2d
Dry Toast	2d
Buttered Toast	3d
Marmalade	2d
Jam or Honey	3d
Tomatoes on Toast	6d
Spaghetti on Toast	6d
Baked Beans	6d
Welsh Rarebit	6d
Buck Rarebit	10d
Bacon (2 rashers)	8d
Kidney on Toast	9d
Sweet Corn	6d

CEREALS.

Puffed Rice	6d
Corn Flakes	6d
Shredded Wheat	6d
Creamed Barley	6d
Honey Grains	6d
Porridge	6d

ALL WITH JUG OF MILK.

GRILLS.

Cutlets (2)	1/-
Rump Steak	1/-
Fillet	1/6
Mixed Grill	1/9
Sausages (2)	8d
Veal Cutlets	1/6

COLD TABLE.

Ham, Tongue, Roast Beef or Lamb	2/-
One only	1/-
Roast Chicken (hot or cold)	2/-

EGGS.

Boiled Egg	4d
Poached Egg on Toast	6d
Poached Eggs on Toast	9d
Scrambled Eggs	10d
Scrambled Eggs (Portuguese)	1/-
Two Fried Eggs	8d
Omelette (plain)	9d
Omelette (Ham)	1/-
Omelette (French or German)	1/-
Egg Mayonnaise	9d

SOUPS.

Soup (see Menu)	4d
Soup Heinz (Tomato or Ox Tail)	6d
Soupe a l'Oignon Gratinee	6d
Consomme (home-made) (hot or cold)	6d
Consomme with Poached Egg	9d
Bovril	6d
Bovril with Poached Egg	9d

More items on the old restaurant menu. (Courtesy of May Arkell.)

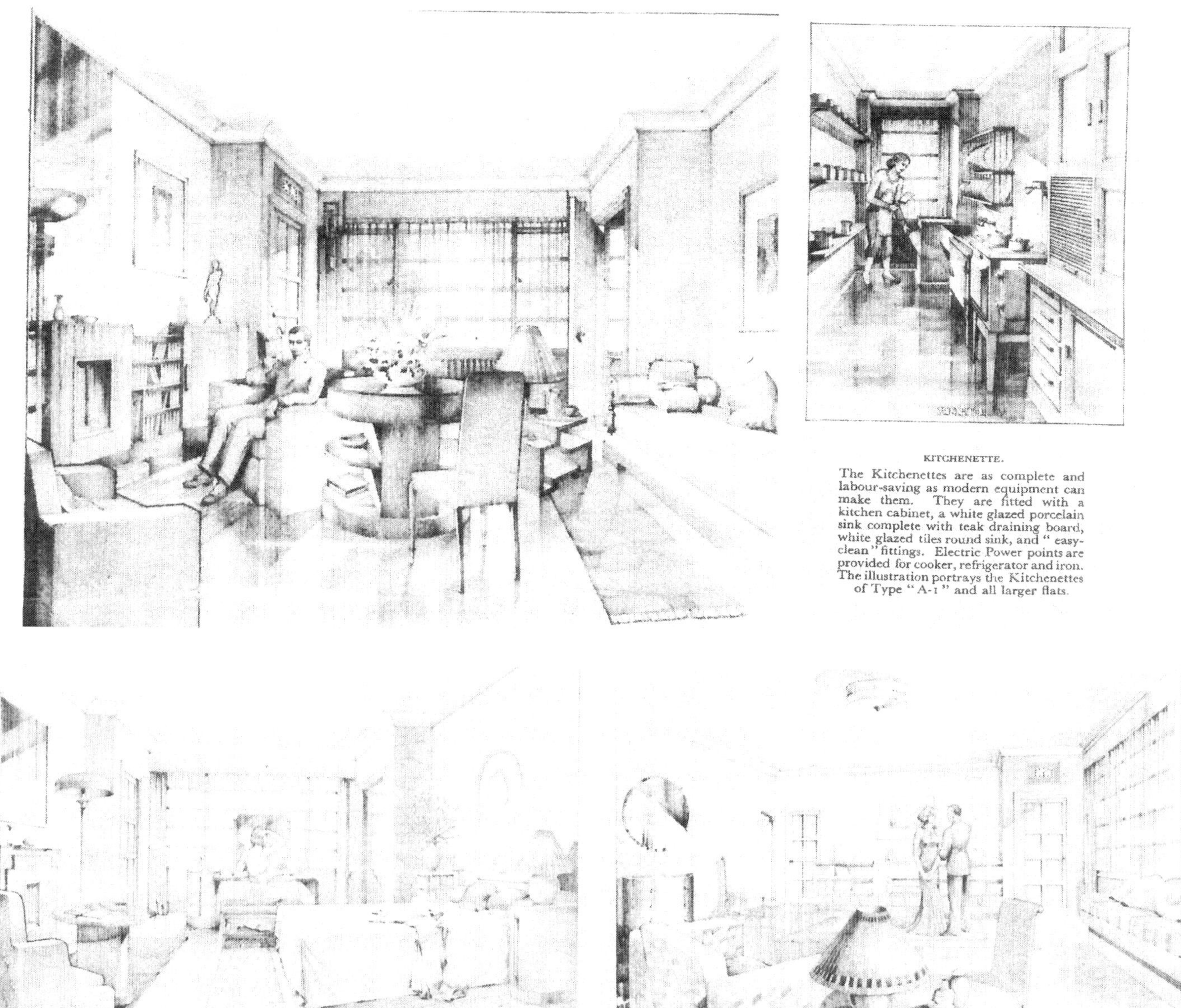

KITCHENETTE.
The Kitchenettes are as complete and labour-saving as modern equipment can make them. They are fitted with a kitchen cabinet, a white glazed porcelain sink complete with teak draining board, white glazed tiles round sink, and "easy-clean" fittings. Electric Power points are provided for cooker, refrigerator and iron. The illustration portrays the Kitchenettes of Type "A-1" and all larger flats.
BEDROOM
SITTING ROOM

An artist's impressions of what the interior of the flats would look like. The rooms appear somewhat larger than they generally are. (Courtesy of May Arkell.)

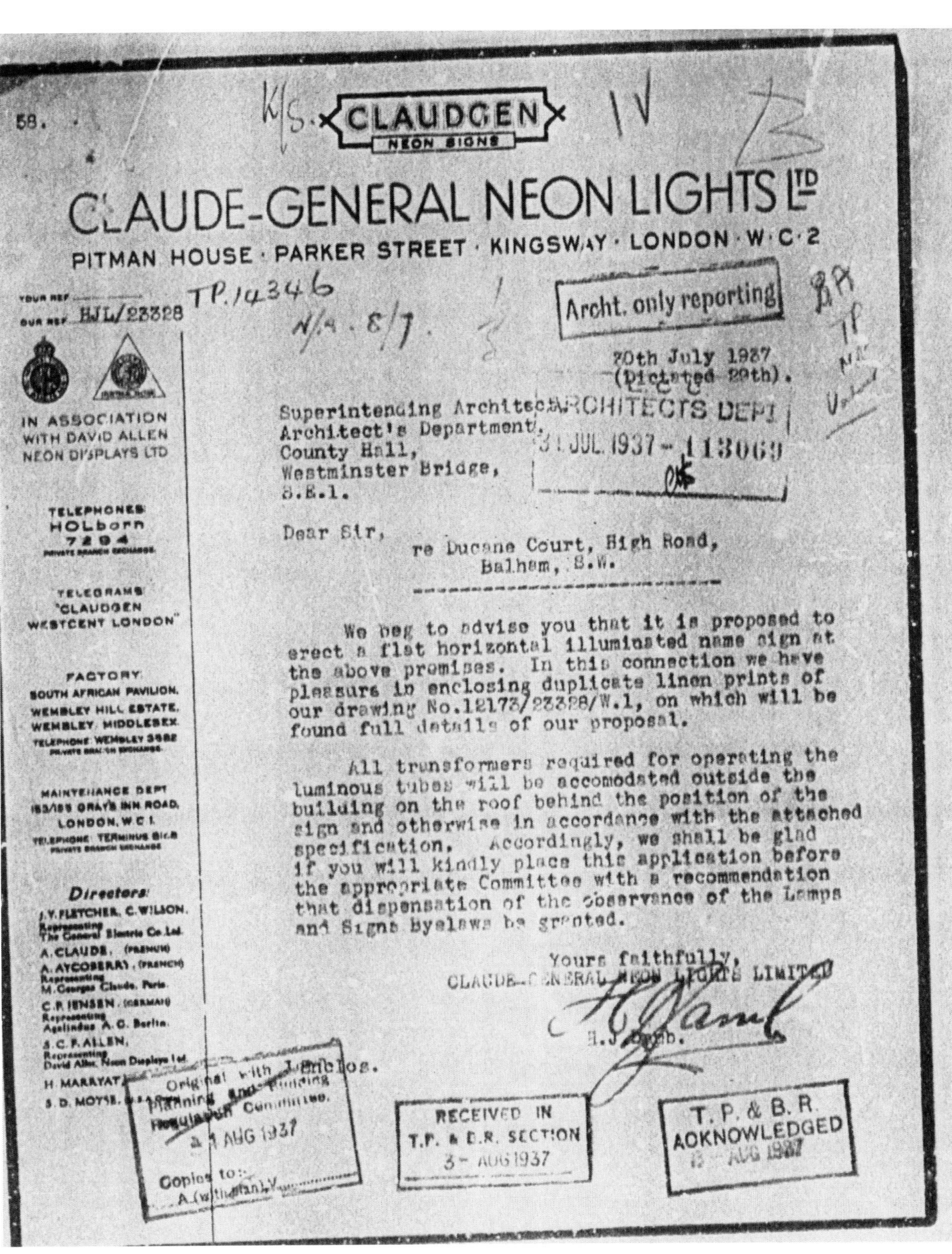

58.

CLAUDGEN
NEON SIGNS

CLAUDE-GENERAL NEON LIGHTS LTD

PITMAN HOUSE · PARKER STREET · KINGSWAY · LONDON · W·C·2

YOUR REF ....
OUR REF HJL/23328

IN ASSOCIATION WITH DAVID ALLEN NEON DISPLAYS LTD

TELEPHONES: HOLborn 7294 PRIVATE BRANCH EXCHANGE

TELEGRAMS: "CLAUDGEN WESTCENT LONDON"

FACTORY: SOUTH AFRICAN PAVILION, WEMBLEY HILL ESTATE, WEMBLEY, MIDDLESEX. TELEPHONE: WEMBLEY 3582 PRIVATE BRANCH EXCHANGE.

MAINTENANCE DEPT: 153/155 GRAY'S INN ROAD, LONDON, W.C.1. TELEPHONE: TERMINUS 81...

Directors: J.Y. FLETCHER, C. WILSON, Representing The General Electric Co. Ltd. A. CLAUDE, (FRENCH) A. AYCOBERRY, (FRENCH) Representing M. Georges Claude, Paris. C.P. JENSEN, (GERMAN) Representing Agalindus A.G. Berlin. S.C.F. ALLEN, Representing David Allen Neon Displays Ltd. H. MARRYAT, S.D. MOYSE.

TP.14346

Archt. only reporting

30th July 1937
(Dictated 29th).

ARCHITECT'S DEPT
31 JUL 1937 - 113069

Superintending Architect,
Architect's Department,
County Hall,
Westminster Bridge,
S.E.1.

Dear Sir,

re Ducane Court, High Road,
Balham, S.W.

We beg to advise you that it is proposed to erect a flat horizontal illuminated name sign at the above premises. In this connection we have pleasure in enclosing duplicate linen prints of our drawing No.12173/23328/W.1, on which will be found full details of our proposal.

All transformers required for operating the luminous tubes will be accomodated outside the building on the roof behind the position of the sign and otherwise in accordance with the attached specification. Accordingly, we shall be glad if you will kindly place this application before the appropriate Committee with a recommendation that dispensation of the observance of the Lamps and Signs Byelaws be granted.

Yours faithfully,
CLAUDE-GENERAL NEON LIGHTS LIMITED

H.J. Lamb.

Encls.

Original with Building Planning and Regulation Committee.
1 AUG 1937
Copies to: ...

RECEIVED IN
T.P. & B.R. SECTION
3 - AUG 1937

T.P. & B.R.
ACKNOWLEDGED
13 AUG 1937

In the 1930s, there was a controversial attempt to install a neon sign on the roof of Du Cane Court. The intention was to proclaim the name of the new building to the neighbourhood. (Courtesy of Wandsworth Borough Council.)

A PAGE OF PRACTICAL AND USEFUL INFORMATION FOR THOSE TAKING UP RESIDENCE AT

DU CANE COURT, BALHAM HIGH ROAD, S.W. 17

TABLE OF TIME OCCUPIED FOR JOURNEYS BY SOUTHERN RAILWAY OR UNDERGROUND.

TO VICTORIA	9 MINS.
TO WATERLOO	15 MINS.
TO CHARING CROSS	17 MINS.
TO LONDON BRIDGE	18 MINS.
TO TRAFALGAR SQUARE	18 MINS.
TO BANK	19 MINS.
TO LEICESTER SQUARE	20 MINS.
TO PICCADILLY	21 MINS.
TO MOORGATE	21 MINS.
TO LIVERPOOL STREET	22 MINS.
TO OXFORD CIRCUS	23 MINS.

BUS SERVICE TO AND FROM WEST-END.

Routes Nos. 32 and 88 pass Du Cane Court every few minutes, and proceed to the West-End via Balham High Road; High Street, Clapham; Clapham Road; South Lambeth Road; Great Smith Street; Parliament Square; Whitehall; Trafalgar Square; Piccadilly Circus; Regent Street; Oxford Circus; Oxford Street; Marble Arch; and on to their respective destinations.

Balham Underground Station to Oxford Circus by Bus, half hour, approximately.

TABLE OF DISTANCES FROM DU CANE COURT.

TO WANDSWORTH COMMON	¼ MILE.
TO TOOTING BEC COMMON	¾ MILE.
TO CLAPHAM COMMON	¾ MILE.
TO STREATHAM COMMON	2½ MILES.
TO MITCHAM COMMON	3 MILES.

SOUTHERN RAILWAY FARES, BALHAM TO VICTORIA.

	Season Tickets. 1st Class.	Season Tickets. 3rd Class.
Weekly	£0 7 0	£0 4 9
Monthly	£1 4 9	£0 16 6
Quarterly	£3 7 0	£2 5 0

CHEAP DAY TICKETS.

Cheap day tickets are issued every weekday to Victoria by all trains after 9.30 a.m. Sundays by all trains. Return by any train on the day of issue. Return Fare, 1st Class .. 11d., 3rd Class .. 7d.

UNDERGROUND RAILWAY FARES.

From Balham to :—	Ordinary.	Season Tickets. Wkly.	Mthly.	Qtly.
Trafalgar Square	4d.	4/-	16/6	45/-
Piccadilly Circus	5d.	4/6	18/6	50/-

BUS FARES FROM BALHAM UNDERGROUND STATION.

To Trafalgar Square and Piccadilly Circus:
Single 5d. Return 8d.

CHEAP MID-DAY BUS FARE.

To Trafalgar Square and Piccadilly Circus 3d. (Approximately 10 a.m. to 4 p.m., Monday to Friday only).

Although every care has been taken to present accurately the information contained in this brochure concerning the flats and maisonettes at Du Cane Court, such information, or any part of it, cannot be taken or accepted as part of any contract between Tenants and Du Cane Court, Ltd.

Some early advertising, emphasising the benefits of Du Cane Court's location. (Courtesy of Estate Office.)

16 Dec 6th 1935 THE BOROUGH NEWS.

South London's Latest Modern Luxury Flats
DU CANE COURT
BALHAM HIGH ROAD, LONDON, S.W. 17
Nine Minutes from Victoria, Nineteen Minutes from Bank, Twenty-one Minutes from Piccadilly. Within One Minute of Balham Tube Station and Balham and Upper Tooting Station (Southern Railway).
DU CANE COURT WILL BE READY For OCCUPATION ABOUT MAY, 1936
Phone: BATTersea 3674
INCLUSIVE RENTALS:
FROM £60 PER ANNUM or 23/- PER WEEK
FOR convenience and accessibility to all parts of London, these flats excel. Just think of this, for instance! There are 495 Southern Railway trains daily between Balham and Victoria, and a two minute service by Underground to the City and West End during many hours of the day. The 'bus and tram service is exceptionally good.
For health, Du Cane Court is ideally situated. The delightful commons of Wandsworth, Clapham, Tooting Bec, Streatham, and Mitcham are all within easy reach.
The amenities of DU CANE COURT include electric lifts, roof gardens, large restaurant with low tariff, central heating, constant hot water, many private balconies, and radio and electric clock to every flat. Electricity for lighting, heating and cooking is available at ½d. per unit, plus a small quarterly rate.
You should call and see the show flats of this wonderful building, which are now open for inspection.
OPEN EVERY DAY UNTIL 9.0 p.m. AND SATURDAY AFTERNOON AND ALL DAY SUNDAY.
If unable to call, use enquiry coupon provided, or send a P.C. for full particulars.
POST ENQUIRY COUPON NOW
CENTRAL LONDON PROPERTY TRUST, LTD.,
7 Pall Mall East, London, S.W.1
Please forward me the Du Cane Court fully illustrated brochure, post free, & without obligation
NAME
ADDRESS
W.B.N 6-12-35
½d stamp if envelope unsealed

Some more early advertising. (Courtesy of Estate Office.)

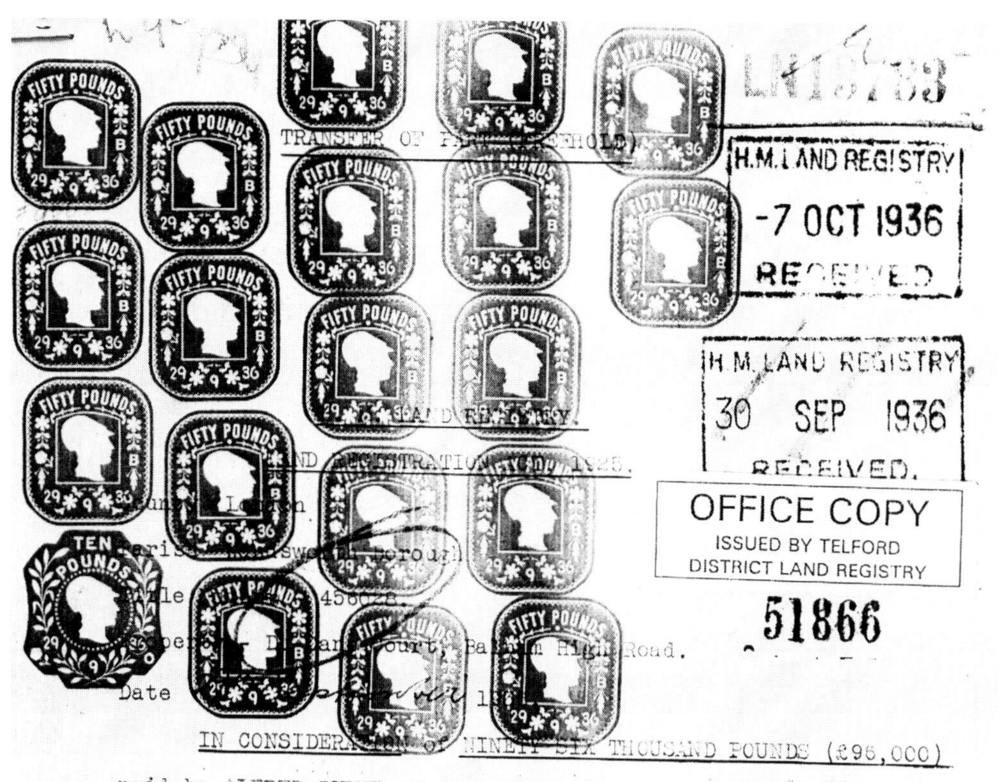

LN[illegible]

H.M. LAND REGISTRY -7 OCT 1936 RECEIVED

H.M. LAND REGISTRY 30 SEP 1936 RECEIVED.

OFFICE COPY ISSUED BY TELFORD DISTRICT LAND REGISTRY

51866

TRANSFER OF [illegible] (FREEHOLD)

LAND REGISTRY.

LAND REGISTRATION ACT 1925.

County London

Parish Wandsworth Borough

Title 456028

Property Du Cane Court, Balham High Road.

Date [illegible] 1936

IN CONSIDERATION of NINETY SIX THOUSAND POUNDS (£96,000) paid by ALFRED BYRNE THOMAS HAMBLETT J.P. and JOE GLEDHILL the Trustees of the ROYAL LIVER FRIENDLY SOCIETY whose registered office is at Royal Liver Building, Pier Head in the City of Liverpool (hereinafter referred to as "the Purchasers") out of funds in their hands as such Trustees as aforesaid to CENTRAL LONDON PROPERTY TRUST LIMITED whose registered office is at 7 Pall Mall East, S.W.1. in the County of London (hereinafter referred to as "the Vendor") the receipt of which sum is hereby acknowledged the Vendor as BENEFICIAL OWNER hereby transfers unto the Purchasers ALL THAT piece of land (part of the land comprised in the Title above referred to) with the block of flats erected thereon known as Section One, Du Cane Court situate on the northwesterly side of Balham High Road and southeasterly side of Balham Park Road in the County of London more particularly delineated and coloured pink red and brown on the plan hereto annexed but except and excluding such portion of the land as is coloured blue on the said plan which it is intended shall be conveyed to the London County Council for the purposes of the Metropolis Management Act 1855 the Local Government Act 18[illegible]

INLAND REVENUE PRODUCED FINANCE ACT 1931

The Royal Liver Friendly Society purchased the estate from the Central London Property Trust over two transactions, the first of these in 1936. (Courtesy of Companies House, and of the Land Registry.)

THE GARDENS AT DU CANE COURT

*

A Growing Love of Gardens

In the 1920s and '30s, the garden began to have a special place in English life. House owners lavished their spare time on growing not only flowers, but also vegetables and fruits. The introduction of 'Daylight Saving' in 1916, coupled with reduced working hours after World War 1, made it easier for the populace to have such a pastime; and even the large apartment blocks of the period must have been designed with this new fashion in mind, for they were often surrounded by lush green spaces and pleasant floral displays.

The courtyards at Du Cane Court were the brain-child of a Japanese landscape gardener, Seyemon Kusumoto. They are attractive, and oriental in an understated way – although they were not always well maintained and, at present, only the external courtyard with the water feature is truly Japanese in conception. Japanese garden features are now quite popular in the UK. Tiny but exquisitely formed bonsai trees can be purchased from local florists, and there are public gardens created in the Japanese style, the Kyoto Garden at Holland Park being a prominent example.

So how deep are the roots of this style in our green and pleasant land? In fact, an interest in Japanese culture was already growing in the early years of the twentieth century [Jellicoe.et.al]. One thinks of Puccini's 'Madame Butterfly' (1904), and of a book – the first of its kind - called 'The Flowers and Gardens of Japan' (1908), by Florence and Ella Du Cane. The two sisters wrote several travel books together, Florence producing the text, and Ella, the illustrations; and, with our own gardens in mind, it is tempting to think that they might have passed on their enthusiasm for this alternative mode of horticulture to significant others within their family.

The author, Judith Conway, has found references to nearly eighty Japanese gardens in England that were constructed before 1935, when work on Du Cane Court was begun; but probably the best documented garden of this kind in the British isles is 'Cowden' in Perthshire. It was created in 1907, after the person who commissioned it, Ella Christie, had spent a year in Japan. There, she had met the writer and artist team of Florence and Ella Du Cane, one of whom may have suggested the name of a capable practitioner for the job (Kusumoto, perhaps?) – although in the end Ms Christie chose someone else.

The Japanese Influence at Du Cane Court

A Chinese visitor to England once asked: 'Why do you have lawns? They may be of interest to a cow, but what is there to stimulate the intellect?' And the same sentiment is expressed through Japanese gardens, where almost everything is imbued with some ulterior meaning. Lanterns are quintessential, and there are two of them in each of our outer courtyards. They symbolize a light source which will illuminate an adjacent pathway. There are even different kinds of lantern. Stacked lanterns (like pagodas) have three light chambers, representing earth, water and sky [Gustafson]; while two of our own have cloud and wave motifs. In Japanese gardens, no path is straight and no two garden sculptures are identical. This lack of symmetry is a key difference from the traditional English garden, and conveys the idea that one's path through life is ever-changing.

There are stone lanterns at Du Cane Court which are quite possibly original artifacts from Japan. However, one or two lanterns may be concrete or bronze, and therefore manufactured elsewhere. Concrete ones can be bought easily enough, but they are more porous than stone, and could chip or crack in freezing conditions. Also, the high alkaline surface will not allow the growth of decorative moss or lichen. Fortunately, a few sprays of buttermilk lowers the Ph level, and adds a film of nutrition on which airborne moss can grow, while vinegar may be applied to help it age gracefully – for in Japan, ancient things are venerated.

I have heard that there used to be an arch made out of wire, in the middle of the southern courtyard at the front of the block; and that all of the courtyards possibly contained ponds at one point, with bridges crossing over two of them. (Sadly, we have only one pond now, which I understand was not completed until after the building was finished.) Bridges are a popular Japanese characteristic, and where they are arched, the partial circle of the reflection is viewed as a phase of the moon. The remaining pond at Du Cane Court is stocked with koi carp, and needs to be at least six feet deep to allow these fish to escape from the cold weather in winter; although a skin of frost on the surface does have an insulating effect.

Koi carp can be very expensive. They breathe through their mouths and may grow tame enough to feed out of your hand, although most breeders say the fish should not be touched in case oils are transferred from the hand to the scales. Heavy metals are toxic to fish, so we must discourage visitors from dropping a coin into the water and making a wish that they will return one day ... mind you, a miniature Trevi Fountain could be a valuable source of income for those residents who struggle to pay their bills!

We have exotic plants such as the Japanese Maple, which may yield pink and green fruits called samaras; and the small, dainty Japanese Anemone. There are also cherry trees and evergreens; and bamboo in one of the inner courtyards. All of these are in keeping with the ethos. When hollowed out, bamboo can form part of a most unusual timepiece, receiving a stream of water until it can hold no more, tipping the contents away, and then oscillating back to the starting point with a tiny knock. In this way it punctuates short periods in a time of meditation, instructing the subject when to leave one theme and turn to another; and it would be romantic to speculate upon whether such a device might once have enriched these gardens of ours.

On the other hand, the trees are now too high, and the lawn too extensive, for the Japanese style. The fountain is really a western feature, although water *is* important in Japanese gardens as well, and would flow from east to west. The onions, growing behind the bushes near the front entrance, and the limestone rocks around our pond, would also be atypical. In Japan, the rocks are made of granite; but irrespective of their composition, they have a salient role to play. They can stand guard like sentinels, but one author I have referenced goes further. For Gustafson, rocks may be seen as the backbone of the landscape, with water as its life blood and the topsoil like skin; whilst the water pump becomes a metaphor for the human heart.

The Japanese do not favour bright colours, as they like their gardens to emanate a certain tranquility; and apparently the text on one of our lanterns means 'a time of great peace'. Perhaps it was an expression of relief after World War 1? Either way, and whatever the vicissitudes of life later on, the grounds worked their magic on an apprentice gardener, Robert Walker, who was only 17 when Du Cane Court was built, - for he would return like a homing pigeon to the site of his former employment every year, to visit his friend, Marion Hopkins, and to attend to the pond that he, perhaps, had once helped to create.

Kusumoto's Other Work

Our landscape designer writes in a 1936 article that the Japanese generate 'the best of nature's handiwork in a limited space' – and this feature surely makes their ideas an asset in any densely populated area. According to the Garden History Society website, he was involved with about 200 gardens in the UK. Among these were several noteworthy projects in England. In 1937, he exhibited a rock garden, with lanterns and dwarf conifers, at the Chelsea Flower Show [Gdnrs.Chronicle], the previous year having reproduced part of the renowned Silver Pavilion Gardens (of Kyoto in Japan), for Mr A.H. Winham's Burngreave Estate at Bognor Regis. His creation was called Kyoto Court, but sadly it does not exist any more.

He also redesigned the Japanese garden at Cottered, near Buntingford in East Hertfordshire (Grid Reference GD1545; English Heritage Register TL3129). Work on the grounds was begun in 1905 by Herbert Goode, and continued until 1937 [HMBC.Gdn.Reg.]. Kusumoto made his contribution between 1923 and 1926, adding an ornamental garden and a woodland of two hectares. The place is open to the public on just one day each year.

Kusumoto was a Fellow of the Royal Horticultural Society.
His design firm was established in 1923, and catered for a range of requirements. At the time of the Chelsea Flower Show (1937), two addresses are given for him: 8 Monkville Parade, Temple Fortune, London NW11; and 64 Hendon Way, London NW2. Kelly's Hendon Directory confirms that he was at the second of these addresses in 1937 and 1938.

What Became of Him?

Our landscape gardener hailed from a country which we would soon be at war with, and we might well wonder what became of him. One person I spoke to felt that he may have been interned. Of course, another possibility is that he went back to Japan. At any rate, the following information, which I obtained through NHS Traceline, shows that he was here at the end of his days:

Seyemon Ruichi Kusumoto. Landscape Gardener, retired. Died 19th May, 1968, at the General Hospital Peace Memorial Wing, Watford. Cause of death: carcinomatosis, cancer of the prostate (Death Certificate, General Register Office).

The widow of the deceased was A.F. Kusumoto – living at 35 Camrose Avenue, Edgware, in Middlesex. According to Directory Enquiries, there are currently no people with his surname living in Middlesex in 2007, and only two addresses are recorded against 'Kusumoto' in London, both of which are x-directory.

Some salient records could have been destroyed, and there is possibly only one photograph of our landscape gardener in existence, taken by a certain Neville Chuck and apparently displayed at Cottered. Naturally, I have written to the owners of this heritage site, and also had the good fortune to speak to the photographer himself. Neville told me that he took the picture in 1962, and formed the impression that his subject was amiable and looked quite young for his years. At some point, Kusumoto may have owned a place in Oxhey, Watford. He married a local girl, and had a daughter; but I have not succeeded in contacting any surviving relatives.

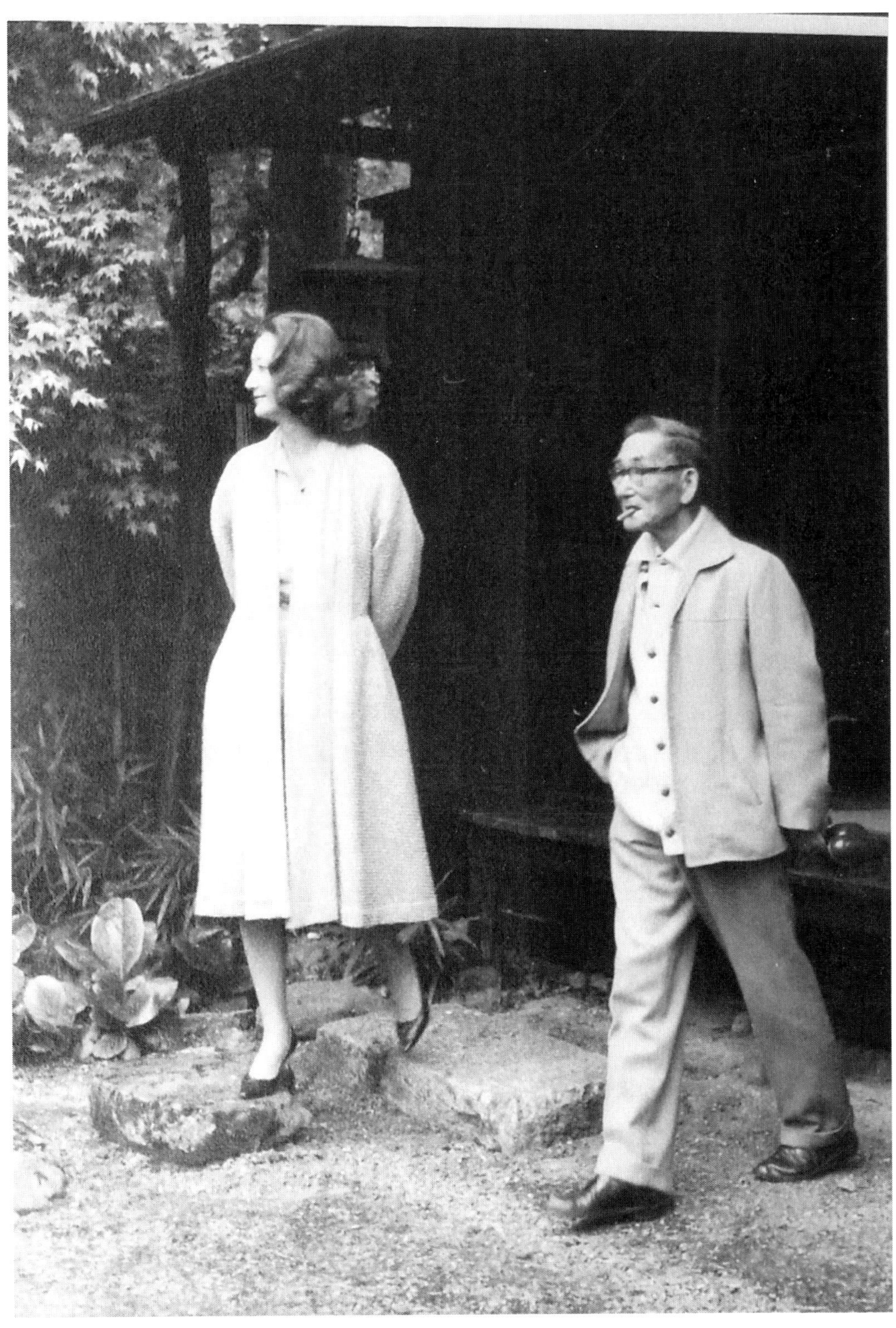

A photograph from the early 1960s of Kusumoto, who designed the Japanese gardens at Du Cane Court. He is shown with his daughter. (Courtesy of Neville Chuck.)

Section of 8 Acre Garden in Hertfordshire.

Established 1923

Phone: ~~EDGWARE 5969~~ & WA. 36086

INTERNATIONAL GARDENS

LANDSCAPE ARCHITECTS & CONTRACTORS

Kays Nursery & Office:
~~122 STATION ROAD, EDGWARE, MIDDX.~~
and at
55 HAMPERMILL LANE, OXHEY, WATFORD.

JAPANESE GARDENS AND GARDENS OF EVERY TYPE ANCIENT AND MODERN

SEYEMON KUSUMOTO, F.R.H.S.

The following are a few of the Gardens I have designed and executed:

THE CHEYNES, COTTERED, HERTS.

DALMORE, WINNINGTON ROAD, N.2.

THE SOUTH WINDS, WHITCHURCH ON THAMES, OXON.

DOWNVIEW COURT, WINCHELSEA GARDENS, HASTING COURT, ETC., WORTHING.

SAN REMO TOWERS, BOURNEMOUTH.

KYOTO COURT, BOGNOR REGIS.

THE GRAND HOTEL, SANDOWN, I.O.W.

CORTLANDS, RICHMOND, SURREY, ETC.

PATRONISED BY MANY WELL-KNOWN PERSONALITIES.

MEDALS FROM ROYAL HORTICULTURAL SOCIETY AT CHELSEA FLOWER SHOW.

Neville G.Chuck Esq,
I5 The Crescent,
Cottred,
Nr, Buntingford,

23rd
30th June,1962.

Dear Mr, Chuck,

Thank you so much for your kind letter and enclosures regarding my visit to the Japanese garden at Cottered.

It was indeed a most pleasant surprise to receive the article and photograph and if it is at all possible I would very much appreciate a further copy of the photograph. Perhaps you would let me know if this can be done and advise me of the cost.

Once again many thanks,

Yours sincerely,

Seyemon Kusumoto

Seyemon Kusumoto,

A letter from Kusumoto to the photographer, Mr Chuck; notable for the information it contains on Kusumoto's other work. (Courtesy of Neville Chuck.)

HC 737042

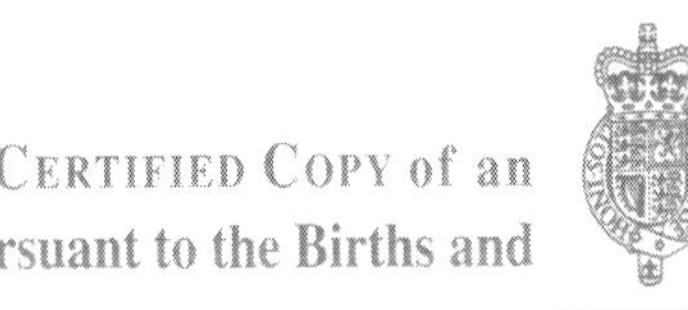

CERTIFIED COPY of an ENTRY OF DEATH
Pursuant to the Births and Deaths Registration Act 1953

Registration District Watford

1968. Death in the Sub-district of Watford First in the County of Hertford

Columns: -	1	2	3	4	5	6	7	8	9
No.	When and where died	Name and surname	Sex	Age	Occupation	Cause of death	Signature, description, and residence of informant	When registered	Signature of registrar
171	Nineteenth May 1968 General Hospital Peace Memorial Wing Watford	Seyemon Roichi KUSUMOTO	Male	73 years	of 35 Camrose Avenue Edgware Middlesex Landscape Gardener Retired	1 (a) Carcinomatosis (b) Ca of Prostate Certified by Michael Davis MB	A.F. Kusumoto Widow of Deceased 35 Camrose Avenue Edgware	Twentieth May 1968	D. Judge Deputy Registrar

Certified to be a true copy of an entry in a register in my custody. .... Walter additional Superintendent Registrar

20.6.2001 Date

CAUTION: THERE ARE OFFENCES RELATING TO FALSIFYING OR ALTERING A CERTIFICATE AND USING OR POSSESSING A FALSE CERTIFICATE. ©CROWN COPYRIGHT

WARNING: A CERTIFICATE IS NOT EVIDENCE OF IDENTITY.

Kusumoto's Death Certificate, supplied by NHS Traceline, courtesy of General Register Office.

A TRIP DOWN MEMORY LANE

*

It is curious to observe how an area changes over time, and yet how, even in distant decades, it already contained the roots of life as one now knows it.

Long ago, before Du Cane Court was even conceived of, Thomas Hardy lived at no.1, Arundel Terrace, Trinity Road. A friend of mine, who resides in 'the Court', even claims a remote familial link to him. Balham High Road used to be much narrower than it is today. The estate agents, John Dean's, which is still a presence in the locality (and always advertising flats for sale in the block), once occupied the site where Abbey National stands; and there was Mudge the watchmaker and Balham High School for girls (since replaced by Irene House). A key source of entertainment was the 'Royal Duchess Theatre', later to become the 'Hippodrome', which every Du Cane Court resident of a certain age will remember. It was situated at the corner of Yukon Road and Balham Hill, and signalled to outsiders the area's burgeoning connection to the histrionic world. A number of well-known entertainers appeared there and the plays of Shakespeare were performed[Ablett.&.Short].

Shortly after the arrival of Du Cane Court came the Balham Odeon, in 1938, which must have been a popular haunt of many residents, and which remained open until 1979. It is now a 'Majestic Wine' warehouse.

Early Days at Du Cane Court

One of the most engaging of our elderly residents was a lady called Paddy Flawn. She led a full life – and was formerly a concert singer, and latterly a bridge player. Debbie King has rendered a charismatic portrait of her through her lively conversation:

'I moved here in 1940 to share with a friend whose husband was at sea,' said Ms Flawn. Earlier in life she had been a hostess for the New Zealand forces club, and would often cook for six on a Baby Belling stove ...

'I'd buy a leg of lamb from Walter, the butcher across the road. He was a character - always drunk. Once we found him in the gutter clutching a ship's mast.' Miss Flawn also recalled the time when she saw a man riding a bicycle along one of the corridors wearing 'not a stitch of clothing'.

'In the early days all visitors were accompanied by a page boy. If we were listening to the radio the Head Porter could interrupt and relay a message from our visitor at reception.'

By all accounts, Du Cane Court operated rather like a hotel. It is even rumoured that there was a seamstress, who might, perhaps, have prepared a lady's frock prior to her evening out. And there was a magnetism about the place, for it was not only the gardener's apprentice who kept returning. A recent manager, Andrew McKeer, told me:

'The present clock in the foyer may well have been the original one, and a specialist would return – even after retirement - to service it, which is just as well, as he was the only one with the requisite expertise. To begin with, it probably ran off the mains, but now it is battery driven.'

The early managers are clearly remembered by Mrs Beerman ...

'In order, there was Miss Summerville, Mr Jackson, and then Mrs Whelpton, who was very businesslike. Miss Summerville was the manageress when I moved in - a wonderful lady, and very well-spoken, who showed us around five flats before we eventually settled on one. She was middle-aged, wore a white blouse and a black skirt, and her hair was taken back in a bun.'

Mr Jackson took over in about 1940 and lived at Carshalton Beeches during the war. Mrs Whelpton was his secretary. Initially she was in charge of the guestrooms.

One commentator says that all of the porters wore a top hat and a morning coat. Another adds some period colour: 'They were dressed in green uniforms which had silver buttons, while the Head Porter wore a black jacket and striped trousers.' Apparently, the porters also had gold braid on their collars, and they were still wearing their green uniforms in 1964. Mrs Beerman found them to be very amiable. One of them was Polish, and his mother would sell newspapers outside the block to businessmen on their way to work in the morning.

People moved in and out quite rapidly in the early days because, at £10 per month for a 2-bedroom flat, the place was too dear for them. Yet there were others who intended to come just for a year, and ended up staying a lifetime.

A Memorable Ambience

Mrs Borris, who arrived in 1938, says her sister owned a big flat here, and it seems that Du Cane Court offered a world where everyone could mingle freely. One day, after meeting the famous comedian, Tommy Trinder, Mr Borris decided he wanted to be on stage; but his mother told him: 'No. You are the main bread winner. You must earn a living.' Harry Roy, the bandleader, was said to be here as well – although no one remembers such celebrities performing in front of an audience within the building's social facilities. (There were talented people here both before and after the war, but for convenience I have written at length about the early celebrities in one place in the next chapter.)

Mrs Borris recalls how happy everyone was then.

'Things have changed a lot,' she says. I was glad of the communal areas for socialising and relaxation, and I think we could have benefited from them today - because you know, dear, there are a lot of lonely people here.'

Jessie Boran, who arrived in 1941, spoke of the dour war years, and yet there was optimism about the future. Marian Hopkins told me that, 'in spite of the rationing, people probably ate a balanced diet and they seemed to be much healthier. And they were so friendly. I have kept in touch with friends I've known from childhood. There were open-topped buses, and the transport service was better than it is now.' It seems life could be quite exciting for her too ...

'When I worked for the Department of Agriculture and Fisheries, I met Winston Churchill, Lord Sainsbury and the Queen Mother.'

According to Jean Evans, 'everyone knew each other and everyone was helpful, but this is less the case now'. It seems there are many who eulogize the past, but whatever we gain in one respect, we may lose in another. Time is a strange phenomenon. When I arrived, it seemed that the population of the building had a high average age, whereas now there are new arrivals who come unburdened by the very years which I have accumulated! Yet if time changes our surroundings, it must change us as well, for to another we are part of them.

The Social Facilities of Du Cane Court

The restaurant is marked on one of the original plans for the building, dated the 4th of February, 1935, just three weeks after the conveyancing of the land. Clearly, it was a seminal part of the design, and was intended to be truly international. The menu offered an English, American and Continental breakfast; scrambled eggs prepared in the Portuguese style, a French or German omelette, and Bovril with poached egg; but the most expensive items were either roast chicken from the *a la carte* menu, or a four course set lunch, - both for exactly two shillings[Rick.Jones].

The restaurant, decorated in green, was on the seventh floor of C block, and it afforded a fine view over London. As you entered, the bar lounge was to your left and the dance floor was at the end.

Jessie Boran remembered courting her husband and dancing there. She told me:

'There was a piano played by Eddy Wheeler, and perhaps a violin and saxophone. The dais was near the window and could support a two-piece or three-piece band. The bar was the venue for wonderful new years' parties. People would join hands and sing and dance in the corridors. And a barman called Jimmy made wonderful beverages (Tommy Trinder would simply have a light ale), but I never saw anyone drunk up there. Then one day Jimmy closed the bar down and made off with the money. I couldn't believe it.'

Apart from the restaurant, the focus for social gatherings was a club of ample proportions on the seventh floor of H block – where there are now three apartments: H71, H72 and H73. The décor was green and black, and the facilities included a billiards room, a cards room, a reading and writing room, a bar, and lavatories; and there was the opportunity to play table-tennis or darts. In the architectural drawings, special provision was also made for the staff. A flat on the ground floor of block B was reserved for the use of the manager; and on the eighth floor, or the roof, there were (besides two tank rooms) a staff dining room, a kitchen and a scullery.

The Prospect of War

In the 1930s, there was growing recognition that private buildings might have to withstand the ravages of war: a daunting prospect, indeed, for previous conflicts had not involved damage to private property, except in the case of invasion. There was much talk about England being unready for this trauma, but, fortunately, a sense of humour is never more apparent than when a dark future is presaged, and there was a delightful quip in one of the journals of the time: Question. Why does a steel frame underlie all modern buildings? Answer: Because in an air-raid, when the bricks fly off, the occupants can still hang on to the joists!

One article [JRIBA.16/10/39] speaks of the part architecture could play in winning the war, and in the peace which followed. Yet there was real concern for the profession, for the first effect of war was said to 'sweep out of sight almost every job in hand or in prospect'. Du Cane Court had been completed just in time. Several years later, the money would not have been forthcoming for such an ambitious venture. But what about the building's immediate future? Well, there was some comfort in a British Steelwork Association advert of the time, which referred to the Ministry of Health when it claimed that 'a frame building is the type that will offer the greatest resistance to blast pressure' [JRIBA.20/3/39]; but with a gas supply to flats at the front of Du Cane Court, some residents might have been concerned by the opinion [JRIBA.8/5/39] that gas mains should be shut off because of the risk of fire.

Apparently, an air attack could involve three main types of bomb: incendiary, gas and high-explosive [JRIBA.27/6/38]. Most steel and concrete buildings of the 1930s were deemed to be safe from the incendiary effects; and furthermore, 13½ inch brick walls or 12 inch concrete walls would protect against splinters from a 500 lb bomb bursting 50 feet away. The first point was good news, but regarding the second – as I have mentioned, the walls were not that thick.

Du Cane Court during the War

In World War 11, many citizens evacuated to the country, leaving Du Cane Court comparatively empty and quiet. In its short tenure it had become highly fashionable, but by the end of 1939 'they were virtually begging people to move in'. The prevailing opinion was that the place was a death trap. The freeholders must have been concerned and, to make matters worse, the Landlord and Tenant (War Damage) Act of 1939 was complicated. In theory, it was drafted so that both owner and tenant may obtain rough justice from a settlement, but essentially the act was biased against the property owner [JRIBA.16/10/39]. So, perhaps in a fit of desperation, the flats were rented out cheaply. Foreign Office juniors moved in; and for the Polish arriving on these shores with nothing, the building became a refuge from persecution - just as England had once been for the Huguenots.

There is a plaque commemorating Wladyslaw Sikorski, leader of the Polish Free Forces; and what is now the Rubens Hotel, on Buckingham Palace Road opposite the Royal Mews, was the site of their headquarters. It is possible that the Polish government (which was in exile) did a deal with our landlords or management, persuading them to take a number of refugees; and there is a rumour that most of block A was inhabited by Polish officers (and their wives and girlfriends reputedly lived in the building as well). Indeed, such was the influx of people from this downtrodden nation, that when the bus or tram stopped outside Du Cane Court, the call would be heard: 'Anyone for the Polish Corridor?'

Inside the Block

Some people lived in their flats during the day, and would hide in the cellars at night. Louisa Wheway, however, chose to remain in her maisonette even during the air raids, for fear that part of the building might collapse and imprison those who were in the basement. There were no dugouts in the grounds, although many houses would have had Anderson Shelters in their gardens; and wardens with 'ARP' on their arms were available to direct citizens to those shelters which lay above ground in all of the roads.

Jean Evans says that in those dark days no bomb ever hit Du Cane Court, and she has no memory of any fire or explosion on the premises. So gradually people began to feel that the block was pretty safe after all. Mrs Beerman and her husband were among those who were blazing a trail of confidence. They arrived in 1940, and from 1945 lived here with their young child. They chose not to make use of any bomb shelter, and besides, Mr Beerman was too tired after a day's work to be bothered going out again.

'We'll be safe here,' he said. In his work as an ambulance driver he saw some terrible things, which hardened the proverbial arteries and made him fearless. His wife would go into the hallway to escape the noise of the bombs, and others would join her. They may have been wary of shards of glass from exploding windows – although at least window frames in 1930s blocks were surrounded by a thick layer of putty, and so presumably they could absorb shock waves better than the conventional wooden frames. Another, more general, safeguard - which tenants could have organized by themselves – was to apply sticky tape and brown paper directly to the panes of glass. Yet windows did not always behave in a predictable way. Some in the vicinity of an explosion remained intact, whilst others at a distance were destroyed[Shaw.&.Mills].

At Du Cane Court, curtains had to be drawn at night, and if there was so much as a chink of light you were told about it. Net curtains were also required; and one resident, who lives in a maisonette, told me that before she came, the glass on the outside doors was painted black. Imagine the scene. You would be ensconced in your living room with the radio on, shut away from the madness of the outside world – like the disciples before the second coming – when, quite unexpectedly, an announcement from the manager, Mr Jackson, would break through the airwaves. He could sound like a prime minister addressing his citizens:

'Du Cane Court calling! Du Cane Court calling! A flat on the second floor in H block has the light on, and the blackout curtains are not drawn. There is an air raid tonight.' In fact, some flats may still have their original blackout curtains.

Fire Watching

A warden's lookout post on the roof would have been a common feature of large residential blocks. From there, he could have taken stock of the local mayhem, and raised the alarm when danger was imminent. Paddy Flawn remembered firewatching at Du Cane Court, and another resident, Sylvia Say, said that her mother was involved.

'She wore a tin hat and smoked like a trooper', said Sylvia with her inimitable smile. Apparently the process was quite well-organised, occurring on the roofs by all four courtyards and in the gardens. Rotas were set up, and those on duty were issued with armbands labelled appropriately. The participants probably used torches for signalling to each other – or maybe just to improve visibility in the dark; and 'hurricane lamps' would have been employed on every floor. When information had to be relayed, a runner could have sprinted to one of the telephones in the corridors. For many Londoners, the immediate antidotes to an impending disaster were heavy sandbags and 'stirrup water pumps'. Firewatchers were essentially dedicated to their own building, and, beyond that, the prevailing ethos was: 'every man for himself'.

Children in Wartime

People today often speak of the effect of a father's absence upon family dynamics; and on this note, the impact of war upon childhood is poignantly expressed by a little story told to me by a resident, Emily Quarman, who survived both of the great wars:

'My father went to war when I was two years old. One day in 1917, when I was only five and busy playing, my mother told me that he had died in service. "Has he?" I said blankly, and carried on skipping. I never saw my father and I never expected him to come home. He meant nothing to me.'

In the Second World War, children were moved to the countryside for their own safety; but by February, 1940, many of them had returned, and, as there were no schools open, they were roaming the streets. Gangs were fighting each other, and there were many acts of burglary and general theft. Set against this background, it is hardly surprising that youngsters were not welcome at Du Cane Court. However, even adults may have struggled to 'tow the line', for managers were stringent in the enforcement of their rules; and, I was told, with Mrs Whelpton in charge you could do nothing without criticism.

A Catalogue of Disasters

On the 14th of October, 1940, at the height of the blitz, the government appealed to everyone to refrain from using the underground stations as shelters, as this 'impeded the flow of passengers' and 'disrupted the service'. The request was ignored [Shaw.&.Mills]. At about 8pm a large, high explosive bomb penetrated the high road, leaving a crater outside Cullins foodstore near Balham Station and piercing the underground, where some 500 people were sheltering. Water mains and sewage pipes were ruptured, and an avalanche of earth and debris swept into the station, killing around 68 people and injuring many others. Apparently, torches were switched on and off in the darkness, and a boat was floated up the tunnel from Clapham South in an abortive attempt to save the day.

Mrs Beerman recalled the incident, and the 88 bus which careered into the hole, and says that the area was cordoned off. Another resident remembers walking past and seeing the windows of the bus sticking up out of the road. A nearby cinema, The Palladium, was shaken by the blast, and a shower of plaster fell from the ceiling, but many patrons who were inside preferred to stay and watch their film rather than leave! One gruesome story I have heard is that there was nowhere to put all the bodies from Balham Underground, and so they were laid out in one of the courtyards at Du Cane Court, – and it may be that several victims breathed their last away from the scene of the accident; although, in fact, it was not until Christmas that the last of the dead were removed. There were no residents among them; and, remarkably, I could only find one wartime casualty in Wandsworth from 'the Court': Mabel Beryl Houghton-Day, who met her end at General Motors in Balham High Road [Hook].

Marion Hopkins was a more recent resident, although she lived in Balham most of her life. As a toddler she participated in a peace march down Balham High Road in 1919, and she recounted some strange experiences from the war:

'I was standing by a cinema one day and an explosion blew the roof off. I was wearing a black hat at the time and felt something drop on me. When I looked, the plaster from the roof had actually turned my hat white!

Once, I struck up a conversation with an unfortunate man at a bus stop. He said he had been a Japanese prisoner of war, and that he returned to find his house was preserved and unoccupied, because he, the owner, was not declared dead; but his wife and child had drowned in the Balham Tube disaster.'

And who could have forgotten the doodle-bugs travelling silently above, which would pause ominously before dropping out of the sky? But the hellish surprises did not end there. The kind of death inflicted could be quite unusual too.

‘Friends of mine were killed by a V2 bomb’, Marion told me. ‘It was not a direct hit – but it drew all of the air out of their lungs, causing them to implode.’

Another elderly occupant of Du Cane Court told how her family had been decimated by war:

‘I lost my husband and two brothers in the First World War. One was gassed, and the other accidentally shot half of his foot off while going over the top of a trench.’ But war was not always the cause of calamity. Some who survived the war could not survive the peace ... One resident had a mother who was killed on the brow of a hill in Wales by a motor cyclist; a sister who fell down in the bathroom, and struck her head and died; and a friend, whose husband asked for a glass of water one day - and then just collapsed!

Amidst the maelstrom of unnatural disasters, some vestige of normality prevailed. Residents of ‘the Court’ had several cinemas close by. These included the Palladium, built in 1914 between Balham Station and Oakmead Road, which was popular with local people before it was sacrificed to the blitz. It could change its programme three times a week, so that patrons might attend regularly without seeing the same film twice. Given the reputation of Du Cane Court in the early days, one might have bumped into a celebrity whilst in the process of going out for the evening to see that very person perform on stage or screen. And who knows? One might also have had a special kind of welcome, upon first arriving in the block. Tommy Trinder, the ever-popular persona with ‘a long face in a trilby hat’, once said to a couple who had been bombed out of their house, ‘Why don’t you move to where I live?’ So they did. On the obverse side of the coin, I heard of a policeman and his wife who left the block for an old flat somewhere else, only to perish in a bomb blast.

Contributions to the War Effort

Wandsworth took a battering during the war, and also made its own contribution to the home front. The Balham Home Guard was created early in the war and by 1941 was of battalion strength [Gower], with their headquarters located at Fusilier House near Du Cane Court.

In August, 1940, the mayor of Wandsworth, councillor W.C.Bonney, set up a Spitfire Fund – and eventually three spitfires were purchased. Each may have had a separate fund dedicated to it, for Sir Alfred Butt, MP, was the first to donate to a fund for the spitfire presented by the community of Balham, Tooting and Streatham.

A resident of Du Cane Court, Corrie Hutchings, once worked for James C. Hounsfield (Secretary of the Balham and Tooting Chamber of Commerce), who was in charge of the money for the local Spitfire Fund, and was involved in the running of a charity shop where clothes were sold, and the proceeds put towards the money for the new aircraft. Apparently, Jympson Harman - Film Critic for the Evening News - lived at Du Cane Court during the war, and his wife (whom Corrie met) was one of the helpers in the shop.

The Flying Cross was awarded to Pilot Officer Charles Raymond Hattersley, who was 26 years of age and the son of Mrs Hattersley and the late Mr Hattersley of Du Cane Court - formerly of Uganda, Africa St.News.30/8/40. Two reconnaissance missions were made, and on the third, young Charles bravely descended to a low altitude regardless of enemy fire, and enabled Sergeant Windle to destroy or damage enemy property and equipment.

At this juncture, I must opine that an historical record need not only be characterized by actual events, but also by those happenings which the reader anticipates, and which, therefore, are conspicuous by their very absence. So ... there was a campaign by Lord Beaverbrook in 1940 to persuade citizens to give up their pots and pans, as the aluminium could be used to make frames for spitfires. One might have said, when one of the famous aeroplanes flew over, 'There goes my saucepan!' But, oddly enough, I found no evidence of this initiative affecting the residents of our block. Neither was there any 'digging for victory' (using the gardens for growing vegetables) here during the war – even though a whole common was turned over to this function elsewhere. And Marion Hopkins remembered a knitting campaign called 'Socks for Soldiers' – but she became a resident long afterwards (in 1977), and she was the only interviewee to mention it.

An Inviolable Fortress

A contemporary aerial view revealed the presence of craters all around Du Cane Court, and everyone who has a stake in the building must be grateful that the Luftwaffe somehow missed it. But there may have been some close shaves. Mr Van Gelder, a current resident who also lived here with his parents during the war, remembers one particular occasion when he saw a bomb moving ominously towards his home. As he watched its progress, he realized that it was on course for a direct hit. But suddenly, the bomb stopped in mid-air and fell to the ground in Elmfield Road.

Mr Pobjoy claims there is evidence of scarring on the building; and argues that when Balham station was blown up, the effects of the blast were carried over such a distance that they left their marks on the brickwork! Whether they did or not, I think we may safely assume that Du Cane Court survived the war pretty much unscathed. As a result, other occupants in the locality felt a degree of resentment. Many may have lived in pre-fabricated houses, which were commendable for their comfort but could not withstand the punishment of the blitz. Their attitude could be summarized thus: 'How typical it is, that a place where the rich live should get off so lightly!'

Fact or Fiction?

In this atmosphere strange rumours began to circulate. Was this block exempt from catastrophe for some reason other than good fortune? Did the Nazis have a vested interest in it? Stories proliferated of German bombers using it as an aid to navigation, of spies at Du Cane Court, and of the Fuhrer wanting to claim it for the officers of the Third Reich when he invaded.

The folklore which surrounds a place may have its roots in fact, or in ideas which seem plausible to rhetorical speakers during those moments when listeners are susceptible to persuasion; and what is merely apocryphal may, through repetition, acquire the authority of truth. But in the same way, there are many who find it exhilarating to destroy any remarkable notion, unless it is countenanced by a handsome dossier of statistics. And so we counterbalance what is frivolous with what is arrogant, and are forced to conclude that neither makes for good scientific method. Yet we may say with confidence that the fact that rumours can arise with such fecundity says something for the place, or way of life, which gives rise to them. After all, would we dispense with fables because they cannot serve as a literal means of explaining the world? All things of special significance become, through our experience of them, figments of our imagination also; and so, in a way, take on two lives ...

The fabled presence of Von Ribbentrop would have churned the concept of Du Cane Court into a fertile soil for the imagination. Apparently one resident, who was here as a child just prior to and during the war, distinctly remembered seeing Ribbentrop's ambassador car by the entrance. The Nazi diplomat was associated with the German Embassy at Carlton House Terrace, and would have left around 1937. Did he have a mistress here, or was he performing a reconnaissance for his Fuhrer, perhaps?

Michael Block renders a succinct, comic portrait of a rather unfunny man; but then it is a peculiar aphorism, much detested by the victims, that unsympathetic characters are the devil's gift to humour. Block writes of Ribbentrop:

'He exhausted his junior officials by making them run about on ridiculous errands. Although he himself was ridiculously disorganised and unpunctual, he insisted that everything be done at great speed! He was, however, a lavish entertainer - and famously devoted to his family.'

Oh, well. Perhaps that last point rules out the possibility of a mistress.

A Geographical Landmark for Navigation?

It is quite conceivable that the Luftwaffe would have used a landmark the size of Du Cane Court to navigate by; but there may not have been any official plan to do so. It is said that the block looks like a swastika from the air – to which I must reply, 'Only on a cloudy day!'

Yet like a small child who craves attention, a legend cannot be silent for very long, and in the blink of an eye an enhanced version is ready for broadcast: 'The entire building was constructed in the shape of a swastika by a Japanese workforce.' Well, we do have Japanese gardens, but as for the rest ...

The reality is that any navigation which occurred may have been somewhat haphazard and done 'on the fly' as we like to say nowadays. The Hinkel Observer and plane commander Otto Jufen described his experiences thus: 'In some respects we felt we were on holiday [...] not too seriously taken up with the idea of attacking England'. He continued, 'I became so engrossed in tracing all the little roads and houses I almost forgot what we were there for'.[Blandford].

Baedekker's maps were widely used by the Luftwaffe, although they actually predate Du Cane Court. Apart from them, Hitler's bombing of England in the first 2-3 years of the war was based on what he learned from travel guides, for there were hundreds of German businessmen and tourists in the UK in the 1930s. This was one of the reasons why he singled out the picturesque city of Coventry for punishment in the Blitz.

The Enemy Within

Du Cane Court was also reckoned to be a hotbed of spies. Now it may be that Londoners have a special fondness for such yarns, for espionage has also been linked in the public consciousness with other blocks of flats in the city. One presumes that the anonymity of such dwelling-places *would* make them ripe targets for spies – and it has been noted that, with its facilities, you could 'lie low' at 'the Court' for quite some time.

One voice which would have heightened people's fears of 'the enemy within' was that of Lord Haw Haw, so-called because of the contrived laugh that would accompany his treacherous broadcasts. Like the manager, Mr Jackson, he could interrupt your radio programme at will, but this time your heart would miss a beat.

'Gaimany callin'! Gaimany callin'!' was the familiar introduction, followed by a joyful account of how the allied forces had lost ground in some bloody battle ... and then the usual sardonic chuckle. Lord Haw Haw had no nobility in his blood, and his real name was William Joyce. My dear friend, May Arkell, was convinced that he resided in the block during the early years of its history; and another resident corroborates this idea.

'Why yes,' May told me, 'his family lived in Balham for generations – although I don't know whether he made any of his speeches from here.' The truth is that he was born in New York and brought up in Galway, although he was not typical of his countrymen [Hastings]. When he crossed the Irish Sea in 1921 he was a fanatical English loyalist, but he was a misfit and became disillusioned. If he had an association with the block, then it must have been before 1940, as in 1939 he went to Germany and spoke to us over the airwaves from a safe distance; but in the end, he had to face the gallows.

The British Secret Service

An elderly Polish woman, living on the ground floor, once informed me that a lady was here in 'ze war', who did important work for the allies in the effort to crack German codes.

'Is she still here?' I asked excitedly.

'No. She doesn't live here any more.'

'So where is she? I would *love* to interview her.'

'She lives in ze grave.' Now, keen as I am to pursue every lead, I humbly draw the line at graveyards and disembodied spirits!

There were other residents involved in counter-espionage, although they did not necessarily live here during the war. For instance, a lady friend of mine worked at Bletchley, where the English succeeded in cracking the German codes; and another lady named Emily Quarman was involved in an undercover operation before the war. Ms Quarman has been something of a star among our residents. She began to study Spanish at the age of 80, and was the best in her class. Following her tutor's advice, she relocated to Alicante – and later returned with a First Class Honours degree. She told me:

'I first went to university when I was 17. I needed to know French - as well as some German and Latin - to get in. The knowledge proved useful, because I visited Germany for the 1936 Olympics. I was concerned that children were being persecuted in concentration camps, and so I became a member of the Anglo-German bund. I pretended to have a friendly interest in Germany, and three or four times met and spoke with Ribbentrop.' I was impressed, but she continued: 'The ice ran in his veins. He had no humanity ... In Cologne, I was to meet a person who had sympathy for the plight of some Jewish children who were coming to London. Hitler was going to let them go, provided they took no money with them. I passed on the information I was entrusted with, but knew nothing of its content. It was obviously high security stuff. Three times this happened. Once, when on a train, I heard Germans speaking to each other in such a way as to suggest they were suspicious of me, and that my life was in danger. That was in August, 1939, – just before the outbreak of war. When I got back to England, a Scottish gentleman said to me, "That was your third trip, wasn't it?" I did not reply and he put a white cross on my rucksack.'

Emily then told me of someone in the secret service who was less fortunate.

'I knew a Pole who taught in the sewers of Warsaw and who was caught by the Gestapo. Rather than submit to their interrogation, my friend chose to break up a light bulb and swallow the pieces.'

Emily also interrogated spies herself.

'Many Germans posed as Norwegians,' she said. 'I would examine their accent, and if they were found to be German they were shot in the

Tower. It's strange, but they couldn't pronounce the letter "a". As with Scottish people, it came out sounding like an "e"'.

Du Cane Court for the Gestapo?

The Luftwaffe photographed every bit of England during the 1940s, so it is likely that Hitler would eventually have become aware of any building in the capital which offered ample accommodation, even if he did not know about it to begin with. However, I could discover no evidence whatsoever for the theory that Hitler and his grisly henchmen had plans to move into Du Cane Court when they invaded – nor for the outrageous suggestion that the Fuhrer actually lived in a flat here, on a secret visit to London prior to the war. Having said that, if the invasion *had* gone ahead, I am sure the Germans would have found such a building as our own to be most useful. But it did not go ahead - so how did the block escape destruction? Was it luck, pure and simple? Certainly, Lady Luck did not favour every block of flats. For example, G.K.Green's Sloane Avenue Mansions was damaged in the air raids.

Realistically, the kind of targets the Germans were aiming for - docks, gasworks, train stations, bridges and airfields – would not have included apartment blocks; except, perhaps, in the case of Dresden and Coventry, where the onslaught was unremitting. In fact, did Hitler even *want* to invade? I have heard that he respected the British Empire, and did not actually want to fight us at all! The blueprint for invasion was called 'Operation Sea Lion'. But the operation was postponed for an indeterminate number of months [Fleming]. Meanwhile, other places succeeded Britain on the agenda - including Gibraltar and Madeira, and especially Russia. 'Operation Sea Lion' may have been a ruse to distract attention from the enemy's real plans.

If one wishes to adhere to a doubtful tale with something more than blind faith, there are questions one must have answered. On the other hand, if one had never chanced upon that solitary article in 'The Builder' for October, 1937, and knew nothing of Du Cane Court at all, and then was suddenly told extraordinary things about it, - one might well infer that the building, itself, had as tenuous a hold upon reality as the very rumours which have made it famous.

This was remembered by a couple of elderly residents, and is what many people expected to happen to Du Cane Court. It is a picture of the infamous Balham Station disaster of 1940. (Courtesy of Wandsworth Heritage Service.)
After the accident, the driver of the number 88 bus said, '... the bus began prancing about like a horse and the next thing I knew was that I was lying in a shop doorway.'
During the war, over 40,000 bombs were dropped on Wandsworth, and about 10,000 on Battersea. Of 76,000 domestic properties in Wandsworth in 1939, 72,701 were damaged or destroyed; and of 28,500 properties in Battersea in 1939, 28,468 were damaged or destroyed. Even though most of the affected properties received 'lesser damage', it may be seen that Du Cane Court got off lightly. (Ref: Shaw and Mills.)

AFTER THE WAR

*

The Changing Face of Things

The post-war years at Du Cane Court got off to a terrible start. On the 2nd of September, 1945, - the Victory in Japan Day, - fire broke out in the restaurant and ballroom, with the result that the area was gutted. In the opinion of Mrs Whelpton, the restaurant should have been on the ground floor anyway. She said that it was too remote and not well publicized. In addition, it must have been hampered by rationing, and most likely failed to make a substantial profit. After the fire, it never truly recovered. However, the pre-war *joie de vivre* was not entirely dissipated, for the social facilities in H block remained open for many years; and Jessie Boran remembered one attempt to excite interest in them, by approaching the community at large - with an advertisement on the buses about joining the 'Du Cane Court Club'.

Perhaps the idea of clubs and dances did not appeal so much to a populace who were still jaded after a second terrible war ... for in 1946 [Daily.Mail.9/11/46], the director of Du Cane Court Ltd, Mr George Alfred Jackson, interrupted the normal wireless programmes for 15 minutes at a time to address tenants on the subject of a ballroom opposite the building; and a petition suggesting it would cause noise and disturbance was signed by 316 residents. On the other hand, a tenant named E.L. Randall said that there would be no more noise from this facility than already arose from the block itself, where 'cars come in and out, cats yell, dogs howl and bark, and the wireless is on until 11pm.'

Obviously, such incidents did not deter people from living here, and one interviewee of mine, Mrs Wheway, who had only just arrived (in 1944) is still here today. Her reason for choosing the area was that all the shops were attractive. The environment also had something cultural to offer; and on March 14th, 1958, notification was given that a branch of The Writers' Club was to be formed in the Borough of Wandsworth [WBN.14/3/58].

The reception area has evolved over the years. Besides changes to the predominant colour - the Head Porter once occupied what is now the Estate Office, and to the left, where the porters are currently situated, was an off-licence which also sold cigarettes and chocolates. Opposite the front desk, beneath the timeless clock, the manager had an office where you would be invited to air your views if you had a problem of any kind.

Mrs Whelpton had arrived by 1939, and she eventually succeeded Mr Jackson. Her husband had died and, with five children to support, times must have been hard for her. She brought a certain toughness and determination to her new role - 'but,' said Jessie Boran, 'she was a fair manager and not without a degree of modesty. When she heard how educated Mr Boran was, she would call at our flat and ask: "Is Mr Boran there? Could he advise me on something ...?"'

Mrs Beerman completes the picture for us:

‘Mrs Whelpton never wore a suit. She was about five feet tall, which was average for her time, slim, with auburn hair and blue-grey eyes, and a pallid complexion. She worked six days a week; and on Monday, Tuesday and Wednesday, she was in the office until 8pm. By the late 1950s, her daughter, Jennifer, had joined her as an assistant; and Mrs Whelpton, herself, was still here in the late 1960s. Apparently, she possessed a smallholding in the countryside, and most likely had the intention of retiring there.

Management Style

It seems that Mrs Whelpton was generally prompt, polite and helpful; and, apparently, she favoured prospective candidates for residency who were known to those already living here. One candidate was a policeman who was getting married and had nowhere to live; and he was eternally grateful to Mrs Whelpton for giving him G25. But she was not popular with everyone. New residents had to supply two references, and she would not take blue-collar workers. Indeed, some of the people living here today would not have been accepted then. Even Emily Quarman had to wait four years to get a flat, and eventually she gave a £50 bribe to the secretary in order to achieve her goal! The net curtains needed to be already up when you moved in – and nylon was not allowed. As for the main curtains, their colour had to be beige. Loud parties were tolerated at Christmas and New Year, but not otherwise. One elderly resident described to me how a slight conflict of interests could easily be aggravated …

‘One day my nephew and a friend of his were leaving my flat. They must have been a little rowdy, because a neighbour of mine said:

“Less noise, please.”

“Sorry, darling,” the friend replied.

This mild familiarity was reported, as my neighbour hadn’t been called *darling* for years! I had to appear before Mrs Whelpton the following morning, and I accounted for the behaviour by saying that the visitor was in high spirits as he had just returned from naval service. I was terrified of her.’

Margaret Whelpton was eminently dependable, hard working and with strong convictions - a valuable ally; but tending to be rather hasty and severe in her judgement if you crossed her. Mr Livingston, a director of National Bank, which purchased the estate in 1967, once said, ‘With Mrs Whelpton in charge, Du Cane Court was the most trouble-free place I ever owned.’ Apparently when she left, ‘everything downstairs was in chaos for a while’.

I have also heard that ‘Mr Livingston was a benevolent man’, and it was very possibly he who visited Jessie Boran one day, and was happy to condescend to a little intimacy in conversation. She told me:

‘The director noticed a painting of a pretty girl in my living room. He said, “I have a picture which looks exactly the same - of my wife!”

Apparently, both paintings had been done in the same artists' quarter of Paris, one street past Montmartre near the Sacré-Coeur.'

Other Staff

The Express Dairy was very handy for tenants. Besides dairy produce it stocked tinned fruits and vegetables, and it also delivered food to your door. In the 1940s two women ran it. Adjacent to the dairy was a grocery store selling tea, sugar, flour, eggs and other general consumables. Opposite these facilities was a door marked 'Wine Store'; and originally, there was a milk machine, where sixpence would buy you half a pint.

Mrs Andow took over the running of the guest-rooms from Mrs Whelpton, eventually moving in. She was short, talkative, and vividly remembered:

'When she was head of housekeeping, she would be in the flat of a dead person even before the relatives!' However, she was well-liked, and may have had a legitimate motive for entering the homes of the recently departed (apart from the remit which her employment gave her), as they actually left her gifts. In fact, she once inherited an entire property!

In the 1940s a certain Mr Bonello was the Head Porter, and later a gentleman named Harry Burden filled this position. He lived in the Porter's Lodge and was 'a big, burly man who would corner people in the lift'; and there was 'Lean', the electrician, so named because he made a habit of leaning on the porters' desk.

The outside of the building had only swing doors, and a commissionaire would monitor people entering the block and help them with their luggage. (Apparently, the father of this gentleman had worked on the disaster at Balham Station.) No one was allowed to move in on Saturday afternoon, nor wash the car on a Sunday. Also, no delivery vans ever appeared at the front of the building. Everything went to the back, unless it was for the maisonettes.

While Du Cane Court has always had porterage, there was no security company to begin with. Nevertheless, most of those who have been here for a long time are of the opinion that the whole service used to be more professional than it is now. Naturally, some have begged to differ, including a certain Suzanna Hughes who came here in 1953. As for Mrs Middleton, she remembers various Head Porters. One of them was sacked for insolence and idleness, and was last seen stacking shelves in Sainsbury's!

Mr Hearse was Head Porter by 1957, and remained so through to the 1970s. He worked at Wandsworth Prison in his younger days, and would not take any nonsense. He used to circumnavigate the building, knocking on doors and informing people that their windows or curtains were dirty, and he would report noise and evict the offenders if necessary. Obviously such heavy-handed 'law enforcement' made a profound impression upon our discrete community, and, long afterwards, a woman named Miss Densum would ask the good-humoured porter, Mr Neil Gray, 52 Sundays of the year, 'Have you noticed the curtains are dirty? Have you noticed the windows are dirty?'

There was a man who mended watches, clocks and radios; a father and son window-cleaning team; and a muscular grounds man, nicknamed 'Blondie' because his hair had turned grey. Many of the staff were residents themselves. Mrs Whelpton (at least by 1956) lived in K001; while Alfred K. Tindale, porter and piano tuner, lived in F64 Reg.of.Electors. There was also a resident plumber and a resident electrician – who were both good at their jobs, although the plumber was young and rather brazen in his manners, and the electrician was an alcoholic (leaning on the desk for support, perhaps).

One character never to be forgotten was Mr Bowdery, the resident carpenter, also known as 'Chippy'. He had an admirable sense of humour and has been affectionately referred to as 'a little dark man who was useful for repairs'. He worked in a big garage at the back of the building which is now 'the lodge', and his wife telephoned me out of the blue one day to fill in the detail:

'My husband first came to Du Cane Court in 1949 and worked there for many years. He rose through the rank and file and had a good career; although it was not without its stresses, for he would mutter about the management company, Keith Cardale Groves, in his sleep! After he died, I put up the money for a memorial.' To this day, there is a seat which commemorates him in one of the front-facing gardens, with a brass or copper plate which bears his name.

Early Residents

Du Cane Court was known for housing nurses, doctors and civil servants. There was a Dr Francis who would rush to the aid of anyone who was sick and in distress. And in the 1950s, there were many solicitors and barristers here too. After the war a British soldier lived here, who had somehow escaped from a German prisoner of war camp and was subsequently shielded by a German family. He had married the daughter and moved to Du Cane Court, and it is a testament to the good will of the place that his German wife was accepted here – although she would bemoan the sacrifice she had made, in renouncing her country and her religion to be with him.

I have also heard of three residents having Swedish wives. Indeed, Du Cane Court must have hosted a veritable melting pot of nationalities over the years. And so, when a tram or bus pulled up outside, the driver or conductor would call out, 'League of Nations!'

The Preece and the Porteous: a Light Interlude

Glancing through the Register of Electors for Du Cane Court took me through a sea of enchanting names, which I could not resist recording; and in the order I observed them, they seem to form a parallel history.

There was a *Nellie Stubbs* and a *Nancy Scraggs*; three *Gambles*, two *Thoroughgoods*, and a *Hilda Baden Crummie*. What a scene to fire the imagination ... with *Sunshine Low* over Du Cane Court, as well as a *Blanche Cave*, *Olive Wicks* and *Violet Groves*. *Mr Love* was in the air, and so was a *Lovelace* and an *Amy Playfoot*; a *Constance Cleave* and (posing like a badly-conjugated verb) a *Margaret Spink*. On the saucy side were *Mr Lusty*, *Gemima Hooker* and *Alice Cockayne*; and, for good measure, a *Maud Dick*, an *Ethel Spurgeon* and a *Dorothy Lovering Cocks*.

Somewhat darker were *Augustus Underwood*, *Horace Clay*, *Lilly Mudd* and two *Coffins*. And posing, like a firm of solicitors for the deceased, were *Knight*, *Rumble* and *Blundell*. Only later did I observe a *Hearse* and a *Margaret Buggy*; although a furness had been available, followed closely by a *Pye*. (Sadly, there was no *Sweeney Todd*.)

To mark the war, in the next but one flat from two *Wheelers*, there were four *Cannons*. And to honour the nation's fallen heroes, there were four *Chappells* opposite the Polish church. But how dramatic was the effect of rationing! Whereas in 1938-39, there had been *Seal* and *Gammon*, later there was only *Helen Niblet* and *A.P. Nutt*, with perhaps a dash of *Spriggs* and *Lemon*.

In C block, and registering what a gamble life had been in times recently past, were the *Hedgers*; while downstairs, with happier-sounding names, were the *Bubleys* and the *Prangleys*; then suddenly, two *Bubleys* popped up higher in the building (evidently filled with helium).

In 1945, more entertainment is provided by *Constance Pratt*, *Pollie Cheatle*, a *Hogg* and a *Unite-Webb*, a *Parzy*, a *Tweed* and a *Mary Crippo*; one *Ethel Pinkey* and two *Littleboys*. In 1950, I observed *Frederick Flude* then *Rhoda Falcus*, while *Agnes E. Cox* made *Gladys Woon*. (I jest – for no one really swooned!) And in the midst of a *Pocock* and a *Krisky* were two *Pilgrims*. A *Leech* on the ground floor was succeeded by a *Bidhead*; whilst one floor up from two *Gulleys* was a *Meryl Spooner*.

From the mid-1950s, leading into the swinging '60s, were a *Burden* and a *Griffin*, a *Thick*, a *Bender*, two *Inches* and a couple of *Hollows*; and in 1960 – perhaps having escaped from an aquarium - a *Sadie Fish*, a *Preece* and a *Porteous*. But that was not the last of the animals, for two *Pigeons* emerged, perhaps to commemorate Du Cane Court's now dilapidated restaurant. Finally, it was the turn of *Gay Pride*. Thanks for the *Membrys*.

One day, after browsing through the old volumes of electors, one or two of which had begun an epic process of disintegration, I looked down at my hands, and was surprised to see an abundance of sticky detritus. Then a macabre thought came to me. It was as if the tenants had not only yielded up some of their vital statistics, but also a portion of their actual remains.

Serious Notes from the Register of Electors

In 1936, only three people occupied Du Cane Court. By 1937, there were still no lower ground floor ('00') flats recorded – although 379 residents are listed, for flats in blocks down to E. Of course, the largest structure in Balham did not sit upon a cushion of air! Rather, the distinction between the lower ('00') and upper ('0') ground floor exists only at the rear of the building, where the ground slopes downwards; and the corresponding blocks, F to K, were not yet completed. The number of electors remained below 700 prior to World War 2, and reports suggest that during the war the population fell dramatically. But by June, 1945, everything had changed. There were 961 electors. So clearly, the place had become popular again, although the size of the registered population is never constant. In 1981, for instance, it was only 729.

Not surprisingly, those with a public face sometimes lived near to each other. There was Andrew Sandham of B04, and Elizabeth Sellars of B01; Tommy Trinder of G002, and Ernest Bubley of G003. (Ernest later moved to C11.) But it is curious to find celebrities residing in relatively cramped conditions. Andrew Sandham shared his maisonette with Kathleen and Joan Sandham; the Bubleys (in 1948) were sharing with someone called Joan Watson; and Elizabeth Sellars shared *her* maisonette with *five* other people! However, I must qualify all of this with the appreciation that my sources were simply lists of people with the franchise to vote, and so I cannot be sure how much of their time they actually spent here. On the other hand, many more people may have lived here than I could ever know, for anyone under a certain age would not have been listed; and, furthermore, no records are held for the war years.

Examining the great 'Register' for signs of celebrated lives is like navigating over a vast sea, hoping to descry dry land, whilst simultaneously realizing that even those hot little islands which *do* exist may be shrouded in a volcanic fog of their own making. This is because successful people often have more than one residence, and may have submitted the one which is *not* at Du Cane Court for the purposes of voting. They may also be known by their pseudonyms rather than by the names they were christened with – witness 'Harry Roy', the bandleader, who was really Harry Lipman; and 'Derek Roy', the comedian, who was actually Derek Thomas.

Early Celebrities

One of the factors that has always given Du Cane Court a degree of prestige is the calibre of the people who have been here. I have heard it said that because so many have called this place their home, a long roll-call of the famous and the infamous is to be expected; and the proximity of the block to the centre of town would act as a catalyst in such an equation. I also concede that there are no Nobel Prize winners in our midst! Nevertheless, I must exhort my reader to compare a few hundred residents with the sixty or so million citizens who are domiciled in the British Isles, and then to ask himself: How likely is it that so many persons who are widely known would have congregated under a single roof?

Mrs Whelpton once said that before the war '75% of the population of the block were show people. Brixton used to be the place for them, then Streatham and then finally Balham.'

It is rumoured that the actress, Hermione Gingold, had a presence here, although she may have only been visiting friends. She was known for her wit, and when it was said of Olivier in one of his roles that he had been a *tour de force*, she famously remarked that Donald Wolfitt, in the same role, had been 'forced to tour'. A latter-day resident, Mrs Macdonald-Ross, met her in the 1930s, and summarized her impact upon private company in a few well-chosen words:

'She was very humorous and could have a room full of people in stitches. But she was also rather brittle – not very generous or warm-hearted, and slightly vain.'

The famous actor, Richard Todd, is said to have been seen around the building, and Margaret Rutherford was reputedly a resident. Indeed, I have heard of one person who remembers seeing her when he lived here as a child. Early in her career she would play rich, eccentric English ladies, and she is affectionately remembered for her portrayal of Miss Marple, Agatha Christie's famous elderly detective; but her most famous role was Madam Arcati in Noel Coward's 'Blithe Spirit', which was shown in the West End of London and subsequently became a film. Edward Kay is a resident of Du Cane Court with an unusual story to tell about her:

'My cousin and his child once met Ms Rutherford, and she was full of praise for the little one.

"What a lovely boy!" she exclaimed.

"I'm not a boy. I'm a girl," came a disgruntled reply from inside the pram, in response to which she withdrew in shock.' Now her flawed judgement would be of no great consequence, except that she adopted a boy who grew up to become a famous transsexual writer (and who would one day marry a black, schizophrenic mechanic)! Another resident of 'the Court' told me that he saw Margaret Rutherford on a bus one day, unclean and unkempt, washed up like the jetsam of life, for she suffered from mental illness in her later years. Evidently, the problem ran in the family. In fact, she inherited her mother's maiden name because her father, William Benn, murdered her paternal grandfather, the Reverend Julius Benn, by battering him to death with a chamber pot. William was later admitted to Broadmoor. Yet to her credit, she transcended this dark past, and became a Dame of the British Empire in 1967.

Another member of our illustrious community, who has received a brief mention already, was Elizabeth Sellars. She was born in 1923 and appeared on stage from the age of 15. She made her first London appearance in 1946 in 'The Brothers Karamazov', which is noteworthy as it may have coincided with the time she was here. She shared a flat at the front of the building (in 1945 and 1946) with several others, including a certain Charles Victor Dhanapala, who owned a large estate in Sri Lanka. Mr Dhanapala was a charismatic resident himself, and he sounded like the ideal flatmate for Ms Sellars. He would give sumptuous parties for his thespian guests, whom he revered; and he would love to have been an actor himself. He had good manners and etiquette and a sense of fun, and he was devoted to anyone who was well-educated.

There may, of course, be other characters worthy of note. For instance, someone I spoke to had a feeling that one of the acting pair - Derek and Terence de Marney – once lived here.

Orchestra, Song and Dance

The bandleader, Harry Roy, was allegedly here. He was born in 1900, and in 1935 married the white Raj of Sarawak, nicknamed Princess Pearl, before teaming up with her in two film-musicals, Rhythm Racketeer (1937) and Everything is Rhythm (1940) [Larkin]. In 1938, Harry Roy and his band toured South America, and during World War 11 he played for the troops in the Middle East. His signature tune was 'Tiger Rag'. Many fine musicians passed through the ranks of his band, which was among the most popular of its time.

I was told that Harry Roy lived in a maisonette in B block with his parents, and that his father played cricket for England. Neil Gray, a porter of long standing at Du Cane Court, who played the trumpet in a ship's orchestra for many years, remembers him well ...

'I met him in later life when he was about 70. He was short, dapper, and had a great personality. He had black hair even at that age, and looked quite healthy, although he drank very well. He played the clarinet ... after a fashion; sang ... after a fashion. It was his personality that carried the show. He would perform at the Embassy Club – a venue where I played myself for 14 years.' And that's not all. The father of a certain Mr Horton, who lived in A41b, was a saxophonist who played with Harry Roy.

Another musical star, Harry Leader, definitely lived here. He came about 1960, and stayed for some time. Furthermore, the hugely popular singer, Matt Monro, was a guest of his. In fact, it is a regrettable possibility that Harry Roy has come to be associated with the block because of a pastiche of 'Harry Leader' and 'Derek Roy', who figures in the next section. (However, the reader will have gathered by now that this book is about legend as well as fact!) Anyhow, Harry Leader was born in London, the son of a Russian Army trumpeter, and his career spanned three generations, from the dance band days to The Beatles. He played with George Formby, wrote hundreds of songs – many of them with his wife, Rona, - and sold millions of records. Leader and his band often featured on BBC Radio, particularly in connection with 'Music while you Work'; and, incidentally, Michael Leader, his son, is frequently seen in 'EastEnders', driving a milk float around Albert Square. Michael has also helped to launch a Brighton and Hove bus (number 630) which bears his father's name. He proudly told me that his talented father could play six musical instruments, and that he would hone his skills on all of them every day.

A resident musician by the name of Joe White played with the Billy Cotton band, and numbered Claridges amongst his venues; and it seems that a Jazz musician named Jim Bray lived here for a long time, before his recent death. Glenn Mitchell, who is known to the British Music Hall Society, describes Bray's distinct appearance and manner thus: 'He was a large man, with a wild ridge of hair delimiting a bald area on his head. He performed with the finest players in his genre, and won the respect of them all. Having a shy demeanour he was very serious about his art, although occasionally he could surprise you with a bright smile. I suppose it was part of what drew people to him.'

George Parkinson (who reputedly had his own quintet) resided here between about 1945 and 1960. And a few of the Tiller Girls lived at Du Cane Court (but not Betty Boothroyd, who since became Speaker in the House of Commons). They famously performed at the Windmill Theatre in London, dancing and singing. They would kick their legs up high into the air in perfect unison, like the 'Can Can' girls, and could be on BBC programs about television history - displayed in a little 'window' in a corner of the screen.

Among our minor celebrities was Anona Winn. She was a singer (and a member of the chorus of 'The Merry Widow') who realized the importance of being versatile, and she was once referred to as a 'human flute' [Daily.Tel.]. Anona was also a radio personality, and one of the original panellists on 'Twenty Questions', which was first broadcast in February, 1947. Tessy O'Shea, a '20-stone Irish singer with a very strong voice' and an unflattering nickname, 'Two-ton Tessy', is said to have been here too. Finally, Sylvia Say, who was an evacuee during the war, told me about her gifted father, who came here in 1939: 'He wrote the words and music for some of the shows in the Hippodrome on Balham Hill. He was Lesley Brightwell – and Balham's answer to Noel Coward.

Comedians

Richard Hearne, alias 'Mr Pastry', was among the colourful characters seen here after the war. He became known for his slapstick comedy, and one of his trademarks was a funny walk. He appeared in commercials and on children's television. One lady I spoke to admitted that she found him amusing, although she could not exactly say why. Richard used to visit his mother, who, it is said, lived in a big flat at 'the Court'. He once raised a petition to enable her to keep her yorkie dog – contrary to the wish of management – and he had a taste for the countryside, owning an area of 170 acres in Kent called Platt Farm[Tatler.and.By.].

Derek Roy is remembered, too. He was short, plump, and wore glasses; and besides being a stand-up comedian, he featured on an amusing radio variety show. He was well-liked, well-known and very vulgar. He lived in B11 and had a large dog which he would take on stage as part of his act. His mother and father also resided here, and they may have all shared the same flat. Then there was Roy Potter, a stand-up comedian who played the bassoon, and - the most talked-about resident of them all - Tommy Trinder. He was born in Streatham and there is a little plaque to him there. As a young man he reputedly worked at Sainsbury's in Balham, yet he went on to become one of the country's most popular entertainers. He would begin his act with, 'The name's Trinder. That's T-R-I-N-D-E-R, pronounced *Chumley.*' This witticism was a gentle dig at the snobs of society, who insisted on pronouncing ordinary names in a fancy way which was utterly un-phonetic. (Today, we have the same social-climbing habit, but with the opposite effect, pronouncing local place names, such as 'Bal-ham' and 'Cla-pham', with their full phonetic glory.)

Max Miller was the king of music hall, yet Trinder (who was here by 1939) clearly saw himself as competition for him, and was sometimes a thorn in the great man's side. His act was similar to Miller's, with the colourful pyjama-like suits, the two-tone shoes and white trilby hat. I understand that he even bought a house in Brighton and became a neighbour of his famous rival, no doubt much to the chagrin of poor Max! Yet Trinder was more than a stage persona. He was a movie star as well, notably appearing in the film, 'The Foreman went to France'. In 1955, he assumed yet another role – Chairman of Fulham Football Club, - and in later years he became a familiar face on television. No doubt he would have been quick to say to everyone who met him, 'You lucky people'.

The Local Man and Popular Hero

A stranger contacted me one day in response to an advertisement of mine. As a youngster living in the vicinity in the early 1950s, he remembered travelling by tram and stopping outside Du Cane Court. He told me, 'When I saw a toy sailing boat in one of the windows, I said, "Tommy Trinder lives there"'. As a matter of fact, Trinder lived at the back of the building, although it is a measure of his achievement that he was a hero even to local children. One resident I knew went out with him in her younger days. She was Ena, the mother of Sylvia Say, and was known as 'the lady of the lampshade' on account of her tendency to wear a sunshade over her eyes. Another person, who lived here in the 1940s, recalls that his father was like a double for the famous man.

'You mean he was his understudy?' I asked.

'Oh no. They just looked identical. One day my mother was going about her daily business, and she was surprised to see her husband buying cinema tickets. She thought, "What is he doing that for?" But in fact it was Tommy Trinder, and her own husband was behind her!'

A female resident whom I spoke to describes a chance meeting with the comedian ... 'The wind blew my silk scarf across my face. A gentleman beside me threw it back over my shoulder and said, "One should never hide a pretty face". It was Tommy Trinder.' I have also been told, 'Tommy Trinder owned an Austin 7, and had a white bulldog called Winston which he took to Wandsworth Common. He would sometimes dress up just to go out for a walk, although his clothes did not always match. Once I saw him wearing a light blue suit and a peaked cap. He could look flamboyant or pedestrian, just as the mood took him.'

Tommy Trinder felt that he was unlike Max Miller in that he could take a joke against himself; and he once said, 'I don't think there is anything that can ever wound me' [Daily.Tel]. Nevertheless, he had his fair share of misfortune. He was robbed so many times that he finally put a sign on his front door for burglars – 'Don't bother ... You've already taken everything'; and after the war, the papers were full of the divorce case between him and his wife. Furthermore, he may have left Du Cane Court in unhappy circumstances. I have heard two stories about this. One is that he was asked to leave because of his raucous parties. The other, that he was made to feel guilty and unwelcome by the manager, because he had a second property somewhere else at a time when others were forced to 'tighten their belts'.

Sport

Although the block is primarily renowned for its theatrical celebrities, it is perhaps through the arena of sport that it has bequeathed to us its most talented sons. One of these was the cricketer, Andrew Sandham, who was born in 1890 and lived here between the 1930s and the late 1950s. He was the first English batsman ever to make a triple century in a test match; and his match aggregate of 375 was the test record until the 1973-74 season. Furthermore, Sandham's 30,000 runs in first class matches makes him 13th in the all-time best list – up to the end of the 1990 cricket season [Frindall]. He teamed up with Hobbs to great effect, but not even his famous team-mate was more reliable. He was also the most unselfish of players, a man of integrity with a good sense of humour.

Andy Sandham came to Du Cane Court in 1938-39, having only retired from first class cricket in 1937 [St.News.9/37]. In an interview, Mr Sandham, senior, said that his four sons started playing cricket as soon as they could walk [St.News.27/2/31]. They defended a table leg whilst their father bowled with a softball, and many were the ornaments and flowers that were knocked to the floor and broken. Mr Sandham senior was, himself, a fine cricketer at club level, and replied with a negative when asked if he was proud of his son. One senses that modesty was instilled into Andrew from an early age ...

'It is only his job. He couldn't do your job, and there are many things I can do that he couldn't.' However, his father went on to express pride that his son was chosen for his county.

'Very few people know that Andy is a first-class mechanic,' added Mr Sandham. 'He served a 5-year apprenticeship as a portmanteau and bag maker, so that if he failed as a cricketer he would have had a trade to fall back upon.'

Ernest Bubley was England's top table-tennis star before the war [Crayden]. Yet he was a small, portly man who hardly looked like an athlete. He occupied G003 from 1948 to 1951, and flat C11 from 1952 to 1976; and apparently he also had a flat in France.

He was left-handed and would play with a rubber-faced bat, and he wore a glove because he was prone to some kind of skin complaint. He played close to the table, taking the ball early, and was a formidable opponent with a perfectly executed backhand and a forehand which was a vicious chop. Ernie's downfall was the introduction of the sponge bat, as the lack of sound and the irregular bounces completely destroyed his rhythm. To confuse matters further, the thickness of sponge could vary, and the bat could even be rubber on one side and sponge on the other. His greatest performance came in the quarter-final of the English Open in February, 1939, when he almost defeated the legendary Victor Barna.

He had his own table-tennis club in Whitechapel in the East End called 'The Manhattan', which was *the* table-tennis club to belong to – but there was more to Ernie than the game by which he made his name. Within the compass of his abilities was an embarrassment of riches. He had a photographic memory, and it is said of him that – if he was blindfolded – one person could select a book from a shelf; another could choose a specific page; and a third might specify a paragraph and ask, for example, 'What is the third word in that paragraph?' And he would know! He was a 'dab hand' at bridge, and played snooker to such a high level that he was able to make breaks of 50 when such scores were rare, even by the champions of the day. He would joke, sing and play the violin in the club at Du Cane Court (after the fashion of Jack Benny), and he once – infamously - appeared on the Michael Barrymore show, 'My Kind of People'. Unfortunately, Mr Barrymore made his guest look foolish, by alluding (rather obscurely) to the fact that his 'flies' were unzipped: 'Oh! I can tell he's a good old Jewish boy!'

Ernie Bubley died on the 21st of January, 1996, at the age of 83. He had led a full and varied life [Crayden]. He was also a man of various moods. At his best he was an extraverted and self-confident character, and also very humorous; but in his later years it seems he may have sustained some kind of injury to his leg, and he became slightly bitter and antisocial.

Stan Hardes was a retired policeman in the block who remembered drinking with Ernest Bubley. Stan was a keen table-tennis player himself, and was Surrey County champion at 17.

Animals at Du Cane Court

Over the years, animals have had their part to play in the history of this building. Long ago, a pair of mallard ducks settled on our pond. Then there were the fish – and there was the *disappearance* of the fish. But this conjuring act had nothing to do with the ducks. A look-out post was set up day and night to discover who the thief was. Eventually, a heron was found roosting on the roof, which would swoop down and help itself to the fish whenever it felt hungry. Apparently, it had escaped from Battersea Park Zoo. The stock of marine life was replenished, but it was subject to other assaults, as small boys used fishing nets to see what they could capture; and some fiasco with herons may have occurred since, for, in recent times, a metal heron was placed in the pond to frighten off intruders. The installation of this inanimate bird was presided over by the well-qualified manager (who collects letters after his name like a Hoover in an early learning centre), with proceedings that were highly officious and slightly amusing: for they involved a military-style parapet of hessian cushions, and a band tied around the edge of the pond. (Somehow, I doubt whether such a precaution would have restrained our little helper, if he had mutated into flesh, bone and feathers, and made a quick dash for freedom!)

I have been told that Du Cane Court did not accommodate pets to begin with. One lease I saw (actually for G01) specifies that no bird, dog or any other animal shall be kept on the premises without consent in writing from the lessors - which may be revoked at any time upon complaint. There were, however, quite a few pets in the building by June, 1950, when an article in the Daily Mail said that 34 tenants had been instructed to get rid of their dogs, or be prepared to leave. The Canine Defence League was asked for advice; and the puissant Mr Jackson, presumably still a director of Du Cane Court Ltd, enthroned his derriere upon the vaunted seat of reason with the words, 'I am a dog-lover myself and won prizes at school for essays on kindness to animals [, and my] company rightly feels that dogs should not be kept in a block of flats'. At one point Derek Roy joined the fray, promising to lampoon the governing powers of the block if they did not stand down from their request; and, with his help, love (if that's what it was) triumphed over reason. But, to be fair, the dog-lovers were not so unreasonable, for when it comes to exercising pets, there is more green space within easy access of those who dwell here than is enjoyed by many house-holders.

Less controversially, Jessie Boran said that her children kept many pets, such as hamsters and canaries, - one of which got eaten by a cat.

No Place for Children?

I understand that there is no provision in the lease for excluding children from the building. However, Du Cane Court has never been child-friendly.

'Of course, dear, they want to skate down corridors,' says Marjorie Loter, who moved here in 1972; and besides a young visitor skating on his paper round, she recalled one lonely little black boy who waited at the end of the corridor to see the sun set. But however forbidding the welcome, this place has always been a source of fascination for children. One lady of mature years remembered herself, as a child, running up the stairs with her friends, onto the roof (perhaps thereupon taking a second to admire the view); and then running down the stairs and out of the building – all before anyone could catch them. It must have been an exciting game!

One of my most fruitful interviews was with a gentleman named Robert Renak, whose company, 'Art for Industry', had supplied illustrations relating to local history for a public house in Balham, called 'The Moon Under Water'. He and his brother lived in 'the Court' as children in the 1950s, and the scale of the place made quite an impression on them.

'Du Cane Court was our whole world,' he said. 'I would play around the garages with my friends, but we got chased off. If we turned on a tap at the back of the building, we would be told off. The porters were like the Gestapo, screaming at us whenever we stepped out of line.' An image comes to mind of Joe, in Charles Dickens's 'Bleak House', always being asked to move on. It seems that Robert would get himself into all kinds of trouble. He enjoyed water, but would fall into one of the ponds and return home soaking wet! And that is not all. He told me:

'The restaurant fell into disuse in the years following the war. A window was broken, leaving one large pane of glass shaped like a fish. Pigeons used to fly in and out. I suppose they had made their nests there. On one occasion a cat jumped out, perhaps in pursuit of the pigeons, and landed on its feet seven floors below – then simply walked away! There were even fights in the place ... and it was left like that for more than a decade. So my parents designated it as strictly out of bounds. As a further precaution, my brother and I were told not to use the lift on the outlandish rationale that if it was ascending, it would just keep on going ... up ... and up ... and eventually out through the roof and away into the wide blue yonder! The deception worked, for I became very afraid of the elevator, although I would use the fire escape instead.

We were not allowed in the boiler room, nor anywhere in the basement, on our own, but a certain Mr Philips took a liking to us, and under his kind patronage such places became accessible. Coal was used in the early days to heat the water for the building, with chimneys belching smoke into the atmosphere. The boiler room became known as *The Dungeon*, or *Aladdin's Cave*. To us, it was a place of enchantment where strange old fellows pitched great piles of rubbish (probably from a skip, or from the dust chute collection areas) into the mouth of a huge furnace, whilst flaming tongues licked the sides of the walls. It was like entering a dragon's lair. Then there was a discrete area behind the garages ...'

'What we call the Secret Garden?' I asked.

'Yes. Only in those days it was not a showcase. It was used for burying dead pets - hamsters, birds and the like. I suppose the cardboard boxes and tissues, into which the corpses were consigned, must have decayed long ago, leaving just the skeletons. A Pet budgerigar of ours was laid to rest in the area, and mother would say, "Don't worry. JoJo has gone to heaven." So one of us would take friends round there to show them *heaven* – although it was really just a place where people dumped their rubbish.'

Robert also remembered the milk cart which stopped outside their front door ... 'There was a large vat in the cart, and the milkman would fill a container from the vat and carry it – exactly one pint of milk, if that was the amount required, - to the resident's front door, and then decant it into a bowl set aside for the purpose. My brother, Lee, once went for a ride in the milk cart, and had the special moment captured in a photograph.'

Romance and Decadence

With husbands and lovers away at war, Du Cane Court acquired a reputation for having some young ladies who were generous with their favours; and this unflattering impression never really went away. Jean Evans remembers the thick 'black out' curtains at the end of the corridors and remarks, 'If you pulled them back fast enough, you could catch people necking!' Robert Renak felt fairly sure that Du Cane Court was 'stuffed full of mistresses and prostitutes', and his father, Mr Jack Renak, told me that when his family lived in K15, they would see a young gentleman park his car, and then leave an hour later ...

'You could set a watch by him. We called him *lover boy.*'

In the 1950s, there was a Mr Whip, who was short, skinny and unattractive – and who somehow won the heart of the then *femme fatale* of the block, a young girl called Ruth. She felt frustrated living with her parents, and so one day she and her unprepossessing boyfriend simply *whipped off* together! Then there was the case of the heating engineer, who got into a rather compromising situation with a lady. And apparently, there was an assistant manager who would get his underlings to maintain one of the freeholder's guest-rooms, so that he could use it to seduce his mistress; and when her husband found out, she left him.

Jessie Boran recalled two men (said to be cousins) who worked at Du Cane Court. One looked after the building and tenants; and the other cared for the gardens. But Jessie did not believe they were cousins - but lovers. And I learned of an eccentric prostitute who lived in the lower ground of H block, who was once espied sitting on her bed, eating winkles and drinking Guinness: doubtless the one was for her reproductive system, and the other for keeping up her strength during live performances. Another resident was going into the lift one day, when she saw a man there with literally nothing on but his shirt. He looked abashed, and she thought he had been locked out of his flat, but he was actually a young porter with a drink problem.

Rumour has it that Christine Keeler, of the 'Profumo Scandal', had connections with the building, although she actually resided in Dolphin Square. Nevertheless, the salacious reputation of the place was by now well established, and it was known in some circles as 'Tart's Court'. Passengers on public transport might hear, 'Anyone for the love nest?' Or, more simply, 'Knocking shop!' (For Du Cane Court is unique, in that it has its own bus stop.) And as if these names were not enough, still more cries would issue forth, such as 'Balham barracks!' or 'Cocaine

Court!' A long-term resident once remarked to me, 'They must think the place is a brothel.'

The World at Large

While Du Cane Court was consolidating its sex appeal, the sign, 'Stop jaywalking - Use the crossing', in a 1960s photograph of the building and its environs, implied a certain innocence compared with today, when crossing the road is a free-for-all. But, in the name of progress, the adjacent thoroughfare was about to change. By the end of January, 1958, work on the widening of Balham High Road between Trinity Crescent and Oakmead Road had commenced [WBN.1/58]. The intention was to make the overall width no less than 90 feet at any given point. Furthermore, there was some talk of the M23 being extended across Mitcham Common and through Balham – and of part of Du Cane Court being razed to the ground to make way for it! Thankfully, nothing like this ever happened, and it may have been no more than a malicious rumour. However, the residents of the building had other causes for concern. Later that year [Wands.Notes.], some news broke about the risk of exposure to radiation in the event of an aeroplane, carrying an atom or hydrogen bomb, crashing into a built-up area such as Wandsworth. Even the Prime Minister could not ignore the issue, and, in the House of Commons in December 1957, he stated that there was no danger whatsoever of a nuclear explosion in the event of a crash. Well, I suppose he *would* say that, wouldn't he?

The new age aspired to be 'environmentally aware', with the establishment of the 'green belt' and of the first national parks, and the Clean Air Act of the 1960s. Clearly, no one wanted to go back to the poisonous fogs produced by chimneys and coal fires: an ugly scenario, to which Du Cane Court had made its own contribution. Thus, on 10th February, 1964, tenants were notified that the modernization of the building's refuse disposal systems would begin in two days.

Physical Changes in the 1950s and '60s

On 22nd January, 1954, the Council gave permission for 44 lock-up garages, but only 38 were subsequently erected. Meanwhile, there was an old lift which could get stuck between floors, and on at least one occasion one or more residents had to be rescued. In the 1950s you could travel in the lift without shutting the door, and so without your extremities fully enclosed. As a result of this oversight, a newspaper boy lost his leg. The remedial action was to attach a weighted cable to the doors, which automatically closed them.

Hilda Middleton remembers the décor in the 1950s. The walls were stuccoed, presumably for sound insulation, although this may have been an elegant feature in its own right; but eventually this, and other classic features, would be lost. As a result of age, maintenance or structural alterations, the built-in radios began to lose their reception. The first examples of this might have occurred as early as the 1950s.

And by 1957, planning permission had been granted for the conversion of the restaurant in C block into four 1-bedroom flats [W.Council], although it was not actually converted until the mid-1960s. Then, in 1964, like a valediction to a bygone age, the council gave permission to turn the locker rooms on the eighth floor, and the club premises and billiards hall on the seventh floor, into dwellings. And so the heart of the building was cut out, and fed to the hound of progress.

Celebrated comedians who lived in Du Cane Court: above, Tommy Trinder and Richard Herne, otherwise known as 'Mr Pastry'; and below, two pictures of Derek Roy. (Courtesy of Max Tyler, British Music Hall Society.)

A still from the film, 'Never Let Go' (1960), featuring one of Du Cane Court's famous actresses of stage and screen, Elizabeth Sellars, and the much-loved Peter Sellers. Elizabeth Sellars was on the electoral register for the building in the 1940s, although she may well have left by the time this film was released. (Courtesy of Everett Collection / Rex Features.)

Harry Leader, shown in close-up, and with his band performing for the BBC Radio programme, 'Music while you Work'. Both photographs date from circa 1960, which is around the time he became a resident of Du Cane Court. He sold millions of records in his career, which spanned three generations. (Photos courtesy of Michael Leader.)

Two delightful photos of The John Tiller Girls, several of whom lived at Du Cane Court. (Courtesy of Doremy Vernon.)

Andrew Sandham, an early resident of Du Cane Court, and one of the outstanding cricketers of the 1930s. He was the first English batsman ever to make a triple century in a test match; and his match aggregate of 375 was the test record until the 1973-74 season. (Courtesy of MCC Library, Marylebone Cricket Club, Lord's Ground, London.)

Ernest Bubley, who lived in Du Cane Court between 1948 and 1976.
He occupied G003 (the flat beside Tommy Trinder's) from 1948 to 1951, and was England's top table-tennis star before the war. (Courtesy of English Table Tennis Association.)

ISSUES OF OWNERSHIP, AMBIENCE AND LIFESTYLE

*

Who Owns Du Cane Court?

From the 1960s it became common for landlords to sell off their flats on a leasehold basis for short-term gains. In this climate of events, a most peculiar question was in the air: who owns Du Cane Court anyway?

We have touched upon this question already, but since it was such a thorny issue – going all the way to the high courts - it might be useful to recapitulate, and to explore the mystery a little further. According to the Land Registry, the Royal Liver Friendly Society had a stake in the building from 1936 to 1972, although the company claims to have only collected the ground rents (which, it has to be said, is normally the action of the freeholder). The Central London Property Trust, which created Du Cane Court, was not finally dissolved until 1986, although the liquidators were appointed in the 1960s. The Trust must have had the freehold originally, for it had the authority to assign a head lease to Du Cane Court Ltd in the 1930s. Between 1964 and 1966, Du Cane Court Ltd acquired mortgages from Westminster Permanent Building Society, and apparently purchased the freehold in 1984, whilst sharing the same premises as the vendor, Keston Properties. But the plot thickens. The original Du Cane Court Ltd became Walrob Properties, only to pass out of existence on 31st August, 1985. Meanwhile, in 1967, the enterprise had been cloned like Dolly the sheep; and the clone remained extant until 1998.

Just to confuse matters further, a Du Cane Court Furnished Flats Ltd was incorporated in September, 1950, and dissolved on the 24th January, 1958, - although one assumes this dealt *exclusively* with furnishings or lettings, and not with ownership. Regalian must have had the freehold in 1974, in order to preside over the leasehold extensions which dated from that year, and which ran to the end of the twenty first century. Anyhow, in the final analysis, one or more individuals have owned the block at any given point in time – who may have been directors of one or more companies. In fact, in the 1950s or early 1960s, four men had dominion over this palatial dwelling place. One of them was Mr Livingston, whose name was displayed over the door of the in-house shop for many years. He may or may not have been the principle freeholder; but he was, at any rate, the leading light of Du Cane Court Ltd, mark 1, which possessed the head lease and therefore had a *form* of ownership.

The court case on the subject of ownership, which I have previously mentioned, dates from June, 1962 [Guildhall Library]. The key events were as follows. In an action of January 29-30, 1962, it was determined that William Livingston, the so-called ‘moving spirit’ behind Du Cane Court Ltd, was entitled to a block of shares, through which he would gain control of the company by a marginal majority. On May 25th, a resolution was passed for the increase of the capital by £150,000 - divided into three million shares of one shilling each. On the same day,

800,000 of the new shares were issued to Livingston's daughter, Mrs Hamilton. The Times Newspaper reported (on 7th October, 1966) that the new shares were withheld, and that General London and Urban Properties Ltd were confirmed as owners of 87% of the company. The opinion of the judge was that Du Cane Court Ltd did not need the new capital for its business, and there were grave suspicions of what the directors might do if not restrained by an injunction.

Flats for Sale

First National Finance Corporation purchased Du Cane Court in 1967, with the money provided by a consortium of bankers, including Hambros, British and Continental Banking, the Ionian Bank, and the Suez Finance Company [Troop]. The new owners resolved to give residents the opportunity to buy leases, initially running to 2035 (which was all the head lease allowed), and in doing so ushered in a new era at Du Cane Court. What was the motivation? Well, it was a quick profit and the properties would, in any case, revert to the freeholders at the end of the head lease; but apart from that, the rent which could be collected had become unattractive because it was subject to government control (and some residents still pay a 'controlled' rent to this day).

Indeed, after the war, landlords could not increase their rents for years. With the Rent Act, the principle was modified to apply only to flats above a certain 'rateable value' - which was the government's estimate of what the property was worth, - but it must have been a bane for any wealthy person who was affected. New legislation also made it easier for tenants to buy their properties, and, by all accounts, the landlords couldn't get rid of them fast enough! Our managing agents, Keith Cardale Groves, kept putting notices through people's doors offering them the right to buy; and the prices for existing tenants were very reasonable, ranging from £1,100 for a studio, up to about £5,500 for an apartment with 6 rooms. Mrs Middleton was offered a lease on her communal flat for £2,200.

'Oh, I couldn't pay that!' she told them.

'Well. What could you pay?'

'£1900.'

'Alright then,' came the placid reply. And so the price was set.

By 1973, the cost of property here varied from £4,500 – to £13,400 for a 3-bedroom flat [Evening.St]; and this pattern of steep inflation has continued. Maybe the pope's visit to Balham in the 1970s acted like a talisman ... for he blessed the Polish church next to the block, where many residents attend mass every Sunday, and it is rumoured that he visited the Polish club at Hamilton House, where the Tenants Association would later conduct its Annual General Meetings.

One commentator, Gray, estimated that only about 5% of all flats in Britain were owner-occupied in 1947 [Hamnett.&.Randolphe]. This has changed dramatically, not least at Du Cane Court, but owner occupation will never be 100%, because many flats are rented out and others are left vacant – even when owned by private individuals of modest means. In fact, some extraordinary research (on 101 blocks in central London) found that the percentage of vacant flats increased, between 1971 and 1981, from 8.8% to 33.2%.

Closing the Roof Gardens

One change at Du Cane Court which was not welcome was the closing of the roof gardens. Actually, they may never have been 'gardens' in the proper sense. Perhaps there had once been a few flower pots outside the restaurant, and elsewhere, – but the main attraction of this open space high above the city streets was the opportunity it afforded for sunbathing without being overlooked, and, perhaps, the chance to see some unusual people with their guard down. Hilda Middleton recalls meeting a gentleman on the roof one day who was called Mr Lusty. He was an old fellow in his 80s, and his family owned a firm which manufactured seats made out of cane called 'Lloyd Loom Chairs', otherwise known as 'Lusty Loom Chairs'. Yet instead of showing off one of these celebrated creations, which are now collector's items, he was perched on an old deck chair that was virtually falling apart!

Opinions differ as to when the roof was finally closed to public access. According to one person, the year was 1963; whilst another, Mary Whiteford, says that when she came in 1969, the roof was still open – although not for long.

According to Mr Bowdery, the roof had to be closed off so it could be resurfaced with dark bitumen and white chip gravel. The pressure of people's shoes, especially if they wore stilettos, would have caused punctures and allowed rainwater to leak into the seventh floor flats. Also, there was vandalism. Once, four lads were playing football up there; and on another occasion, children were scraping the surface and sending a shower of gravel over the side of the building. But Emily Quarman tells a more dramatic story. She says the real reason for closure was a Czechoslovakian throwing himself off the top of the building! And no doubt that bureaucratic monster, 'Health and Safety', did the rest. Really, as if someone with dire intentions could not just as easily jump out of a window! And what about Alderbrook Primary School - with a playground on its roof? No worries there, then ...

I, myself, wonder if the roof was declared 'out of bounds' because of a plan to build another floor at the top of the building.

The Benefits of Roof Gardens

Lord Rogers has praised roof gardens abroad, and he has a vision for London [Griffiths]. At the moment, turning your roof into a legally usable outside space often involves a lengthy battle with town planners. Taking up the baton, the Mayor of London, Ken Livingstone, published a paper some time ago encouraging homeowners to use their roofs to create a greener capital. Furthermore, a television programme broadcast on the

29th of March, 2000, focused on the Mayor of Chicago's determination to make *his* city more green. In his opinion, even the tops of skyscrapers should have plants. The concept is clearly gaining momentum, and has impacted upon the law - which in Basle, Switzerland, specifies that all new flat-roofed buildings must be covered in some form of vegetation; while official guidelines in Basle highlight the value of roof gardens for endangered beetles and birds. The effect of soil on roofs is also to insulate buildings and to make them warmer in winter. Iceland, known for its cold climate, has turf roofs on some of its old churches. But, quite apart from the benefits of insulation, or the joy of seeing a little floral colour, a green roof on Du Cane Court would supply Balham with an extra pair of lungs.

The Development of our Gardens

With their public space under threat, the residents of Du Cane Court started to take action. A Polish lady whose flat overlooked Balham Park Road noticed that there were few, if any, flower-beds opposite her. She asked if flowers could be planted to improve her view, on the proviso that she would pay for them. She actually paid about £200 – which must have been a lot of money in those days, - but ironically the grounds were soon afterwards apportioned to the development of a school. Another Polish lady, in a frenzy of activity in the 1960s and '70s, planted evergreens in one of the inner courtyards, and these have now grown to an imposing height. Hedges were planted around the outer courtyards in the late 1970s, or early 1980s, delivering more privacy for sun seekers. And yet another lady, Mrs Watts, converted, in the 1970s, an area behind the garages, that was formerly a rubbish tip and pet cemetery, into a delightful patio garden.

Flooding

All those who love horticulture must, in the final analysis, be glad of our wet climate, which keeps England green and fertile. But in the summer of 1973, there was a tremendous deluge of rain. Some roads were knee-deep in water, and a river ran through the grounds of the building. Even Balham High Road was flooded. The Head Porter, Mr Hearse, and an assistant descended to the boiler room, with the intention of switching off the power – but I understand the torrent of water was such that the stalwart pair actually ran the risk of drowning. One resident was astonished to find that water had navigated up through the pipes, and into his flat on the fifth floor! His bath was almost full, and there was gravel on the living room floor from the kitchen sink.

The next day, carpets were hanging out everywhere to dry; and the water mark was a foot or so high around the garages. In total, the hot water supply in the block was stemmed for about 10 days. Clearly, some serious action had to be taken to protect the area in future, and so a new storm sewer was installed by the water board near Bedford

Hill. But inside Du Cane Court floods still occur, and in severe situations certain pungent fluids may steel upon private wash basins or baths. However, we cannot blame the elements for all of these problems, for there is also the phenomenon of forgetful neighbours who leave their taps running. A little Irishman called Mr Rooney was one of the victims. The water seeping down from the flat above him mingled with his light fittings, and caused an explosion. Then one day he heard his doorbell ring. When he opened the door, standing before him was a buxom black lady with two bags of shopping. She lived below him, and had come to complain that water was penetrating *her* flat!

Emily Quarman, whose experiences of espionage in the war have been described, was flooded 14 times.

'I forgave the offender because he fought at the Battle of El Alamein,' she told me. 'Then one day he turned on his hot water and nonchalantly went out shopping. When I protested, he had the effrontery to bring a camera down to my flat in order to check if there was any damage. So I took him to court and sued him for £400. It never happened again.'

The most distasteful example of flooding was related to me by a good-natured friend of mine, who must have required the forbearance of a saint to refrain from strangling someone! He says:

'I awoke one night to discover my bed was warm and damp. When I switched on the light and investigated, I saw that sewage was leaking through the ceiling and down the walls.' Well, we have all heard the story about the gentleman who spends an evening at a wild party, and awakes the following morning to find a beautiful damsel - whom he does not recognize - lying next to him in his bed. One can even imagine contingencies such as this arising at Du Cane Court over the years ... but one would never expect one's bed to he warmed by a stranger's effluent!

The culprits were two pieces of scaffolding which had blocked the natural flow through one of the waste pipes. The manager said: 'It's not our fault.' When describing the incident to me, my friend tempered his wrath with the comforting thought that his flat is one of the few which is properly earthed. (Never mind that it was *im*properly soiled.) The 'cherry on the cake' is the disturbing information I once received that the owners of the building (then Belgrave Properties) were no longer able to obtain financial cover from their insurers, with regard to any damage caused by leaking stack pipes.

Like the Body Politic

Occasionally, when I relax in the quiet evenings and listen to the sounds of this huge building, I imagine that it resembles the human body. The 1930s obsession with curves and horizontal roofs gave it a rounded torso and a flat bald head, like an abbot. The sturdy joists are its skeleton, and -like the ribs of an athlete who is in fine condition – they are occasionally almost visible, at least in the foyer, where great, muscular boulders lure the roving female eye ... while all is encased within a thin layer of brickwork and glass, that hopefully breathes like a membrane.

The heart is the boiler room. Certain pipes are its arteries and its veins, with the radiators among the extremities. The stack is the intestine, clinging to the outer wall like a colostomy bag, and wishing it were a sweet and endearing little creeper: a grapevine, perhaps ...? And, as in any giant creature's digestive system, there is a great gurgling and bubbling of fluids, especially beneath the baths, that is sometimes accompanied by an unwelcome calling card; but never fear, for Mr Muscle acts like a dose of Andrews Salts.

The fabric of the building, like the living tissues of a body, also plays host to an army of parasites – including silver fish, carpet beetles and exotic ants – which are rarely seen and even more rarely heard, but are forever plying (forever unsuccessfully) their wicked trades to bring about 'Sick Building Syndrome'. Then there is the eternal cycle of building work, like the rounds of hospital treatment for the infirm (although this building is anything but 'infirm'); and, as in a hospital, the customer has little control over the proceedings, and perhaps even less over the outcome! Furthermore, he may reluctantly feel himself becoming a ward of 'the Court' as he grows older. But every inhabitant has at least the certainty of service charges, like death and taxes.

GOVERNANCE, CHECKS AND BALANCES

*

The Tenants' Association

Now that the tenants of Du Cane Court had a real stake in their future, it seemed only natural to inaugurate a Tenants' Association to represent their interests. Lucy Slater founded the new organization in 1971. It still exists, and is composed of a committee of about ten people and, perhaps, several hundred members. The leading lights of the committee are the chairman, the membership secretary and the treasurer, but there are others who play their part, including liaison officers who move between the committee and the residents, especially with an eye to canvassing new members.

Up to the mid-1980s membership was much higher than it is now - and on one occasion was about 500, - but by 1989 it had fallen to 380. There were far more owner-occupied flats in those days, whereas now it is an oft-spoken concern that those with short tenancies do not know the rules of the lease.

The recruitment drive for the Association has sometimes been quite aggressive, and I remember receiving one letter myself, probably in the late 1980s, which was so full of vitriol as to imply that membership was not a matter of choice but an obligation, and that the responsibility for all manner of ills could be laid at the doors of those who failed to sign up. Admittedly, the joining fee is only £5 even now; but this personal attack was a bolt out of the blue, and so I concocted a letter to the effect that it would be a peculiar act of masochism to pay even a tiny fee for a service which consists partly of abuse. However, for the sake of diplomacy I refrained from sending it. Of course, everyone has his own opinion. By providing succour to the Association, many have no doubt felt that they are fulfilling a civic duty; although, if they are acting under duress, they may derive no more pleasure from their involvement than 'jailbirds doing time'. Others there are, who revel in the moments of verbal combat and the dry bureaucracy.

To be fair, the Association can be helpful to residents, and operates in an open and democratic way. Any candidate for the committee may stand for election; and there is a small box in reception, into which residents (including non-members) may 'post' their feelings on the key issues of the day. The Association audits the service charges, and has the power to veto the management's choice of a service provider, if it finds another company which can perform equally well at less expense; and it has the right to insist upon at least three quotes for any major works above a given fee. It may countenance the needs of tenants in a dispute with the landlords, or at least perform the role of an impersonal mediator. So, in recent years, it was renamed the *Residents' Association*, to ensure that it does not appear to favour leaseholders. Unfortunately, I have heard that the new name divests it of any legal authority! Thankfully, this is not true. But it is true that membership has its privileges. Recent perks have included a 10% discount at

Chadwick's, the organic butchers by Balham Station; and a 20% discount on bills incurred at Du Cane Dry Cleaners.

The committee has been involved in many events over the years. It used to orchestrate trips to the Houses of Parliament, with assistance from the local MP. Upon arrival, the visitors would be shown around the House of Lords, and then treated to a cocktail reception before sitting down to dinner.

It was also involved in the creation of a Pet's Register. A block of flats would not generally be regarded as a suitable habitation for many species outside of *Homo Sapiens*; but as the years go by, the rules are less stringently enforced. Mavis, a portly old woman with a walking stick, used to stand in one of the courtyards with a Burmese cat on her shoulder, whilst smoking a pipe of herbal tobacco. I knew an elderly Polish woman who rescued stray canines, and displayed a message on her door, 'Beware of the dog', although the creature alluded to would have been unlikely to nip your ankles. One resident kept an iguana in the bath, and the bathroom was always hot and steamy like a sauna, in order to simulate the humid conditions of its natural habitat. Another keeps two tarantulas ... and a former manager once assisted in the rescue of a pet rat. Finally, in what sounds like a classic case of overcrowding, a single flat was reputedly home to a husband and wife, four children, two whippets, one or two hamsters, and one or two budgerigars!

Not every action of the Association has been successful and popular. It once opposed the shop's application for a liquor licence, but the proprietor, Kulbushan Chopra, proudly surmounted the resistance to become, at 23, the youngest person in the vicinity to obtain such a licence. Nevertheless, its opinion has been sought from time to time with regard to local issues. In the 1970s, Balham was chosen as the site for a pioneering experiment in traffic management. It was reckoned that every newborn child had a one in ten chance of becoming a road casualty before his sixteenth birthday; and a letter, dated November 25th, 1976, was sent to the secretary of the Tenants' Association, inviting representatives to a Round Table discussion at Brierley Hall, United Reform Church, in Balham High Road.

An Exceptional Committee

The committee has contained some pretty unusual characters since its inception. Among them was Wilfred Watts, Chairman of the British Spiritualist Society, who once appeared on television with Kilroy, claiming to have communicated with his dead aunt. Perhaps one day, when he has become a spirit himself, he will return to us for a while and answer some of the big questions.

But I must tell the reader about one particular gent, who was an old pretender to the chair. When he was chewing over a matter of some import, he would poke his tongue into his cheek as if it was not an organ of speech but a gobstopper. He fought plenty of battles, and (to borrow some words from Laurence Binyon) at the going down of the sun we will remember him, but he, along with others, must remain unnamed and entirely unidentifiable. 'Mr X', as I shall call him, often chased the younger residents who created any kind of disturbance. Upon the door being opened to him, he'd pucker his face in a manner which nicely erred on the side of humility. At the same time, he would gesture with his hands in the fashion of a musical conductor guiding his players through an understated classical movement, - whilst asking the offenders, in his very best Oxford English, to 'keep it down'. He once patrolled the entire length of C block with a spray can in his hand. When asked what he was doing, he replied, 'Somebody's cooking fish!'

But it was not only our oily friends who aroused his sensibilities. He also complained that his sleep patterns were interrupted by a blackbird – although it is more likely to have been a rook, for the blackbird's song is one of the loveliest and most varied in nature, – and he was observed running down a corridor whilst holding aloft a torch, as if he would light the Olympic flame. Unfortunately, while Mr X may be exonerated for displaying courage in the pursuit of his goals, he sometimes wanted in temperance. He once obtained an airgun, and made his way up to the roof with the intention of silencing the feathered creature permanently. I don't know whether he ever fired it – but curiously, a friend of mine received a note from the RSPCA one day about pigeon shooting. The postman had put it through the wrong letter-box, for it was meant for Bill Carrick (now deceased) who was *not* Mr X. And, while we are on the subject, another friend was sitting outside her flat one sunny afternoon, when a bullet suddenly whistled past her head into the nearby bushes. She reported the incident, and wonders if it was some kind of target practice.

Sad to say, the disposition of Mr X evolved over time. The veneer of polished manners was worn away, revealing not solid, dependable oak, nor rich mahogany, but a rough and ready composite that left its splinters in anyone who rubbed him up the wrong way. In fact, he could coin a devilish insult that was so colourful as to be almost a work of art.

Many years ago, a certain significant other was also involved in some (innocent) escapades, but in the end fell out of favour with Mr X. One day they argued and some hair was pulled, prompting the exclamation to someone standing near by, 'Sir, get the police! Mr X has assaulted me ... Assault! Assault!' Then, about five minutes after the hue and cry had died down, the victim showed a virtuous stoicism by opening a conversation with the manager's assistant, in honey-sweet, mellifluous tones: 'Hello, my dear. How are you?'

Venues for Meetings

In the 1990s the former 'gardener's store', which had fallen into disuse, found fresh employment as a venue for the regular committee meetings. However, for the Annual General Meetings, which received a much higher attendance, the venue was Hamilton House, home to the Polish White Eagle Club. It is rumoured that the name 'Hamilton' was derived from Lady Hamilton, whom Horatio Nelson would visit on his way to Merton Abbey where he worshipped; and the sea captain did, in fact, dedicate a building to his sweetheart, even though they were both already married! The site for our meetings is not old enough to have been that building, but the folklore delicately sets the scene for other shady deals which were *not* motivated by love.

The social facilities proffered by the building were previously employed by the '211 Club' (so called, because the address was 211 Balham High Road); and local legend, like a garland, encircles the place with startling claims: that it was opened by the famous actor, George Raft, who had connections with the underworld ... and attended by the Kray brothers on a particular evening when one or both of them murdered an adversary.

Extraordinary General Meetings

Whilst no inhabitant of any underworld – not even Pluto – has condescended to attend the Association's Annual General Meetings, the latter have nevertheless been graced by some colourful personalities. I am told of an attendee, tri-lingual and a journalist by trade, who wore yellow leggings, and draped herself in scarves and other finery. She stood up at the meeting one year, and surprised everyone by exclaiming, 'The Tenant's Association should print its newsletters in French!' After a moment or two of stunned silence, she added, 'En Français! Not everyone speaks English, you know.' There was a fit of giggles in the auditorium, and so – hoping that any emphasis would equate to an enhancement of gravitas – she simply repeated her request. (Nowadays, Balham is so ethnic that such an incident might pass without comment. Mind you, I was told she wanted the newsletters not only in English and French, but in a total of fourteen languages, which even today sounds rather excessive!)

Then there was the fateful day when Mr X was simultaneously expelled from the mouth of the committee, and the rear end of the meeting area. Oh, bad turnip (or brave renegade), whatever was the matter? The man, himself, takes up the story:

'I was grabbed by two thugs in the entrance of Hamilton House. My left arm was twisted behind me and my hand forced back at an acute angle. Had [my friend] not slapped one of them, I dread to think of what might have happened.'

The Fall Out

What has been described was uniquely cruel, for the victim was by now rather elderly and infirm, but there was more political intrigue to come. An equally ambitious pretender twice tried to disband the Tenants' Association, and once inquired if a rival association would be recognised by the manager; but the manager very sensibly replied that his visitor should become involved with the existing one.

'Ah! But of course!' the questioner must have mused, with Machiavellian joy. 'If the existing one is dissolved and I create a new one, then I (with my reforms) will be the leading light.'

The wish was at least half granted. On 15th February, 1987, there was a resignation statement from the entire committee. Well, I suppose their tasks were fairly thankless anyway. After all's said and done, such contributions are made out of charity – or, at least, are not for monetary gain. The atmosphere must have been gloomy, for there was even a statement saying that the committee were 'appalled by porters openly and publicly abusing tenants'. To their credit, the committee had found time, before their resignation, to investigate the 'unexplained excess' in the landlords' charges, which may have been 'as much as 50% of the general service charge for that year' – and which is a subject I shall return to later. But the problems didn't end there. A couple of years after this, on 1st June, 1989, there was an amazing letter from Paddy Flawn to Mr Page, the director of the management company. It speaks of the 'events of last weekend when we nearly lost all our staff', and adds, 'Had Mr Shew gone, the others would have gone as well, not to mention our housekeeper'. It seems that, in the 1980s, the whole system was crumbling.

Bureaucracy and Leases

Sometimes the system of leasehold gives birth to the most defective of situations, where ownership is passed about like a football. So it was that Regalian Securities, our landlords between 1974 and 1984, ran into problems with a penthouse of theirs in Petty France, Westminster, which comprised a maisonette and a self-contained flat. In 1936, a gentleman took on a lease for the entire property. In 1973 he assigned the lease to his son, who sublet the maisonette to a family friend, who, in 1975, assigned the sublease to yet another person! When the original lease ran out in 1978, the son invoked the protection of the Rent Acts with regard to the whole property. Lord Denning presided over the appeal by Regalian in 1981, in which he ruled that the Acts only protected the son for that part of the property which was occupied.

And the great god of legal proceedings said to his pages, 'Go forth and multiply!' And they did ...

In 1978, Thwaytes Solicitors acted for the prospective purchaser of a flat, and of garage 29a, at Du Cane Court; and were oblivious to their sexual *faux pas* as they observed that 'consent for the erection and retention' of the garage was due to run out on 1st February, 1983. (Evidently the world of bricks and mortar runs contrary to the human condition, where the sexual franchise, which is procured through reaching a particular age, cannot later be rescinded.) In spite of this, the client intended to buy a long lease on the garage which would not expire until 2036. I understand that it was, in a manner of speaking, relatively 'young'; and the purchaser was hoping that it would be 'permitted to be retained' (tactfully worded, so as not to give any offence to the garage, which is clearly a sentient being, and might have baulked at the prospect of being terminated whilst still in the prime of life). The District Surveyor replied that it was not possible, but that the situation could be reviewed in 1983 for a further five-year licence.

On 30th March, 1983, Mr Milligan-Smith, Manager of Du Cane Court, wrote that consent was urgently required, as there were three sales of garages being held up. Unfortunately, some of the garages now required maintenance, as the concrete door posts were cracked or breaking; and, not surprisingly, the District Surveyor would only give his blessing for three years ...

So we move the clock on to 1986, when the Chief Building Control Officer was refusing to renew garage licences unless repairs were done! Really, when one reads of 'the council, in pursuance of its powers', one might fantasize about a leaden-footed herbivore chasing its runner beans – with neither hunter nor quarry going anywhere fast!

Finally, on 3rd March, 1987, the deputy of the aforesaid Officer stepped in with breezy confidence, writing that the procedure for granting the garages permanent status was 'purely an internal paper exercise'. A letter from Brian Parker of Keith Cardale Groves soon followed with the words, 'We are most anxious to gain this status'.

Never mind, Brian. When it comes to the law, what's nine years of anxiety between friends?

Landlord and Tenant

All leases may contain a clause stating that the lessor is entitled to enter the property and forfeit the lease in certain situations; but the Protection from Eviction Act stipulates that the landlord must go to court first [Jankowski]. Nowadays, the law somewhat favours the leaseholder over the freeholder, for the courts have held that a landlord who contracts to provide a service should do so, even if the lessee is in arrears with the service charge.

Tenants may request that landlords pay their own legal bills, and, when variations were applied to certain leases at Du Cane Court in 1993, this is exactly what the landlords had to do. Furthermore, most lessees in this block should enjoy full security under the Rent Act when their leases have run their course – because most leases were granted prior to 15th January, 1989. However, I cannot speak for those granted after this date.

Types of Ownership

The leasehold system is really rather archaic, and seems like a contemporary offspring of medieval serfdom. In spite of the sympathies of the law, a leaseholder has little control over his environment, and he is living on someone else's land as if he had a tied cottage, – except that a tied cottage comes free with a farm-hand's work, and a leasehold is anything but free.

There are those at Du Cane Court who would prefer a form of freehold: perhaps a condominium, where each tenant owns part of the building, with shared ownership of the common parts; or a cooperative, where every flat owner has a stake in a single corporate entity which can be mortgaged. The problem with the second solution is that if vacancies are created by people leaving, they must be 'bought out' by those who remain [Paul].

Gaining the Freehold

Curiously, the knights of the cities are more sympathetic to a new system of tenure than the knights from distant rural shires [Fishburn]. So why has a major change not occurred? Well, the ground has shifted over time, but, circa 2000, the condition was that two-thirds of tenants must be in favour of gaining the freehold in order to make it possible – and that half of these should be owner-occupiers [Barry.2000]. Unfortunately, such conditions may not be easy to fulfil in a place the size of Du Cane Court. I know that, in the 1990s, one of our architect's sons – John Kay Green – and his fellow tenants had to fight a hard battle to gain the freehold of their properties; and, in that case, there were only a few tenants involved (Kay Green and Others vs Twinsectra Ltd, 1996).

Many years ago, a key member of our committee, Gloria Blackhurst, saw an opportunity for us to gain the freehold. Unfortunately, the apathy she encountered deeply disappointed her. The thought has crossed my mind that those around her were in collusion with the landlords; but assuming that all accounts have been honestly kept ... landlords of large buildings sell to each other, so why not to us? It is more likely her fellow committee members were dissuaded by a vision of internal strife, wherein everyone is proposing a different constitution. Anyhow, whenever a block of flats comes up for sale, the leaseholders must be given *first refusal*, or the first opportunity to buy. So, every few years there should be a fresh chance for us to stake our claim.

Devil's Advocate: Is the Freehold actually worth having?

The costs of freeholds are calculated on annual ground rents, and many have been purchased by holders of long leases in London for less than £900. Unfortunately, anyone who has a short lease must also pay to the vendor half of the 'marriage value', which is the amount required to 'top up' the normal lease to its full complement. For the owner of a two-bedroom property at Du Cane Court in 2007, with less than 30 years left on its tenure, this could cost about £76,000. The same principle applies when buying a 999-year lease: settling the 'marriage value' is an additional expense. But the consolation is that one would not have to get two-thirds of the population of the building to agree to anything.

In the middle to late 1990s, Mark Pitman (of Belgrave Properties) was happy to offer us the 999-year option with a peppercorn ground rent. The idea was for groups of 10 to 15 people, all with long leases, to operate together, each paying £3000. It was a generous offer – although it was also an attractive deal for the freeholder, rendering a quick and easy profit to his estate; a profit which, although small in proportion to the underlying asset, could not be bettered until long after his demise. I might add that a satisfactory lease extension (of around a hundred years) should be easy enough to organize for a small fee, anyway, so long as the existing lease has at least 80 years left to run.

However, David Young, a member of the Association of Residential Managing Agents, comments (not of any particular block) that of all tenants offered extensions to their leases, only 7% had responded positively; and one article in The Times even states bluntly that the problem is not leasehold extension but service charges, which can sometimes amount to extortion [Thomas].

Most leases at Du Cane Court run until 2099. Will any tenant of 2007 still be alive then? Of course, if a property is retained by a family, and passed down through the generations as an heirloom, then a longer lease becomes attractive.

So much for human life. What of the life expectancy of the building? A recent presentation (19th March, 2004) at the Balham Society on the history of the local Heaver Estate, revealed that 84% of the houses built in Balham in 1860 are no longer here. That was a period of 144 years. Du Cane Court was completed in the late 1930s. In 2099, when most of the existing leases run out, it will be about 160 years old. How much longer than that will it remain standing anyway? There may be wars or 'acts of God' which we can do nothing about. On the other hand, it is built more solidly than the average house; and, furthermore, one hopes that the block will not be *allowed* to fall into a decrepit state (until such time as it is beyond hope), for any popular building which maximizes the use of prime land as well as it does, will continue to be an asset to the community.

THE PASSING YEARS

*

Management 1970s -1990s

There have been various management styles over the years. Mr Hearse, Head Porter in the early 1970s, was affable and decent – although he would not stand for any nonsense. Mr Milligan-Smith was *his* boss, and his style was the opposite - *laissez-aller.*

After Milligan-Smith, the next manager was Mr Parker. He had an intense, serious personality, and was assisted by a mysterious young secretary from the East called Rebecca, whom I can vouch for personally as being well-organised and polite. Following in the wake of Mr Parker were three female bosses, whose employment was presumably far too brief for them to distinguish themselves. Then there was Gary Hopkins, manager in the early 1990s, who was a slim fellow with an interest in yachts; but he was only in charge for a year or so, and could be forgiven for not sailing into the sunlight of our memories.

He was succeeded by David Clark, who was remarkable for his professionalism and efficiency. If you wrote to him, the reply might have been already sitting on your mat before you rose the following morning; although sometimes he was made weary by unhappy residents. A friend of mine, Derick Malet, has praised him for being 'the first of the reforming managers'. Next came Andrew McKeer, who had a buoyant spirit, and was amiable and helpful (although perhaps rather laid back for some people's tastes). He also had a good sense of humour, and once famously remarked that the departure of his voluptuous assistant would leave a hole that was difficult to fill. This may apply not only to the space which her corporeal presence occupied, but to the expansiveness of her personality; for, like many creatures of the wild, she was rather intractable, and would be sweet-natured only if handled with great care. For some reason, the elderly population of 'the Court' seemed to elicit the most kindly responses from her.

How Times have Changed

My interviews with long-term residents revealed something of human life as it used to be. Emily Quarman, whose talent for languages has already been noted, once told me:

'I was the fastest 100-yard sprinter in my county as a teenager, and confused the opposition in hockey by playing left-handed. I must have been born happy, and I must have been born left-handed.' You'd think her mother would have been happy as well, having such a talented daughter, but Emily says, 'I would get a rap over the knuckles to change my handedness.' Thankfully, such a punishment would never occur today.

I also spoke to a lady who'd had a career in publishing.

'The business is completely different from when I was working,' she told me. 'There are now fewer opportunities, and publishers are less interested in literature than in money.'

Another lady in her nineties reveals something of the uncertainty of life between the wars:

'My uncle hid his sovereigns under his bed. He didn't invest in banks, because in those days even banks could just collapse. One day he died and passed on his savings, tax-free, to his children. It was two or three thousand pounds, which was a considerable sum before the war. People had a different attitude to money in those days. For example, when my family and I moved into rented accommodation, we redecorated the property of our own accord. The landlord responded in kind, saying that we'd added value to it, and charged us no rent for three years.

Single parent families used to be rare, although my own mother died when I was young.' Apparently her father was a disciplinarian. He was probably terrified that she might have inherited his free spirit, for she told me, 'When he was eight years old, he saw a Royal Horse Artillery procession on the edge of the family estate. He was so enraptured that he decided to follow it, and left home! The servicemen looked after him well, and he became a mascot for them before joining the force properly; but his family never knew where he was. Finally, much later in life, his wife told him that he should contact them.'

Some Results from the Census

(Note: At least for the purposes of the 1991 census, Du Cane Court was in Nightingale Ward. However, to some extent this is academic, and any data on Balham Ward can tell us something about the surrounding area.)

When I examined statistics from the census, some interesting facts emerged. The shifting boundaries for Balham radically altered the size of the population between 1931 and 1951, from 53,982 to 14,806. Yet for both years there were significantly more women than men; whereas in 1971, among persons in Balham aged 25 to 29 in private households, the males (581) outnumbered the females (551). Whether the gender distribution was the same across other age groups, I cannot say; but I can confirm that in 1991, Du Cane Court was following the first pattern, having appreciably more females than males. The effect was especially marked in blocks H, J and K where, collectively, females outnumbered males by almost 2 to 1 (155:87). I imagine Du Cane Court is attractive to women because, with round-the-clock porterage and security, they feel safe here.

On the subject of ethnic mix, one may think of this block as reflecting the diversity of the surrounding area. However, while Balham Ward in 1991 was only 76.2% white, across Du Cane Court it was just over 90%. This was with the exception of block A, for which the statistics are combined with other properties outside the building. Perhaps there is a tendency for those of the same racial group to congregate together, and so the concentrations of different races become self-perpetuating, or – to air the putative opinion - maybe economic advantages within the white population mean that it is predominantly they who can afford to live here. Either way, we often do not realize how lucky we are at Du Cane Court: for as recently as 1971, of 4,576 dwellings in Balham, 439 had no hot water, 509 had no bath and 430 no inside WC! And even in 1991, 21% of homes in Balham Ward had no central heating ...

But the local economy has improved over the years; and in a 10% sample from 1991, 31.3% of employed residents in Balham were in 'banking and finance etc.'. This is hardly surprising, with all the banks in the vicinity. What's more, in a 1991 sample of economically active people living in Du Cane Court, there was only one resident whose work was clearly identified as below the category of 'skilled non-manual', and no one was in the armed forces.

In society at large there is an increasing number of single people, swelled by divorce and by a tendency to marry late in life. This is reflected at Du Cane Court, for the 1991 census shows that over the whole building (apart from block A), the percentage of men who were single, widowed or divorced was 80.3%; and for women, the figure was 84.5%.

I have one more observation I wish to make. It is often said that the general population is aging, and this pattern emerged with interest at Du Cane Court in 1991 – especially in blocks B to E, where, out of a total of 272 persons, 101 were of pensionable age or over.

DU CANE COURT TENANTS' ASSOCIATION

30 November 1971

Dear Tenant,

You will no doubt recall that you received a copy of the Minutes of a meeting of the Castelnau Tenants' Association together with the notice of our own General Meeting on 25 November.

I announced at that General Meeting that a circular had been issued by the newly formed Federation of London County Residents Associations and, as it is of interest to all of us at Du Cane Court, it was decided that all the tenants should receive a copy, which is attached. We are maintaining a close liaison with this Federation as its main problems are somewhat akin to ours.

Most of you are probably aware that the Du Cane Court Tenants' Association is now officially in being and, as Chairman, I can assure you that we shall make every endeavour to the best of our ability to look after your interests as tenants, whether leaseholders or rent payers.

This letter will probably be the last to be distributed to all tenants of Du Cane Court, as in future only those who have joined the Association will receive notices. It is imperative that we should be in a strong position and therefore may I please request those of you who have not already joined the Association to do so soon.

Yours sincerely,

J.T. KING

Chairman

A proud moment for the new leaseholders of Du Cane Court, who at last had their own Association. (Courtesy of the Tenants' Association.)

cc
M Townsley D34
H Stewart D34
S Emmanuel E53
D Yzelman E411
N Smallman H24
V. Nnoka D58
M Tillman G62
G Owen D74
B Murrell +1 G35
A. Alsader D62
C Jarrett +1

HOUSE OF COMMONS
LONDON SW1A 0AA

From: TOM COX MP

Hilary Tothill Scott
Du Cane Court Tenants Association
Du Cane Court
London SW17

8 February 1996

Dear Hilary Tothill Scott,

Further to my letter of 4th December, I write to confirm that you and your group are visiting the House of Commons on Thursday, 22nd February.

Will look forward to seeing you at St Stephen's Entrance at 10.15am.

Kind regards.

Yours sincerely,

Tom Cox

TOM COX

PLEASE NOTE ST STEPHEN'S (NOT ST GILES'). Please ask policeman at car park entrance if in doubt

Unfortunately I am unable to attend so please introduce yourselves to each other and be PROMPT. Mr Cox will come out of the entrance very punctually and cannot wait for latecomers

I hope you will find the tour as interesting as I did. Mr Cox is very informative and is always happy to answer questions

Hilary Tothill Scott

With the assistance of Tom Cox, the local MP, the Tenants' Association has been helpful in organising trips to the House of Commons for those who were interested. (Courtesy of the Tenants' Association.)

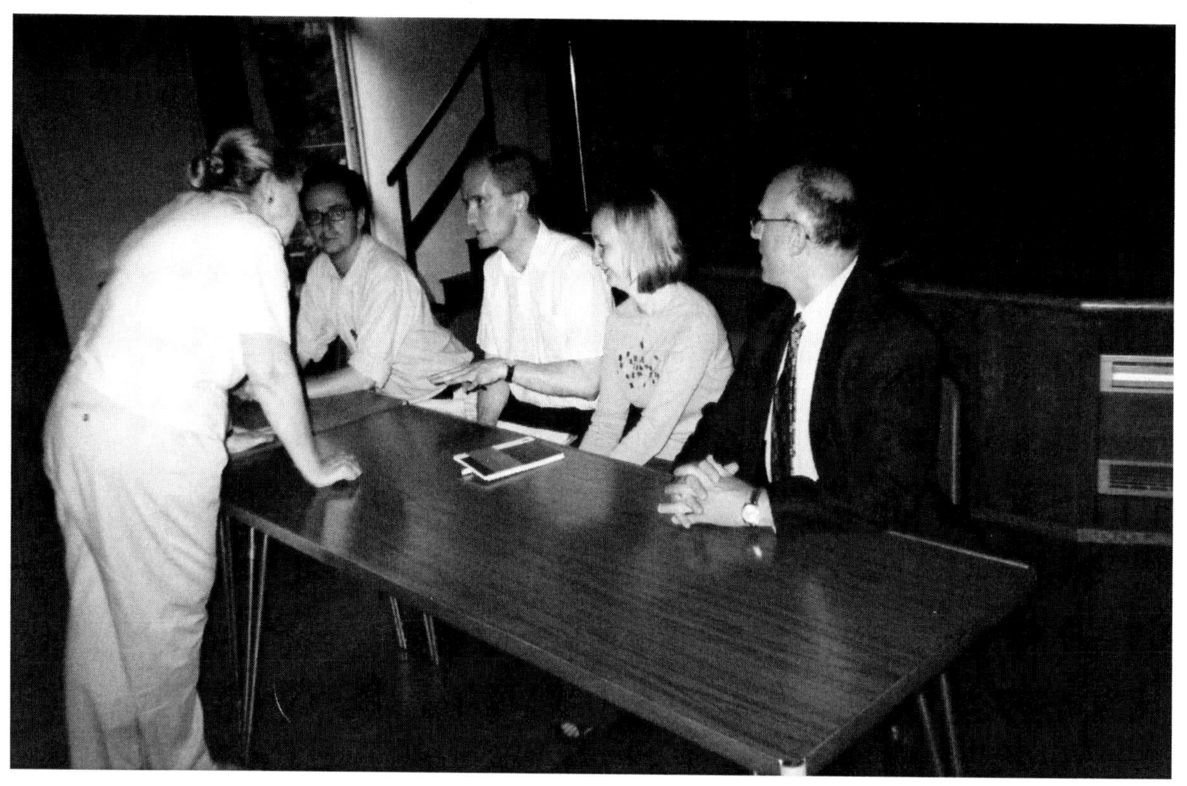

A recent photo of the committee answering a query, at an Annual General Meeting held in Hamilton House. (Photograph taken by the author.)

Hamilton House, where the AGM is held. (Photograph taken by the author.)

THE SPIRIT OF A COMMUNITY

*

In contemporary society, the state has tended to subsidise married couples and families through a variety of allowances. I suppose the assumption is that if people live in stable groups, the community as a whole is more cohesive. Yet still, there is a tendency these days to remain single - in spite of the economics of sharing, – and a network of friends living under the one roof of Du Cane Court, though they may all be single, may become like another kind of family.

They say that those who are happily married live longer, but what of those who are unhappily married, or working their way through a convoluted and interminable divorce settlement? In a large, well-maintained block, you have the vicarious delight of emerging from a chrysalis of silence and total privacy into a social butterfly, and all in the space of a minute or two. One could say, 'You have the best of both worlds'. And regarding the first of those worlds, the realm of privacy, there is the following story. A resident was once privileged to accompany the former Prime Minister, Edward Heath, on his yacht. Unfortunately, the boat sank and a member of the crew drowned. Shortly afterwards, our reception was swarming with reporters who wanted to speak with the lucky survivor, and the situation became so hectic that the Head Porter, Mr Hearse, told them: 'Get out, or I will phone the police!' And the whereabouts of the hunted man were not disclosed.

There have also been times when the community spirit was put to the test. Years ago, a lady became notorious for making strange visits to our little shop. The protocol was as follows. She would collect a large quantity of food and leave it all on the counter, like a squirrel about to stock its larder for the winter, before realizing that she had insufficient funds with her to pay the bill. Then she would apologize and promise to pay later, which she never did. And so everything would have to be put back on the shelves – until her next visit, when the whole tortuous process began again!

Du Cane Court has been compared to a village, although in the eyes of some this is a mixed blessing. If you are the ingenuous type, a shallow fabulist may pluck your barely ripened thoughts, grow them (as if *in vitro*), and then, with a wickedly sharp tongue, syringe them into the agenda for his next scandalous conversation. But I jest, for most people are far too busy with their own business to worry about yours; and – given the size of the building – two neighbours may not meet for months if they do not plan to. When they finally do - there is the shop, the reception area and the garden. Sadly, the facilities on the seventh floor are no more, but residents of all ages have been quite resourceful at providing their own entertainment.

As long ago as the 1950s, there was a group who would organize games and other social events. Years later, entertainers would come together and put on a show for residents at the White Eagle Club. And within the environs of Du Cane Court, there was in the 1980s a little debating society with a pleasantly esoteric name, *The Knights of the*

Round Table, which met in the reception or in the gardens, and behind which a certain Mr Rooney was perhaps the prime figure. (Dear reader, you have met this gentleman before: he was the little Irishman who was once visited by a large black lady, on the premise that she was receiving his water and therefore had an interest in his plumbing.)

'I see you people have been trying to blow up London again!' he was once rebuked during 'the troubles'. But being a man of acute intelligence, he, also, was quite able to break the ice with a shard of banter – before sitting back to enjoy the perturbed ripples undulating just beneath the surface. Most others, who moved about 'upstairs' with less dexterity, would have to content themselves with *staircase wit*: literally, the witty repost that comes to mind only after one has left the drawing room. But then – allow me the embellishment, - the staircase wit of today is the drawing room wit of tomorrow.

Kindness between Residents

Many have attested to the spirit of neighbourliness at Du Cane Court. Often, tenants will visit their neighbours in hospitals or in care homes. One pleasant old lady told me she had never come across anyone bad here in 60 years. She said her home was comfortable, safe and quiet. Indeed, such is the sense of mutual trust at Du Cane Court that residents do not always chub lock, or even shut, their doors. I must also note the camaraderie amongst the old or infirm, which might inspire the following kind of tribute after Sunday service, 'Did you see Mrs Boran sitting in the front pew, with her silk dress and beautiful hat? Even at her age, she still looks marvellous.'

And beyond the exchange of pleasantries, there is devotion. A certain friend, with the presidential surname of Jefferson, was proud that he had worked on the trams in his prime, and was a simple man at heart with his own brand of nobility. One day, a young neighbour of his had her door broken down in a police raid for illegal drugs. With the girl in tears and it being too late to call out a professional, he performed a utilitarian repair on it - so at least her home was not exposed while she slept. That his Christian act was undertaken at night would have been no problem for him, as he was a creature of strange habits, sleeping by day and working under the cover of darkness; or, if not diligent in the *wee small hours*, reclining in an armchair in the flat of his next-door neighbour and reputed girlfriend, an octogenarian who was losing her mind.

Unfortunately, he suffered from a rare condition known as 'coeliac disease', which meant that he had to be on a strict diet – excluding wheat and other sources of gluten, – and this may have had consequences for his energy levels. Nevertheless, he helped his friends with any practical job. Painting and decorating ... carpentry ... it was all acceptable to him, with the fee set by the customer; or with no fee at all, as when he varnished a bureau and a sitting-room table for someone I know. He was a perfectionist, slow and deliberate, taking up to a few months to make a cabinet. And when the favour was returned with a meal, he became very slow indeed. One woman who catered for him told me his timescale: 'three hours to consume a bowl of soup, and five hours for a solid meal!' Sadly, after the fashion of many good people, he had little interest in his own welfare, and in the end he was found by a close friend, drowned in his bath and gradually turning purple, with a cigarette in his mouth and a can of coca-cola by his side.

Another story was related to me by a young lady named Dolores. A neighbour of hers in his mid-90s was a friend of the person who had previously occupied her flat. She didn't change the locks after she moved in, and sometimes she would return home to find, say, a cardigan draped over a chair, or a pair of slippers on the floor. Apparently, the old man had happy memories of the place, and he just wanted to reminisce. So she 'adopted' him – in a manner of speaking - and when he had a heart attack he would leave his own door ajar, so that she could look in on him and check he was sleeping peacefully. I think this is a rather sweet tale of endearment, but sometimes 'sweet familiarity' can be taken too far ....

Sylvia Say remembered a neighbour of hers who used to work at Harrods, and who was often in transit between her home and the department store. Once, this individual pushed her way, uninvited, into the bathroom of Ena Brightwell, who was Sylvia's mother.

'What are you doing in there?' she was asked.

'I'm going to the toilet. What do you think?' came the reply. And another time, she wrapped her silver knives and forks in the folds of her corset, and left them outside Ena's door! Stolen property, perhaps?

Porters and Residents

A huge range of faces have passed through the ranks of our porterage and security teams, and, with such a huge Polish population, it is hardly surprising that, until recently, we had a Polish porter. His name is Roman. He is advanced in years, and was in a labour camp during the war. Perhaps because of this, few things ever really faze him, and to this day he retains a relatively youthful complexion. He was an admirable servant of our community for many years; and he commanded respect, in spite of a small stature - and a healthy surplus of hair which, in the eyes of one resident, stood on end like the spines of a hedgehog. With him manning the desk, you knew you were safe. Although if you were a stranger, you were lucky to be allowed past him without some verbal screening; and, with comical effect, even a resident might have to account for himself! His colleague, Neil, always had a bright smile and an engaging little story, freshly prepared like an all-day breakfast that sustains you through the hours ahead. Indeed, being sociable by nature, and having played in a band (in his earlier days) for Roy Castle, Cilla Black, Arthur Askey, Jimmy Tarbuck and Danny Le Rue, he had a deep well of experience to draw upon.

With their close scrutiny, exercised over many years of faithful service, the two of them got to know where everyone here lived, and eventually the multitudes became known by their flat numbers. Thus

Roman or Neil might observe (although these examples are merely contrived), 'There goes K51, on her weekly trip to the hairdressers'; or 'Poor H58. She turned 90 last week. She thinks she knows where she is, but she really doesn't have a clue.'

The Craig brothers were another unusual double act, although only one of them was a porter here. Some time ago – in the late 1970s or '80s – one or both of them were involved in a haulage business, and would store furniture at the bottom of the fire escape in D or E block! (A fire hazard, perhaps?) One wonders if they also had anything to do with the 1930s van, which sat in an overgrown garden at the back of Du Cane Court for a whole year.

Although it is possible that *certain* porters have, on occasion, been slow to assist the younger residents with a problem, unless they are attractive females, kindness is usually shown to the elderly. One beneficiary said, 'When my electric fire ceased to work, one of the porters checked it out and gave me a new one; and whenever I need something from the shop, I just ring downstairs and they will bring it up to me.' Another told me, 'If I cannot reach a light bulb to change it, a porter will change it for me.' And we have a muscular groundsman called Graham, who will help with heavier jobs like shifting furniture.

The residents cherish their staff, and at Christmas time they shower them with cards, presents and bottles of wine. One person even gave them a television set. What is more, the grounds themselves bear witness to the various personalities who have graced Du Cane Court over the years: with dedications on wooden seats, and, in one case, a memorial which takes the form of a rock.

A Motley Neighbourhood

The community of Du Cane Court tolerates diversity. There are those who have zestful parties - including a girl with braided hair who takes her pet rabbit out on a leash; and there are the senior citizens, one of them so bent with age that the lock on her front door had to be lowered to waist height before she could get into her flat. A friend of mine describes a particular woman as having a mop of hair 'like a buzzard's nest', and a smell to match! And what of an immaculately dressed fellow with a very red nose and arthritic fingers, which have curled around so cruelly that they are beginning to resemble claws? Indeed, the pattern of former ages has been reversed, for to be well-groomed and in fine apparel has become the preserve of the octogenarian of sound mind; whilst the younger inhabitants often have a dress sense like a postman's lost bundle: and both, inevitably, must miss their mark. But by what margin did a particular lady miss the mark when, wearing little more than her knickers and a handbag, she was on her way out of the building with the terse remark, 'I'm just going shopping!' Our trusty porter, Roman, had to rush out and retrieve her - although she was actually quite lucid!

One day two friends of mine saw an unusual lady stepping out of the lift. She was around six feet high, and wore a hat and probably high heels. The verbal exchange between my friends was as follows.

'Oh! My dear, isn't she glamorous? But it's a little late for the catwalk,' said May to Alan, or 'A Local Area Network', as he is otherwise known.

'The catwalk?' whispered Alan. 'It's a man!'

Once upon a time our unnamed neighbour, who is a sexual shade of grey with perhaps double the normal equipage, made the acquaintance of an equally outlandish person from the community at large – whom I have nicknamed 'Shake 'n' Spread Better', on account of his being 'all a-tremble' in the local betting-shop, so transfixed was he by the horses racing across the television screens. This second character also had the singular habit of leaning so far back in his locomotion, that his spine would surely have been married to the unforgiving pavement were it not for the protrusion of the oval stomach, which was smaller than the cricket ground of the same name, but just large enough to counterbalance his posture. Evidently, he had picked up the 'shade of grey' in a local bar, but after a brief interaction inside 'the Court', he realized that he had backed the wrong horse entirely.

'Get me out of here! Get me out of here!' he exclaimed, before issuing forth, stomach first, into the Balham air, like a thoroughly fed up duck which was just ripe for the cull.

Strange Mannerisms

A neighbour of mine moved several years ago to an especially grand dwelling on the first floor. It has a spacious lounge, a dedicated dining room, a utility room, an ample hallway and two bedrooms. His windows are as numerous as a spider's eyes, and through them he watches the comings and goings of the natives – as is, no doubt, customary in the tiny Dorset village from which he hails; and it is a pleasure he shares with his friends when he has them round for a magnificent Sunday lunch. Yet unlike a spider, which actually responds more to vibration, very little escapes *his* eyes. If you went shopping at 1pm and returned at 3pm, he would know. But it is all good-humoured and harmless enough.

Like Mr Turveydrop in 'Bleak House', he, also, has a *School of Deportment*, although the examples he calls to mind are more in line with Monty Python's 'Ministry of Funny Walks'. His love of humour is like a marriage. It must remain pure in order to be genuinely savoured; and even a touch of seriousness is eschewed as if it were an act of adultery. With very little prompting, he will launch into his impersonations like a man possessed.

'Who's this?' he says, imitating a cleaner who walks like a gorilla. 'And this?' he adds, synchronizing his movements to those of a pigeon-toed lady, who would steady herself with outstretched arms like a jumbo jet approaching the runway. 'And this ....' he continues, utterly remorseless, pretending to be a woman with her nose in the air, who is pulled along by a tiny dog so effortlessly, she might have been gliding. 'And Sanskrit ...' he would introduce the last in his 'gallery of the absurd', and the only example which does not involve locomotion: a lady who studies the said language, and who twitches her neck when spoken to, as a peripheral response to the ebb and flow of the conversation.

Well-Connected Residents – And a little Trivia

When reflecting on the building and its people, one may well infer that all roads lead to Du Cane Court. There is a theory that no human being is more than several 'points of separation' from any other, but here you could be forgiven for thinking that one or two points will suffice.

A thoroughgoing gentleman named Edward Kay has spent some time tracing his family tree, which took him on a virtual tour of discovery to a successful family of watchmakers in Germany. Another charming resident who is in her nineties, named Claire Macdonald-Ross, has the maiden name of Meakin. This is also the name of a Stoke-on-Trent pottery firm, no longer trading, which used to make colourful bone china; and it is possible the firm was founded by one of her ancestors.

Michael Grade's cousin lives here, as does one of the participants in the so-called 'reality show', Big Brother; and an Egyptian resident, Nouran El Naggar, is proud to have had a father who is celebrated in universities throughout the Middle East for his books on military strategy. The great grandson of P.G. Wodehouse once had a flat on the seventh floor; whilst another inhabitant of the seventh floor (recently deceased) possessed familial links to various areas of human endeavour. Her name was May Arkell, and she was blessed with a charming facility for making the most of what life had to offer. She was known as 'the duchess' in the local butchers, because she lived life exuberantly and would add a touch of grandeur to her surroundings. When thinking of the pond, and of the mini-supermarket which was formerly a dairy, she would set a rendezvous with the question, 'Lake side or dairy side?' May's aunt was the 'Gainsborough Lady', and she was keen to explain to me what this meant.

'Her image became synonymous with the British film company, The Gainsborough Pictures. My aunt would appear at the start of each film - like the lighthouse for RKO, or the lion roaring for Metro Goldwin Mayor, – nodding her head, as if she was an eminent lady giving her seal of approval to the entertainment which was to follow.

My father helped to found the first fire service in Claygate. My husband, Keith, worked for the Commercial Union, and became the Inspector of Insurance for the square mile. Originally, Commercial Union was known as the "Hand in Hand". It used the logo of the traditional freemason's handshake, and this same motif had to be manifest on the door of any building which was burning, otherwise the place was not insured and the fire service would ignore any cries for help.'

May's husband also had a distinguished ancestor ...

'His grandfather was a wine taster - and Arkell Breweries in Swindon, Wiltshire, belonged to the family.'

The Manager of the Caprice Restaurant once lived here. And yet another resident, Dolores Maia Bingham, has had her artwork displayed in the Royal Academy and in the Mall Gallery. Her brother is even more remarkable. He has been British Light Middleweight Boxing Champion, and he twice challenged for the World Championship. While on the subject, I might add that the art of boxing is alive and well in echelons of society where you would not expect to find it. Charles Jones (architect, and Chairman of the Residents' Association), is one of a number of white collar workers who have taken up the sport in their spare time. He has an amusing but rather catchy nickname, 'The Pink Pounder'. His exploits were featured in two programmes on 1st October 2003: 'Richard and Judy', and 'Real Life Heroes for Six Minutes'. In the second of these, we also learned about one of his opponents, who is a classical musician by day.

Du Cane Court is not short of military connections either. Admiral Mungavin lived here, and a resident now in her nineties, Louisa Wheway, told me that her father was Major York. She says:

'In the First World War, my father's commanding officer was General Du Cane, and my grandfather was General Pipon, Governor of the Tower of London. I was christened in the Tower, and lived there from the age of three weeks – for about five years - in the King's House, now known as the *Queen's* House. It became an alternative royal residence, and I believe Queen Mary once came into my nursery and exclaimed, "What a dear little girl!"

My grandfather was in control of the Yeoman Borders, or Beefeaters, and of the ravens. They say that when the ravens leave the Tower of London, England will fall. In fact, speaking of birds, I kept a jackdaw in my bedroom, and then a pigeon. In the end, the walls had to be stripped because of all the bird dung.'

A resident who hails from Scotland has a cousin, Sir Ronald Scobie, who was the General Officer in Command in Malta, serving under Sir John Du Cane, Governor of Malta. Sir Ronald was clearly popular with the Maltese, whom he was instrumental in liberating. On one occasion he heard the Maltese crowds calling, 'Bisco! Bisco ...!' - and when he asked about this strange vocalization, his assistant explained, 'They are calling for you: "Scobie! Scobie ...!"'

Another engaging neighbour, by the name of Mary O'Connor, had an uncle who introduced pineapples to Mauritius. In fact, there is a walk named after the venerable Charles O'Connor; and the headquarters in Pamplemousses Botanical Gardens were once his offices. Also with links abroad was Jessie Boran from D block. She entertained me one afternoon with a glass or two of spirit and some good *crack*, to use a well-worn Irish term. Her home was very comfortable. In the hallway was an Austrian crystal chandelier, while the dining room contained an example of English crystal and a lovely walnut table, - 'so my young relations know to be careful,' she said. Jessie was proud of the family name, 'Boran', and a plaque on the wall commemorated it.

'Ireland was one of the first countries to develop a system of hereditary surnames,' she explained. 'The surname *Boran* is an anglicized version of the Gallic name, *O'Bodhrain*, deriving from *Bodhar* which means *Deaf*.' (And, trust me, she was!) 'My husband was from County Kildare, and my father-in-law was part of the administrative services in India with the British army. He had the dubious distinction of being the first man to be shot in Ireland by the IRA, in 1916.'

And what of jurisprudence? A certain Ms Dewe is the daughter of the Detective Chief Superintendent at Scotland Yard, who eventually apprehended Crippin; and she would write to the press and radio whenever untruths were told about the famous case. We have also had a Ms Gully, relative of the infamous Dr Gully, the man who was believed to have poisoned Charles Bravo at The Priory, on Tooting Bec Common, during the Victorian Era. However, I do not know if these two ladies still live here.

Finally, if I may allow myself two tenuous 'points of separation', the decorator who laid the kitchen tiles in an enviable ground floor apartment at Du Cane Court, also did the tiling in Prince Philip's private apartment. So, indirectly, we have a royal connection as well.

Different Perceptions of Du Cane Court

Because it is so imposing and has numerous associations, Du Cane Court is erroneously perceived to be an abode for the rich and famous. The following true story perfectly illustrates this feeling, and the delusions of grandeur which may accompany it.

An old lady knocked on the front desk with her walking stick.

'Can you call a taxi for me?' she asked.

'Can't you call one for yourself?' the porter replied.

'*I* pay service charges,' she said, overcome with a sense of her own self-importance. 'So can you please call a taxi for me?'

'Where do you want to go?'

'Worcester.'

'That's a long way. Are you sure you can pay?'

'*I* live in Du Cane Court. Everybody who lives in Du Cane Court is rich.' But the porter was treading carefully, and parried:

'Madam, I can only call a taxi for you if you're sure you can pay.' There was a pause, as the woman retreated to consider her options. Then the conversation began again.

'Can you call a taxi for me?'

'Where do you want to go?'

'Cumbria.' But after some further deliberation, Essex was decided upon. So a taxi was called, which arrived in due course.

'My brother will pay for me', said the lady. The porter rang him up. Sure enough, it was her brother, but he would not pay for her and did not want to see her.

There are moments when it seems that nearly everyone knows somebody who lives (or has lived) here; and our ample gardens are so accessible from the high road, that the locals tend to think of the estate as being part of their collective heritage – and as an extension of their public space. Thus it came to pass that a West Indian woman settled with her child on a garden seat of ours to enjoy a picnic. Roman, the ever-ready self-styled protector of 'the Court', attempted to drive them away.

'I'll come here if I like!' the woman stated indignantly. But she never came back. Really, though, she was the least of our problems. Duncan Scobie once saw a Somali urinating against a hedge on our grounds, and attempted to break the intruder's moment of light relief by swearing at him. This antidote had the desired effect, for the stranger made himself decent (unfortunately wetting his trousers in the process); and a rejoinder came from an old lady, poking her head out of a window two floors up, who shouted, 'Stop swearing on a Sunday!'

Nevertheless, the relationship between us and the surrounding community is not usually abrasive. There are, for example, charming moments of innocence, as when a child plays hide and seek in the bushes, or when he exclaims 'Goodbye!' and then runs along inside the perimeter wall, only to be reunited with his guardian a few seconds later in the high road.

Many people harbour rather odd impressions of 'the Court'. One occupant said that her hallway with rooms leading off it had been likened by one of her visitors to a railway carriage; and another, who lived in a studio flat when he first came here, told me, 'When I dream about Du Cane Court, I never visualize it as it truly is. I see blocks of toilets (or cubicles) in a public corridor, as if I was at a swimming-pool.'

DEGENERATION AND THE PARALLEL UNIVERSE

*

The population of Du Cane Court may have been youthful and vibrant once, but by the 1980s many tenants were growing old; and since then, one or two pillars of our community have reached their century. The building came to be viewed as an old people's home, and, on one occasion, a gullible young lad arrived, wondering if he could have a job caring for the elderly! Nowadays, young adults are returning here in force, yet I must temper this observation with the unpalatable truth that I, myself, have grown older; and in the currency of human life, we tend to make ourselves the gold standard.

The erstwhile porter and friend, Neil Gray, once told me an entertaining story about the lady who lived in K06:

'She had not been seen for some time, and the lot fell to me to investigate the matter. Her flat is just above ground level, so I had to go up a ladder and climb in through a window. I could hear that the television was on, and with some trepidation I entered the living room. And there she was, sitting in front of "the box". But she wasn't dead, nor was she surprised to see me. She simply turned around and said, "A cup of tea and two sugars, please!"'

Unfortunately, the outcome of such investigations was not always favourable ... and, during his employment here, Neil found several cadavers – one of them not long dead. She had a peaceful expression on her face, as if her separation from this world had been a painless affair. On another occasion, a deceased person was found who had – in a manner of speaking - not been 'at home' for some time. As a result, maggots were crawling under his door and the whole place had to be fumigated. Meanwhile, yours truly had opened his *own* front door, and was about to sally forth for a meal with none other than the indefatigable Mr Gray, when a putrid smell filled the air. A moment later, the ill-fated Mr Bhatt was rolled past, seated in a wheelchair and with a blanket over his upper body.

Jessie Boran and Gene Evans referred to their part of the building as Death Row.

'The roll call,' explained Jessie, 'includes Mrs Telford, Brita Hardy, Mr Bellman on the other side, Johnny Johnson, Edward Kay's flatmate, Gene's husband, and my own husband. You know, three people died in one week!' And now, sadly, Jessie has joined them.

One virtuous lady cares for residents whose mortal light is flickering, and, whenever she is seen with someone, onlookers presuppose that there is a grim prognosis. She has been called 'The Death Watch Beetle'. In an environment such as this, death mingles with life in an organic way. Thus, two tenants set off one day to perform a final valediction – involving the dispersal of the ashes of a recently-departed loved one. Unfortunately, the bereaved lady was dithering: 'Shall I? Shan't I? This way? That way?' And the whole lot was eventually flung into a head wind, with the result that her kindly companion, who was not strategically well-placed, got one or two bits between his teeth.

And thus, a sweet Chinese lady, who wears an exotic straw hat and is phonetically challenged, keeps her husband's ashes in an urn.

'That's Woger', she declares happily, if anyone should care to ask.

Senility and Madness

May, as an elegant and lively octogenarian, once said of her great age, 'I go to bed hopeful and wake up grateful' – to which I responded, 'I go to bed grateful and wake up hopeful.' And so we have a moment of prayerful reflection, or of anticipation, depending upon one's age. Yet to articulate any philosophical idea, even if it is quite simple, requires a degree of coherence – and coherence has sometimes been an asset in short supply. Indeed, it has been proposed that 'there should be a conveyor belt between Du Cane Court and Springfield Hospital'.

One day, a deranged old woman reported that a horse and carriage had just travelled past her window. Now this would have been fairly implausible anyway, but just to compound the issue, I am not even sure which floor she lived on! For those who believe in ghosts, there used to be a coach-house in Balham Park Road. But you would need a whole army of phantoms to account for the array of strange behaviours seen at Du Cane Court over the years. What about the crusty old survivor from World War 11 who once stood in reception with his trousers the wrong way round, and complained, 'I can't find my pockets'? He was always about to go to the Isle of Wight to fight the Germans, and would spend all day by the porters' desk.

'I know what you two are up to,' he would say, slowly and ponderously, whilst eyeing the staff with suspicion. On other occasions, he sat in Abbey National for hours, concerned that his money was going to be stolen. But new heights of eccentricity were reached when he summoned Neil to his flat to get rid of a few people, dressed in blue suits, who refused to leave.

'But there's no one in here!' said Neil.

'Yes there is. They won't leave.'

Eventually Neil feigned belief in the illusion, and ushered them out rather brusquely, 'Shoo! Shoo!'

'Thank you!' was the grateful response. 'They've all gone now.'

Also remembered is an old lady who once came to the front desk, with an apparently straightforward problem.

'I can't get into my flat,' she said. So a porter accompanied her – perhaps with one of the spare keys which porters often hold at the behest of residents. Not long after, she reappeared with the same words on her lips: 'I can't get into my flat.' And, a second time, a trusty porter performed his service with perfunctory speed. But by the time he had returned to his station, she was already there waiting for him.

'I can't get into my flat,' was her perpetual request – made fourteen times in one day! In the end, the porters were about to toss a coin to decide who was going to murder her.

'Why don't you just *go* somewhere?' Neil suggested to her, and then expanded on the idea: 'Take a long walk to the other side of the world ... or to Somerset, perhaps?'

She obediently left, only to return in half an hour.

'How come you're back so soon?' she was asked. 'You can't have gone very far.'

'I went to Somerset.'

'What? In half an hour? There and back?'

'Yes. I went to Somerset, but there was nobody there!'

Sylvia Say remembers a lady living on the fifth floor of H block, dressed in a long, flowing velvet cape. Apparently, she was seen dancing with a candle on her head. I do not have the reason for this euphoria, but I can report that she set fire to her bed. Then, with the room in flames, she was emptying her food cupboard out of the window. Nothing that came to hand was spared: jars of spaghetti, eggs, flour, sugar ...! Next, she was chucking out saucepans of hot water. Charlie, a short plumber who was dodging the cascade, shouted up from the ground, 'Pack it in!' Eventually he started laughing; and later the lady was taken off to Springfield.

There have been many fires over the years, and Sylvia recalls a visit from an Inspector Sparks of the Fire Brigade! In another case, an old Polish lady left a cloth or handkerchief on the radiator, which caught fire. The rescue services arrived and asked her to open her front door, but she refused, and so they had no alternative but to smash the door down. In a state of confusion, she may have thought the Gestapo had come for her. Then there was the case of an elderly couple who were using candles to light their flat. One day, the flat was lit up in more ways than one, and a crowd of spectators gathered in the courtyard to see a thick pall of smoke belching out of the window. In the end the place was gutted, and an old man who was retrieved from the wreckage died later in hospital. It is a relief that we have 'fire doors' in the corridors, which will prevent a conflagration spreading, although, to the best of my knowledge, no domestic fire in Du Cane Court has ever spread beyond the flat where it began.

Claire MacDonald-Ross nursed her husband for many years when his intellectual faculties, which had so majestically distinguished him in academia, went into decline. And then, the day before he died, the mind which had been depleted by tobacco, alcohol and senility, was quite suddenly infused with a total clarity of thought. This, coupled with the succeeding period of health and happiness in her own advancing years at Du Cane Court, she took to be a divine concession for her long and arduous devotion. So miracles can happen.

Another elderly neighbour, Philippa Wanek, said that with age you do not change, but become more of what you are. This is an opinion I share, although maybe senile dementia can generate behaviour which was not there to begin with. And so we come to a bald, plump lady, who walked about barefoot and earned the sobriquet, 'Queen Victoria', because her image in advancing years bore a striking resemblance to that sovereign. She would stop all and sundry in their tracks, then ask if they could spare any money for some spirit. Thus, in addition to the condition of Alzheimer's, she was permanently inebriated. But what goes in must come out, and I once saw her pause for a few moments in the high road on her way to the shops, whilst a cloud of steam ascended from beneath her dress. The pity is that she had once been a cultured woman.

For some reason she *took a shine* to Neil, and came to the reception area early one morning to speak with him.

'Would you like to *see* me?' she asked.

'Not before breakfast,' came the modest reply. Once, she pulled her nightgown over her head and posed the question:

'Do you *want* me?'

'No! No!' he cried, in some distress. And at about 7.30 one morning she even proposed to him.

The most outrageous claim about her is that she drowned some kittens in the bath, but I would question this – for, in spite of her fearsome aspect, I think she was harmless enough. Eventually, she was installed in the local asylum. Then she escaped, and was later seen, much to everyone's astonishment, wandering nonchalantly around Du Cane Court – only to be swiftly removed again.

And so the insanity continued, but it was not always the old who were affected. May Arkell once espied something flapping in a dust chute room in C block, and realized that it was a big man with a sheet over his head. A security guard with her interest at heart gave the command, 'Stand back! Stand back!' as if the feared character had a gun. Following the command, the man himself stood up, opened his sheet, and proclaimed, 'I am Jesus'.

May was ushered away to a safe place and told, 'don't leave until you have phoned me, and I will escort you down to the reception area'. In fact, the offending party was a local artist whose paintings used to be displayed in a nearby establishment, and who was quite religious even in his lucid moments. But on that day, he entirely lost his hold upon reality. He ran naked around the corridors with a bird cage on his head, before being collected by an ambulance. May Arkell later came to see him in Springfield, but not before he had symbolically set the bird free. Hopefully, he, himself, is now also free ... of his unfortunate mental illness.

Oh, Pandora! Whatever have you hidden in your Box?

According to the lease, flats at Du Cane Court must be redecorated every seven years, but some flats look like they have had nothing done to them since the day they were first occupied! They may have yellow net curtains or faded wallpaper, which hangs like an unwashed dermis requiring exfoliation; perhaps coupled with a pungent smell reminiscent of a hamster cage.

Against this background of physical decay, an extraordinary story came to light. In October, 1985, a spinster, Ms Netta Verga, who had lived a very private life, died at the age of 77. Her sister and sister-in-law came to her flat to sort out her belongings the day after the funeral, and discovered a mysterious old briefcase in the cupboard. If I may paraphrase, Ms Marjorie Heale described the event thus, 'Standing at the bottom of the suitcase was a brown paper parcel wrapped up in string. A stench came up and hit me. I peeled back three layers and after we looked in, my sister said: "There you are, it's a skull"'. In fact, it was the mummified body of a newborn baby, wrapped in a blanket. The solicitor who later attended the scene remembered an object which was black and seemingly charred, like a block of wood; and there was a feeling that, instead of reporting the matter, the sisters of the deceased could have put the remains of the child down the dust chute, where they would have disintegrated quickly.

At the inquest, the pathologist, Rufus Crompton, told the court that the baby was either stillborn, or had survived only two or three days. The corpse was between 40 and 70 years old; and it is tempting to propose that the birth may have occurred out of wedlock, causing an acute sense of shame and a need for secrecy ... but the coroner admitted that the incident remained a mystery.

Clearly, a powerful effect may be wrought upon the female psyche by living in a building where humanity is departing this world in great numbers, but where there is no new life being born. One lady has been observed pushing an empty pram around the grounds; whilst another, for whom having a child was everything, finally gave birth – only to suffer post-natal depression, and throw herself off the building when her baby was just one year old.

Suicide and Misadventure

Du Cane Court has had its fair share of tragedy. There was the lady nurse who inhabited one of the two dwellings on the roof, and who had suffered a leak in her ceiling which (apparently) was not being dealt with. No doubt this was just one of her problems. At any rate, she must have been very unbalanced, for she made a terminal decision. She bought some bleach – or other descaling fluid – and drank it; and must have died in agony. When her corpse was found, it had a white face with blue lips; and Rebecca, the manager's assistant at the time, suggested very pragmatically, and plaintively, 'Why didn't she just take a holiday?'

It is also said that someone in one of the two penthouses committed suicide by swallowing razorblades; but I suspect the teller of this tale had simply heard about the other misfortune, and reinterpreted the effects of corrosion to be injuries from sharp blades.

Several individuals have either jumped, or fallen, from the building and plummeted to their deaths. One was near the garages, to the rear of the estate. My friend, Derick, stepped outside on his way to work one morning, and there the body was, sprawled out in front of him. Another casualty was a woman from Springfield Hospital, found by the side of the building, near the Polish church of Christ the King. She was lying flat on her back, with her Wellington boots on and her 'nightie' still in place. And in the 1980s, there were two so-called 'sky divers' who landed in one of the front courtyards.

Thankfully, not all suicide attempts have been successful. A neighbour, Pat Grimshaw, was relaxing in the living room of her apartment one day. She was not living on the ground floor, so imagine her surprise when a huge black man, with a baseball cap and blue overalls, suddenly appeared outside her window! He climbed a ladder all the way to the roof, before threatening to jump off. He, also, was from Springfield; and I wonder if he was the same man Philippa Wanek observed, on a small balcony near her own flat. Ms Wanek solicited the help of a porter, and - with one of them holding on to each leg - they managed to haul the person she'd seen back to safety. He was only 18 years old, and was apparently distraught because he was guilty of theft.

Until 2007, the last case of anyone falling from the building to an untimely death was believed to have occurred in the 1980s; but that it should happen at all is deplorable. So what had become of the community spirit ... burrowing like a legless lizard beneath a veritable sandstorm of disasters? Well, I have previously painted a gregarious aspect into my picture of life here, and I am loath to entirely replace it with the gloom of the present section. Therefore, I must say that there will always be some incongruous flat-dwellers, who blend into a social scene no better than water into turpentine; and that their sadness may never be diminished if they will have nothing to do with others. And I should add that not all individuals described were Du Cane Court residents. But even if we overlook these exceptions, disappointment with life at 'the Court' was not always the cause of the problem. One person accidentally fell through a window. And another case was quite unusual. An old gentleman was thought to be throwing clothes out of a window, which actually turned out to be him, fully clothed and falling to his death. This may have been 92-year-old James Ridge, a retired engineer, freshly released from hospital after a stroke, and still suffering from dizzy spells. The story goes that he was apprehensive about a move to an old people's home, scheduled because he could no longer look after himself [St.&.Toot.News].

I have also heard that elderly residents were made impoverished by sudden rises in the overall service charge in the 1980s, and that they had to sell such valued artefacts as furniture and jewellery in order to levy the necessary cash. As a result of this episode, there were apparently one or two suicides. Many could not bear to leave Du Cane Court, and May Arkell, who was among them, once said, 'The only way they will take me away from here is in a body bag.'

So then, in one humble section we have witnessed both the ending of life – and a deep attachment to one's home; and we have discovered how these disparate things can be strangely connected.

CONFLICT, SECURITY AND DECLINING STANDARDS

*

Unfortunately, the community spirit of Du Cane Court has not always been one to die for. There was the moment when two old ladies fought over a garden chair, and one almost fell into the pond. And in another dispute, the owner of a flat put the tenant's possessions outside by the perimeter wall, for every passing stranger to help himself to anything he wanted. On one occasion, a man and a woman – initially with stardust in their eyes – fell so badly *out* of love with each other, that the man scrawled some unwholesome message in blood (or red paint) on the lady's door.

Sharing is integral to the way of life here, and in some respects the place could be compared to a commune. It engenders love and enmity, friendship and rivalry; and any subtle combination thereof. One type of accommodation was even referred to as a 'communal flat'. This was the size of a one-bedroom apartment, but designed for two people to share the hallway and bathroom, while each retained a separate bedroom and kitchenette. Years ago, an outrageous character lived in one of these communal flats, and it would be hard to imagine anyone less suited to sharing. Madame X (I shall call her this for the purposes of my narrative) was of North African origin. She first attained notoriety when she stole the iron gate, which served as an entrance to the newly formed patio garden behind the garages. There had been a move to lock the gate, and thereby prohibit general access, and her argument was that the garden should belong to *all* of the residents. Her principle was right even if her theft was not, but in the context of this narrative it was the only thing she can be praised for.

To begin with, Madame X owned a studio flat, but she wanted something larger. At the time, there was a 'communal' occupied by a frail old man whom I shall call Mr C, who had one room vacant on account of his 'opposite number' having died. So our anti-heroine swooped, like a bird of prey, to purchase the property for herself, and, with the managerial blessing of Mr Milligan-Smith, the old man became her tenant. Of course, this was not good enough for her. She wanted him out, so that she could live there independently or sell for a profit; but, as a sitting tenant, he had every right to stay put. And so her reign of tyranny commenced. She tried to prevent welfare services from reaching him. She would also throw open the bathroom window, in order to subject the old man to the cold air. One day there was a small fire in the flat, and Mr C was found lying on the floor. There was talk of arson, and some of the resulting mess *did* appear to be contrived, yet the police were not interested. Madame X refused to give Mr C his own set of keys to the property, and so he could not come and go as he pleased; and his liberty was further curtailed when she had the effrontery to lock him in with three visitors! The police were contacted again. This time they responded, and the culprit was taken to court. Her plea was that the old man held homosexual parties in the small hours of the morning – and, furthermore, that he had to be kept under lock and key, or else he (and an elderly friend of his) might have raped her. This was in spite of the fact that he had been knocked down by a bus, and depended upon a Zimmer frame for his mobility! A sensible lady, who was incarcerated with him for hours, defused the tension at one point by saying, 'Well. I haven't been raped by anyone yet!' And she later gave evidence to the effect that he posed no danger to anyone.

Meanwhile, the indomitable *Madame* was having none of it. She screamed, and the magistrate threatened to send her down for contempt of court. At one point, when it seemed that she would receive seven days' imprisonment, she even threw herself into a heap on the floor; but, in spite of her histrionics, she was not above sticking her tongue out at an officer of the law on her way out of the courtroom, as if to say, 'They have heard my plea for mercy!' In the end, she was found guilty and fined.

Crime and Du Cane Court

One day, while I was walking around Balham with a friend of mine, I saw three notices with details of serious crimes in the vicinity – including murder. Apparently, different areas of London were assigned crime ratings a few years ago, and Balham was assigned an '8' out of a worst possible rating of '12'; but a policeman named Stan Hardes could remember very little crime within the estate, during the many years of his residency. There have, apparently, been cases of wife-beating; and at least one case of a woman beating her man, who sustained a gash on his forehead. Yet the woman was passionate not only in her anger, but also in her love of animals. So when the police turned up, she complained about a dog chasing her cat down Balham High Road!

There are no known cases of murder inside the block. However, a resident of Middle-Eastern extraction *was* tragically slain elsewhere. She would pilfer from the local shops, and was once cautioned for making off with a leg of lamb from Safeways. She also had grandiose ideas, and told a friend of mine, 'You could be an escort and earn £1000 a night.' Another briefing was delivered outside a clothes shop: 'I can get you any dress you like for one third of the price.' Clearly, she felt that women should look their best. She had a strong personality and, although she was portly, it is said that her face was beautiful.

'In France, the police never bother about shoplifting,' she proclaimed with confidence. But, for all her spirit, she came to a sad end in Bordeaux – murdered at the age of just 27.

Our Security over the Decades

Ms Hockman told me that Du Cane Court was much cleaner when she came here in 1950. Later on, there began to be a problem with vagrants. They would enter the building secretly, and sleep in the lifts – which were also used by children who did not live here, to ride up and down as if they were attractions at a fair ground. More serious issues emerged, but they were not necessarily the fault of the vagrants or the children. In the 1960s, there were 22 burglaries over a short period of time; and in about 1964, 14 car batteries were stolen simultaneously. One day a resident even noticed that the driver's seat in his motorcar had gone! Also, the inner courtyards had no exterior lighting until the late 1960s, and, as a result, 'muggers' were lurking in the shadows.

Among the most dramatic events to have affected the nation in the last 30 years were the riots of 1981. One infamous evening, during the course of that year, lots of vehicles were transporting black people from Brixton, and they appeared to be receiving their orders from a van near Du Cane Court. Come midnight, many windows were smashed in the vicinity, and one electrical shop was damaged. Sadly, the proprietor had not taken out insurance. At Du Cane Court, the common wisdom was, 'Lights out, and all men stand together in a strong defensive wall ... Then, at the blow of a whistle an emergent leader will beckon everyone forward.' Fortunately, the mob never did enter our art deco stronghold, but one of my friends, Derick Mallet, says that he will never forget the awful sound of breaking glass. Later, those porters who had stood boldly by their station were reimbursed out of the Tenants' Association kitty; and Mr Swindale, the corpulent Head Porter who had been absent all night, was now among them and hoping for a share of the profits. He used to wear a 'morning coat', and perhaps he felt that a little sartorial elegance would win him public favour. If so, the strategy did not work on this occasion, for he was told:

'We can't pay *you*. You were in your flat.'

'No ... I was around', he replied vaguely.

'Then why did your wife say that you didn't know of the events until after they had happened?' came the rejoinder. There was no answer to this.

The impact of the civil unrest in the Thatcher years, combined with the earlier incursions upon our peace of mind, brought about changes which were long overdue. In the late 1970s or early 1980s, the front doors of flats were fitted with minute spy holes, which gave paranoid inhabitants an excellent (and secret) view of any predatory persons lurking in the corridor. Also, as a general precaution, the various entrances to the building were locked, and a special key was issued to residents at a cost of about seven or eight pounds, with a telephone number printed on it which you could ring if you required copies. Then, on the 8th of June, 1982, an entry phone was installed on the porters' desk; although, ironically, on the 26th of April, 1983, a 'new rash of break-ins' was referred to. At one point, a Neighbourhood Watch scheme operated; but this kind of thing is no substitute for common sense, and it follows that your address must not be given out to all and sundry. In 1996, it was established in our code of practice that a visitor should know the flat number of the person he has come to see; and that, if he asks for the address, he may legitimately be refused. Furthermore, we now have Closed Circuit Television cameras, and, whereas there used to be one security guard on duty at night, there are now two: one to man the desk, and one to regularly patrol the premises with his dog.

Unfortunately, and in spite of everything, we have had a couple of mishaps in recent years: some cigarettes stolen from the shop, and £1000 or so disappearing from a Yuletide collection box. However, David Clark once told me that, in the course of his managerial office here, he knew of no burglary above the ground floor, and of only four at ground level. When viewed in the context of 676 dwellings, these misfortunes, and even the worst excesses which have been described, appear considerably diminished. One may well opine that one's flat is unlikely to be at risk, except from an inside job; and the odds of this are reduced if the clientele are respectable.

A Personal Opinion on Safety

Over the years, various measures have been introduced to enhance our security, and residents, by and large, would have been grateful for all of them. But I cannot help feeling that some of what makes Du Cane Court a relatively safe haven is unconnected with the actions of the staff on our behalf. For instance, in any given corridor, the only indication that you are beside somebody's home is the presence of a door in the wall. And, if there is no strip of light under the door, a blackguard cannot assume that the place is empty. The darkness might only mean that the occupant is not in the hallway. And if the intruder should knock and receive no answer, is the coast really clear, or is the old hermit-crab as deaf as a post? No windows are present to reveal the interior of a dwelling, and whether there is anything worth taking. The intruder has no inkling as to the size of the place, with the possible exception of a second, unlabelled door further along the corridor; nor does he know whether the home owner has an enviable car, since the garages and parking bays are separate from the apartments, and there is no obvious way of cross-referencing the two.

By contrast, there are many fine houses around Balham where the net curtains are absent, or where blinds are left open during the summer months to let in the light. Thus do the ostentatious rich advertise their wares to a faintly jealous middle class – and to a burglar, who can assess the value of everything, and monitor what times of day an expensive car is out of the driveway.

At Du Cane Court, a thief will have no bushes to hide behind if someone should amble past at the precise moment of his break-in – a contingency not that unlikely, given the number of residents here, – and any suspicious behaviour may be reported at the front desk. Then there is the issue of navigation. Firstly, if our token blackguard has a particular flat in mind, can he find his way there without getting lost? Secondly, how quickly can he escape? Imagine negotiating hundreds of yards of corridor and several flights of stairs, clutching some heavy furniture or a Sony music system! The alternative is to exit through a window; but if it's 50 feet above the ground, he would require a long ladder, a strong stomach, and a stroke of desperation. Meanwhile, anyone might be watching his escapade. Even on the ground floor, he could attract a large audience! Of course, the building is not impregnable, but one hopes that the average opportunist would simply say to himself, 'Why bother?'

The Public View of Balham

In the 1970s, Peter Sellers coined a new phrase, 'Balham, Gateway to the South'. The residents of Du Cane Court may even treat it like a badge of distinction, yet the 21 minute film, 'Gateway to the South', was not flattering. It told the story of two holiday-makers who arrive in England without an itinerary, and decide to visit Balham. The film was directed by Micky Dolenz in 1981, and was loosely based on a script by Frank Muir and Denis Norden. Many of the citizens of our community, as imagined by the director, bear a striking resemblance to Robbie Coltrane, which is to be expected, as he is playing them all! Balham certainly looks worse for wear, as well it might, since much of the filming was not even done there! 'Gateway to the South' has been screened more than once at the Balham Festival, and it gently pokes fun at a place the audience is fond of. Foolish people who do not live here are duped by it, and have labelled Balham according to their misconception ever since. Nevertheless, the butt of all the jokes continues to be a popular choice for relocation - so maybe the last laugh is on them.

An occupant of our building cites the words of an ebullient friend of his: 'I lurve de Bal-Ham!' And Arthur Smith, the radio and television celebrity, has described the biggest building in the area as 'magnificently unfashionable'. Yet he says it with tongue in cheek, for he lives in Du Cane Court himself.

Declining Standards?

The aforesaid work of cinematic art may have been a fantasy, but some residents have complained of declining standards at Du Cane Court, even while the local area is being gentrified. A common remark is, 'I used to know everyone in my corridor, but now, because of all the subletting, I hardly know anyone'. It is said that one person bought four flats here, and rented them out to Wandsworth Borough Council – who subsequently employed them as temporary housing for the poor. Such actions provoke a degree of snobbery from the older residents, who feel that the quality of the clientele is being compromised (although if they are sitting tenants, they, themselves, will be handsomely subsidized).

This idea was prevalent in 1989, when a very young mother and her baby were ensconced in Du Cane Court, and a letter of complaint was submitted. Wandsworth Council Housing Department replied to this letter, and the chairman of the Tenants' Association then made public this reply – which caused great distress because it gave the woman's flat number, and so was an invasion of privacy. The chairman was requested to remove the offensive letter; and early next morning, the entire notice board was missing! In the end, the whole furore was to no avail anyway; for there was a further letter, on 2nd December, 1989, this time to the (then) manager, Mrs Davies, saying that the Rent Office now had six flats let out to council tenants.

In the 1980s, our Express Dairies closed, and there was no shop on the premises for two years. And standards, from time to time, have fluctuated in more obvious ways. For instance, washing might be left hanging out of windows to dry. In fact, the Du Cane Court Tenants' Association once received a long list of complaints: dogs barking, dogs' excreta, clacking footsteps in courtyards, noisy chatterers, cuckoo clocks going off, - and, finally, unwrapped vacuum cleaner dust and cigarette ash, shaken and tipped down the dust chutes. There was also a problem with unauthorised vehicles using the narrow lane in between the building and the garages, but at least this was addressed, with the gate next to Balham Park Road being closed in the 1990s.

Problems with Noise

Sound, like rumour, travels fast. Thankfully, it can also get lost on its journey, so that what one person hears, others are oblivious to; and, on the whole, the place is remarkably quiet - almost silent in fact. But as the devil has the best stories as well as the best tunes, I shall focus, for a while, on the exceptional cases.

The odd bevy of night revellers has been known to blaze a trail of 'noise pollution', on its slow and convoluted journey through the building, like the slime in the wake of a snail; whilst protected, all the time, from any prying eyes by a shell of oblivion. Sometimes the revellers can sound so near: as if, at any moment, they would pass like spectres through the solid wall, and straight into one's private living space. We have all this, and acute sensibilities too ... The width of each corridor is only 4-5 feet, and mostly the front doors face each other. So if you knock on one door - in the morning or late at night, - two or three other doors may open, and quizzical faces might peer out at you with the sleep still in their eyes, as if you had roused a family of dormice from hibernation. How do these mammals cope? Some of them may hear a faint humming noise in the winter months, especially noticeable at night and probably arising from the boilers – or from studio flats with fridges in their living rooms. One man, whom I know personally, objects to wind chimes.

In a meeting on the 8th of July, 1985, concern was expressed about passenger lifts being used to convey household objects such as baths and basins; and, on one occasion, the weight of a bath caused a lift to break down. On 25th April, 1989, a letter from Keith Cardale Groves stated that some residents were moving in and out of the building at the weekend, even though the lease specifies that furniture may not be moved after midday on Saturday. Clearly, the problem did not go away, and it seems that some leniency was inevitable. Thus, in a letter dated 13th July, 1995, the manager, David Clark, wrote, 'We have always advised both staff and security that if people come long distances they should be told the rules[,] but not prevented from using the goods lift or going to the lockers on a one-off basis.' Well, I suppose a degree of diplomacy was called for, considering the gravity of other issues which can arise. For example, on the 10th of June, 1985, there was the following complaint with regard to a young man using a sledgehammer on the roof to break up the parapet: 'Is it any wonder that rain has come through the ceiling of the flat next door. I was left with at least three barrow-loads of rubble on my balcony.'

Other incidents are less severe, but still noteworthy. One resident remarked upon a sound like that of a dead body being dragged across the floor. Another once heard a woman above his head stomping about, so he walked upstairs and knocked on her door.

'It sounds like you're carrying piles of bricks from one end of the room to the other,' he told her. The bane of his day answered slowly and deliberately:

'Well – maybe – I - am.'

Then, there was the humorous tale of the rhythmic hammering. Now this was no workman either, for it transpired that, when a certain couple were love-making, the bed frame kept striking the wall. The embarrassed porter baulked at the prospect of confronting them; and so the bed, like a ship carrying seamen through a typhoon, continued to rock ... to and fro ... to and fro ... for two and a half hours!

Hence we come to the subject of revenge. An individual I know got so fed up with his noisy neighbours that he would press a hooter, which reputedly made the walls tremble! In self-defence, he claimed that it was a burglar alarm, which was automatically set off in the event of a disturbance to the peace. Once, there was an argument in Balham High Road, between a couple and a single woman. The latter was complaining about noise, and so the couple put live frogs through the woman's letter-box. Unfortunately her cat tried to eat them, and as a result became violently ill and died.

A Safety Valve

One of the many advantages to living in a block of flats is that there are civilized mechanisms in place for settling disputes. Basically, you are not alone. At Du Cane Court, leasehold rules exist which everyone must comply with. The windows should be curtained. The flooring of every property must be carpeted with an underlay: the only exceptions being the floors of the kitchen and bathroom, which are concrete. Walking on a carpet with underlay is said to be 22 decibels quieter than walking on wooden floors, and the subjective difference is equivalent to wearing earplugs.

In times of crisis, the whole community can speak with one voice through the Tenants' Association. If a neighbour causes trouble, you may note it in the 'Incident Book', or write directly to the manager. Or, after you have tried to reason with the culprit, you may request that a porter pay a discreet visit. Any of these methods could engender a peaceful settlement – because, by invoking the help of a third party, you introduce an element of detachment. Of course, if you protest too often, the channels of assistance might not be so forthcoming. Also, I have observed that criticising staff to a manager may provoke a counter-attack, which subtly makes the critic feel as if he is part of the problem. Now the defence of one's staff is a noble attribute, but when it is blind it can only obstruct the course of justice. However, as the problem diminishes, the Estate Office might well grow in one's imagination into a miniature Court of Appeal, where all claims are thoroughly investigated, but where the burden of responsibility and the admission of guilt are publicly withheld. In one case, a notice regarding the payment of a fine was sent to someone, on account of an unreasonable disturbance arising from that person's flat. When the manager was asked if the money would be passed on to the 'victims', he stated that 'there is no allowance made for fining in the block'. Clearly, the words, 'do not let your left hand know what your right is doing', come to mind.

Changing Attitudes at the Desk

I have heard it said that a vote against the wearing of uniforms, at a Tenants' Association meeting during the 1970s, may have led to a deterioration in service. Apparently, the tenants were paying for the suits to be cleaned, and this was deemed to be a superfluous expense - even though it arose only once a year. One senses a misunderstanding of basic human psychology. Common apparel in the workplace respectfully conceals differences in personal wealth, and fosters a sense of collective identity. Furthermore, it is easier to have pride in your job when you have to dress up for it. One day, Ms Grimshaw was unhappy with the laying of new carpets in her flat, and asked for them to be removed. In response to her request, two small, scrawny workmen, wearing torn jeans and with rings in their noses, turned up and threw them out of the window. A couple of floors below, a resident looked outside and was surprised to see carpets falling through the air!

On one infamous occasion, the contract for the entire security company was terminated; but not before one of the team had made extensive use of the telephone at the front desk to make private calls, and another had employed the desk, itself, as a footstool, as if he was at home in his living room. Now the duties of the night are – by common consent – quite distinct from those of the day. However, their similarities are considerable as well; and so, for a while, I shall employ the word 'porter' as a generic term.

So what *is* a 'porter'? Judging from the Latin root of the word, his work should entail some willingness to carry ... but the assistance required is not usually manual. Perhaps you want a message to be passed from the day staff to those operating at night? This seems easy enough, as they all work at the same desk; and yet, because they hail from different companies, they may as well be standing on either side of a ravine. In fairness, a culture of misunderstanding often prevails, as the following dialogue between a woman and a night porter clearly shows:

'A dog is barking and it won't let me into my flat.'

'I can't do anything about it, madam. The dog handler is patrolling the courtyard. He is just doing his job.'

'How would you like it if this happened where *you* live?'

'Madam. This *is* where I live.'

In another dispute, a tenant made the mistake of saying, '*I* pay your wages'. Of course, this is indirectly true, but to say it merely inflames the situation.

'Well then you should be ashamed of yourself!' was the sharp rebuke, for the wages alluded to were not extravagant. Our predicament is succinctly expressed by a recent manager, David Clark, who said, 'You pay for everything, but you own nothing': ingredients which might well be regarded as a recipe for friction. Yet there are some who have successfully steered clear of conflict for 35 years or more, and Neil was once moved to praise a paragon of virtue with the words, 'I don't understand it. You *never* complain' - to which the passive response was, 'What is there to complain about?'

Occasionally, one may ask for too much. A parcel left at reception is accepted; but if *everyone* deposited a *large object* simultaneously, the allotted space would be overflowing. On the other hand, why react to an imaginary predicament which will never occur? Pessimism is a fine oar to paddle with, when the objective is to reach an easier job description. At least, one *assumes* there are job descriptions, or has the mythical cartographer forgotten to include them on the map!

If a man enters a shop and buys a pair of shoes, but is unhappy with the service, we may say that for his money he still receives a pair of shoes. The spirit shown by an employee in smiling and being attentive to him is a bonus. But the spirit of benevolence and courtesy which may be said to characterise a porter's business is not secondary, but primary. It is not something extra, which is given away free with what is purchased. It, very largely, *is* what is purchased. So, in the second case, if you subtract the intangible quality away, what are you left with?

However, a balanced criticism must be softened with fair praise. Innumerable residents have bonded with their staff. They confide in them, and are happy with their services. Furthermore, after living here for many years, they may come to depend upon acts of kindness, and to almost look upon the kindest members of staff as part of their own extended family.

PLANS, ALTERATIONS AND OBJECTIONS

*

Everyone who lives in a large apartment block knows that a regular cycle of maintenance is essential, and that a little harsh noise or commotion is *par for the course*. Yet much of the building work undertaken at Du Cane Court would appear to have been anything but essential. Between 1957 and 1975, planning permission was granted for seven additional flats through either conversion or change of use. In 1974, a spectacular request was submitted by Ayrton, Hooper and Jackson – to build another 20 penthouses on the roof! They claimed that parking space for an extra 21 cars would be provided, but there were other issues: the strain on the hot water system, loss of light to flats in the inner courtyards, and the reality that the building already transgressed the rules on height restriction. There were 53 letters of objection and a petition signed by 507 residents.

In 1987, planning permission was given to turn the carpenter's workshop into a lodge, and a storeroom in H block into a flat; and, in January, 1989, to convert a redundant storage tank on the roof into a two-bedroom flat – and to erect a conservatory to go with it. This time, there were 34 letters of objection, and a petition with more than 300 signatures. But plans were already afoot prior to 1989, for on 11th November, 1988, a gentleman named A. S. Maw disapproved of the term 'conservatory', writing that there was no intention of raising delicate or exotic plants, nor of promoting a school of music, art or drama on the roof. What a shame! Meanwhile, other voices were raised in protest. On 11th October, 1988, a certain Andrew Russik, who has been a writer of theatre reviews for the Independent, and scripts for BBC Radio and television, wrote to say that he found all of the work a great inconvenience. And on the 25th of October there was a letter from W.H.Davis, who referred to three years of refurbishment and an 'utter disregard for [the] welfare, health and safety of residents'. The workmen were also accused of dropping masses of debris and broken glass from the scaffolding. Clearly, news got around, for, on 1st August, 1989, even Tom Cox, Labour MP for Wandsworth, penned his concerns about the number of conversions taking place here. And it is reported in the internet record of Hansard that, on Friday, 6th March, 1992, Mr Cox spoke the following words in the House of Commons: 'If ever a group of tenants has suffered the abuses of despicable behaviour by landlords and their agents, it has been those who live in Du Cane Court.'

The former Chairlady of the Tenants' Association, Gloria Blackhurst, related to me some of what she, herself, has had to endure. She recalled a disconcerting day, many moons ago, when she had a premonition of danger awaiting her or her son, if either of them opened their front door and walked under the scaffolding outside, where manual labourers were going about their business with their usual sense of abandon. And her prescience may well have saved their lives, for that very day a substantial glass missile crashed against the front door of her maisonette, and would easily have impaled anyone who was unfortunate enough to be in the way. On another occasion, she was in her kitchen when she heard a loud 'Hello!' emanate from an unfamiliar voice inside her home. 'Have you got a dustpan and brush?' asked the alien voice, which she traced to an intruder standing at the top of the stairs, not far from the remains of one of her windows. Evidently, the background noise had masked the sound of his break-in. The man continued, 'I had to push the old window in. It's got a crack and needs replacing.' Gloria could not remember any crack, but dutifully paid for the replacement window. She notes, with wry humour:

'The outfit responsible for the incident was – or became known as - the Balham Glass Company. To begin with, their shop in the high road was rough and uninviting; but, after benefiting from the lucrative assignment at Du Cane Court, their premises (all of a sudden) appeared quite opulent.'

The round of maintenance and change continued, and sometimes it was a case of trying to put 'new wine in old wineskins'. Hence, on 12th February, 1987, there was an application for flat D02 to be used as an employment agency for nannies. The old telephone kiosks were (at some point) converted into storage units; and, on 16th August, 1989, it was reported that the landlords had reconstructed many of the air-raid shelters, and at the same time created several large storage rooms - which appeared to be let to a neighbouring firm of solicitors, or to any other local business which might need them. Now this contrasted with the formal position once expressed to me, that storage areas were not to be made commercially available to anyone outside the building, as this could compromise security. However, some things remained the same. Audrey Barry opined that a pale turquoise paint, applied to the walls of the first flat she bought here, may have been part of the original décor.

Post-Operative Planning Permission

Before I resume my story, I should say that planning permission is something one may apply for many times, and, even in the face of obstacles, is often granted in the end. Waiting for it may cause a degree of tribulation for someone who is working to a tight schedule; and wisdom is but a feather in a whirlwind of haste. And so we set the scene for a controversy, to which four microfiche cards are dedicated - out of a total of twenty held on Du Cane Court (circa 2000) in the council records.

To open the saga, Mark Pitman, of Belgrave Properties, wanted to divide G01, a one-bedroom apartment, into two studio flats. There was a reply from the Borough planner on December 3, 1990, to the effect that such an action would require permission. The warning was ignored, and, when the work was completed, one Gemma Turner bought flat G01B on 4th January, 1991. Then, on 7th July, 1992, planning permission for the work on G01 was refused. So Gemma had the novelty of living somewhere which, officially, did not exist. (Ah! If only we could *all* live in places which do not exist, the present housing crisis could be solved overnight.) Subsequent to the above refusal, a certificate of lawful use was granted on 31st March, 1995; but as late as the 20th of December, 1995, the council would still not revoke its original decision. And Nationwide Building Society was faced with the same dilemma regarding G01A. What a mess!

Apparently, a dwelling house becomes lawful if it has been used as such for four years, and so this tale of woe hopefully had a happy ending for the leaseholders. But a certain Mr Andrews weighed in with a shocking claim: that there may have been as many as 20 other conversions in the building with no apparent record of planning permission!

Cracks in the Walls

All new tenants must sign a lease, by which they promise not to alter the external appearance of the block. Yet what happens to the fabric of the building affects us more. After all, who would prefer invasive surgery to a simple change of clothing? A certain A.S.Agate wrote, on 16th August, 1988, that because of the extensive roof traffic of men and machinery, cracks have appeared on the seventh floor. Indeed, I have, myself, observed cracks in the walls of the corridors, which are so deep that I was tempted to seek out any doubting Thomas, that he might insert his fingers into the wounds and believe! They have since been filled in, but this is cosmetic. I have been told that a steel frame moves in the wind. I also understand that thermal expansion may be partly to blame. This is because steel heats and cools at different rates to concrete; and, furthermore, London is primarily founded upon clay soil, which expands and contracts with the weather. Such intelligence is no less disturbing for being communicated with great aplomb, but at least there is good news too. Apparently, in a brief investigation, some bricks were once stripped away to reveal a pristine joist; and so we must assume that the frame of the building remains strong.

QUESTIONS OF FINANCE

*

A Kind of Egg Soufflé

Here's a recipe for bitter relations: whip the bad eggs, squeeze the lemons, and then keep whipping and squeezing *ad infinitum.* Put another way, one invites professional detachment and courtesy, and is disappointed if one of these twins should decline. Read on, and you'll see what I mean.

In the 1980s, the leaseholder, Jennifer Whelpton, daughter of the famous Mrs Whelpton and inheritor of her feisty nature, felt the service charges to be unreasonable, and one third of the residents agreed with her. She refused – or was unable - to pay her portion of them, and she won 'her day in court', proving that this particular egg could not be whipped. During her tenure here, she was never asked for the maintenance fee again. But it was a mixed blessing, for later on she had to make good her debt out of the proceeds from the sale of her flat. Perhaps one can understand this, but what about the tenant who received a requisition to attend court for not paying his service charge – after he *had* paid! He went to the Estate Office to clarify the situation; and apparently kept saying that that he *had paid,* but the message was not getting through. (Evidently, it is not only the partitions between flats which are made out of breeze block.)

Once, when I was working abroad, I rang the manager's assistant about my outstanding service charge on a studio flat, and was authorized to settle the bill on my return. But upon arriving home, I found an ominous letter waiting for me on my doormat, which promised that if nothing was done within seven days, legal action would follow; and three to four days had already passed since the date on the letter! When I spoke to the assistant about it, she said:

'Well, you must pay on time.'

'But we spoke about this, and you said that payment at the end of the month was acceptable,' I replied. 'Otherwise, I would have sent it earlier. The landlords have no business threatening me.'

'It wasn't the landlords who sent the letter.'

'It wasn't ...?'

'It was me.'

'*You* sent it?' I could hardly believe my ears.

'Yes. The new landlords are very strict about prompt payment, and requested that I send the demands out.'

I let the issue rest, knowing that my adversary never approached the front line, unless driven there on a full tank of neurosis. So it seems that tyranny – and other species of emotional dysentery – may follow from the mild poison of incompetence. And there is more. What a charming stance to adopt: tell a mildly errant resident, 'your property may be at risk', and then soften the blow by saying, 'this is just a standard letter we send out'. And so we recall our colourful communications with the landlords' solicitors, who used to be Edward

Lewis, hereinafter known as the persona, *Fast Eddie*, - for their pens were always at the ready. I began to rent out my studio flat from 15th June, 1996. It was not clear to me at the time, but £129 was required for a 'licence to underlet'. I was somewhat surprised that I had to pay for this right, but I duly paid, nevertheless. A couple of years afterwards, I received a letter (dated 10th September, 1998) requesting another £125 plus VAT, with the words, 'It has been brought to our attention that you are subletting the above property without the landlord's consent'. So I explained that I had the licence, only for the issue to arise again in 1999. This time *Fast Eddie* wanted £30 plus VAT for the cost of keeping his records in order. I was somewhat disgruntled and felt that his bureaucracy was *his* problem. Nevertheless, I paid up. Then in July 2004, the tenant in my studio applied for a parking disk, and the Head Porter proclaimed in writing that I had no licence to underlet; and again, I referred to my existing licence. I once asked the manager if I needed to pay every year for the privilege of subletting. He told me that payment was only necessary when a new tenant moved in; and I'd had the same tenant since 1996. (Shall we call this a dispensation?)

Thankfully, renting a room in one's flat is not attended by such problems, for in this jurisdiction English common law overrides leasehold law.

Fast Eddie has been a 'pool shark' (in a famous film, 'The Hustler'), and a tennis player, Eddy Dibbs, - although Edward Lewis, the unusual variant who scored legal points over unsuspecting tenants assumed, for the purposes of the above correspondence, the gender of a *woman*. Since then, a new firm of solicitors called Middleton Potts has taken over the running of the landlords' legal affairs; and one hopes that the whole system is now able to consolidate information and act sensibly upon it, without being too severe. As for *Fast Eddie*, he came unstuck in the most peculiar way. Andrew McKeer once told me that a senior partner (and not the lady spoken of) had been convicted of sexual harassment. Well, at least we weren't subjected to that.

Financial Scandal

In the mid-1970s, there was a scandal which would have been a fine conversation piece for anyone living at Du Cane Court who was privy to the information. It was alleged that a married employee of Ayrton, Hooper and Jackson (our managing agents at the time) had misappropriated a large sum of money raised through service charges, to fund a relationship with his mistress. The case had gone to court, and important documents were seized and held in Southampton. As a result, the Tenants' Association was unable to perform an audit for that year. The company at the centre of the furore collapsed in 1978, although it later reappeared as Hooper and Jackson; and it is now a firm of estate agents trading locally under the modified name of 'Jacksons'. Keith Cardale Groves, who had previously managed the building, took over the reigns again and held sway for a few years (although in 1981, it was reported that there was an admission of 'a deplorable lack of management activity'). They were actually a satellite endeavour of a large general accident insurance company; and, in the mid-1980s, it must have seemed like they were about to preside over a large general accident ...

They were attempting to collect a 'special fund' towards the refurbishment of Du Cane Court, including repairs to the roof. As a result, the yearly maintenance charge doubled to one million pounds, and someone displayed a statement on the notice board, to the effect that he or she would only contribute £10 towards the special fund, and make good the balance later on when the tenders were in. At the time the block was about to change hands, and there was no certainty that, in the end, the money would be spent in the way that was promised. There was also concern over the amount of interest which would accrue from such a colossal sum, if collected in advance. Some residents withheld their portion of the special fund and were threatened with legal action, although none was taken. And on the other side of the equation, a certain Mr Evans, in a letter which was read out to a small assembly on the 10th of June, 1985, threatened to embark on a legal injunction to get the major works stopped. *Touché*! Also, several tenants had asked for a rebate on the fee levied for the gardens, since they couldn't be used anyway - and some of the flower beds had been wrecked. Then, on 11th March, 1986, it was reported that there had been a meeting in the House of Commons with Labour MP, Tom Cox, who felt we had a case against the owners for unreasonable charges; but he also realized that, if we took action, we would have to pay for the defendants' legal bills as well as our own!

In 1986, our landlords were Swallow Securities, and they had already been embroiled in a controversy ten years earlier. A 1976 bulletin (from the Conference of Private Residence Associations) carried the story that the trustees of Harrow school had provided their head lessor, Swallow Securities, with a lengthy schedule of dilapidations relating to Maida Vale Block. So it must have been with some relief for all concerned that, on 14th August, 1986, Du Cane Court was sold to Olayan Europe Ltd. Such was the change of ownership, but was the new governance respectful and wise? Well, the new manager, Mr Parker, opened meeting number 146 on November 18, 1986, by describing how he had spent his first two and a half months in office investigating complaints, and looking into ways in which the service charges might be reduced. Clearly, some progress was made, for, in a meeting the following year, we were assured that Olayan Europe Ltd would allow any tenant to see an independent building surveyor, free of charge.

But more stormy weather lay ahead. In 1987, there was a management 'buy out' within Olayan Europe, and the outfit became Belgrave Properties. Also, a new Tenants' Association committee was formed, but it was fairly ineffective and no audits were done for that year. Then an action group emerged to fill the vacuum, and an enormous dossier of information was compiled to countenance its claims. Finally, a complaint was made to Tom Cox, who raised a question in Parliament regarding the management of leasehold blocks.

Apparently, some years ago during an audit, it was discovered that approximately £70,000 had mysteriously 'disappeared' from the accounts! The landlords must have been quite embarrassed, as they went into hiding for several days to examine the matter. To their credit, they *did* eventually account for the money; but, for a while, it must have seemed that the chickens had come home to roost.

Against a general background of mistrust, it is not surprising that the holding of a large fortune, in lieu of some unforeseen expense arising in the future, – a 'sinking fund', as it is euphemistically called, – has never been authorized for Du Cane Court. However, in the late 1990s, David Clark introduced the humanitarian concept of spreading a large bill over several years – rather than bankrupting the poorer residents with a requisition for a single payment.

Service Charges: A Bone of Contention

An interviewee of mine once told me that she saw an interesting television programme in the 1960s. It was about extortionate service charges, and it particularly struck a chord with her because the television camera rotated 360 degrees around one of our inner courtyards. Furthermore, mention was made of First National Finance, which purchased Du Cane Court in 1967.

The general management fee here is about 10% of the overall service charge, and (on top of this) the manager - who, I understand, is usually a Chartered Surveyor - also has the right to levy a percentage of the cost of any major works for his or her personal services. So there is a vested interest in increasing our bills, rather than in reducing them. Yet we have not always had the manager's undivided attention, for he or she used to be responsible for more than just Du Cane Court. And there are other points of contention. To the chagrin of one or two members of the committee, we have for many years been charged rent on the Estate Office. (Bear in mind that we all pay ground rent on the building, anyway.) Parking bays are no longer free (although there is free parking at the front of the estate); and, officially, there is no parking provision for visitors. The service charge on a small one-bedroom flat (without a hallway) may differ widely, depending upon whether it is the result of a conversion - whereby a contiguous cleaner's room has been purchased. And finally, when the flats were first sold, in the 1960s and early 1970s, the service charges were collected retrospectively; whereas the new leases, issued from 1974, protected the landlord from arrears, and specified that payments would have to be made in advance.

One lady, who lived on the upper ground in E block, was evidently a little bit 'touched' by the burden of the maintenance fee. She was now in her dotage, and was once accompanied by a kindly porter to her flat. He turned on the light, and she exclaimed, 'Service charges! Service charges!'

'But, madam, someone will fall and break a leg!'

'I don't care about them ... service charges!'

Mind you, a friend of mine hit upon a novel way of dealing with one of these monstrous bills. She put it through her shredding machine. (It was an accident, of course.)

In the end, perhaps it is better to pay up thoughtlessly, as if you were taking Imodium in the face of food poisoning, for what is not processed cannot hurt you ... well, not for a while, anyway. At a Tenants' Association Meeting in March, 2001, it was reported that 49 people were in arrears with their service charges. Mercifully, there is no known case of a tenant being evicted for not paying these charges, - although there *are* cases where building societies have forestalled when a mortgage is not paid. The wheel of law resembles the wheel of fortune, and, being servant to all and slave to none, is subject to many machinations.

Value for Money

Two letters in May, 1987, expressed suspicions about the cost of structural changes being passed on to the tenants; and one of them, from Kossuth V.L. de Zielve, a Consultant Engineer, even asks, 'Why should lessees pay for any maintenance on a property which they do not own at all?' This is a provocative question, indeed, but we must presume (in the absence of irrefutable proof to the contrary) that the costs of alterations to flats owned by managers and landlords were never passed on to the lessees – for that would have been illegal. However, there are times when I have been tempted to alter the famous Monty Python sketch about the Romans, to: 'So what have the landlords ever done for us ...?' Except that, unlike the Romans, they really haven't done much for us. We have skilled practitioners to thank for the architecture and the gardens, and ourselves to thank for the sense of community. All the freeholders ever did was 'milk the cow'.

On the positive side, various jobs are transacted seamlessly - without any intervention from the residents, -including maintenance of the external face of the building, the corridors, the reception area and the gardens. The buildings insurance and the heating are also supplied. There is 24-hour porterage and security, and there are on-site plumbers and electricians; not to mention the parking arrangements, which have already been discussed. Of course, it is difficult to access the absolute value of all these things, but there is a real benefit in terms of convenience.

The heating may be increased, free of charge, by installing larger radiators, and only the initial outlay is the resident's responsibility. It is supplied for seven months of the year, day and night, and, ironically, the temperature always seems to drop as soon as it is switched off! On the other hand, when it is on, it can be overpowering; but, then, if you wish to exercise any control, you must purchase a valve for around £50.

Hence, a popular alternative is to open the window. (And so the cool air comes in and solves one problem, while noise goes out and causes another!) It has been observed that our situation is similar to that of small conurbations in the old Soviet Union, which were subject to the behaviour of a central generator, switching the temperature on or off in every home, regardless of what the occupants wanted! 'How strange,' you may say. But the received wisdom is that the arrangement cannot easily be changed, since it is defined by the terms of the lease, and a deed of variation to hundreds of leases would be prohibitive in terms of time and money.

In auditing the service charges, the committee sometimes refers to an *equalization fraction*. In the lease, each flat is assigned a 'fraction', or percentage, of the overall service charge. All of the percentages should add up to a 100 – and yet when I last heard, they added up to 102! This was due to the dividing of larger – mostly one-bedroom – apartments into smaller flats, especially studios: whereby, in each case, the two resulting service charges, combined, exceeded the original fee. One might add that the sum of the two freehold values far outweighs what the source property, alone, would have fetched on the open market ... and these advantages, notwithstanding anyone's feigned look of surprise, are surely the reasons for making the alterations in the first place!

There are many who take a dim view of various proceedings within Du Cane Court, and one such person, erudite and now sadly deceased, who secreted a famous mountaineer in the double barrel of her surname, earned herself the sobriquet from yours truly, 'Scott of the intellectual Antarctic'. She spoke of her impressions with a caustic tongue, as if they were engravings which required not the precision of a scalper, but the generality of an acid; although really, underneath the façade, she was a gentle person.

Some members of the committee are also as watchful as hawks for any discrepancies in the accounts, and even the discovery of the tiniest of mistakes gives rise to so much jubilation, that I am reminded of the biblical parable in which there is more rejoicing over the return of one lost sheep, than over the faithfulness and unerring virtue of the whole of the rest of the fold.

An Economy of Scale

The term 'economy of scale' very well describes why life at Du Cane Court should not be expensive. Imagine a series of bungalows, each with a separate roof to be maintained. Now picture this building, with a lower ground, an upper ground, and seven other floors – all nestling under the same roof. Then ask yourself, when the time comes to repair the roof, whether you have economy of scale?

Now imagine maintaining the walls and common parts of a shared building, as opposed to caring for the same facets in nearly 700 detached dwellings. Is there not economy of scale?

And when 1200 large windows need replacing, surely an excellent deal could be negotiated and passed on to the tenants. But *will* it be?

Whereas every house has its own heating and hot water supply, there is, for our grand mansion block, just one system served by several oversized boilers. Furthermore, in a communal living space, everyone benefits from each other's heating: to the right, to the left, above and below. And what about the economy of maintaining an acre or two of green space for the relaxation and rejuvenation of residents – rather than 676 separate gardens?

Of course, there is the other side to consider. Unlike in a house, we have lifts to maintain and salaries to pay. And aficionados of 'the Court' would point to the expensive apartment blocks in the city, which have yearly bills equal to or greater than ours. For my part, I *could* reply that they may also have special features, such as swimming pools, tennis courts and gyms [Barry.99]. However, there are fine public amenities within easy reach of us. So why reinvent the wheel?

UNFORESEEN PROBLEMS SUDDENLY ESCALATE

*

The Changing of the Guard

From the end of the 1980s, there were three female managers who passed through the ranks in quick succession: Fiona Lambourne, Marina Davies and Karen Maw. One Paddy Flawn wrote on October 4, 1989, that she was strongly opposed to Mrs Davies becoming manager, as the latter was effectively part-time. On the other hand, I have heard that Mrs Davies was the most promising of the three bosses, and more helpful than Mrs Lambourne. The prevailing opinion is that Karen Maw was inappropriate for the job, although apparently she was very charming. One commentator said of her, 'She would record everything in a little book of yellow notes – and then do nothing!'

On 1st April, 1991, concern was expressed about the employment of a female security guard ... yet any male chauvinist was shown to be an April Fool, for it was also reported that 'a marked improvement in the keeping of the incident book has been noticed'. In the end, whether the women were competent or not, and whether any of them had outside commitments, or were victims of circumstance, I cannot personally say. But certainly, some unfortunate incidents were coming our way which no one would wish to be held accountable for. Thus, on 30th June, 1990, a certain Sylvia Woods wrote, 'I have been asked by several concerned residents to place on record the incident last week [Tuesday, 26th June] when a block lift (no.1) arrived at the ground floor and then immediately crashed into the basement; fortunately without apparent injury to me.' And there was worse to come.

Inside the Boiler Room

The heating system was originally coal fired, and then it ran on oil, before it was changed over to natural gas in 1976. There were four boilers. Numbers 1 and 4 used both oil and gas, and were manufactured by Ray Autoflame of the USA.

A letter from Keith Cardale Groves, on 5th July, 1982, outlined plans for a new system, which apparently were not followed through. And so, David Kut and Partners, Consulting Engineers, visited the site on March 7, 1983, and one week later they noticed that heating had been lost to blocks D and E. They wrote, 'We left the valves set correctly. To prevent further tampering, we recommend that you arrange for the wheel heads of the valves in question to be padlocked together.' As if this wasn't worrying enough, they went on to say, 'While on site we drew samples of water from the heating system [, and found] that they were heavily contaminated with black oxide sludge [... Things are] corroding internally, the black sludge being a form of rust. If allowed to continue untreated [,] permanent failure of the system will occur.' The feeling was that with new valves, part of the apparatus could be cut off and flushed out.

By 1990, gas leaks had been reported, and a gasket needed replacing; but when Gloria Blackhurst (from the committee) investigated, she found that, actually, it had not been replaced. Only one boiler was now fully functional. Of the remaining three, one was partially functional, one was not operating at all, and one was being used for spare parts.

Calamity Strikes

'The incident occurred between 5.30am and 6.30am,' said Kulbushan Chopra, the owner of our little shop. 'As I walked through the doors of the foyer, I heard an almighty bang, and even sensed a slight tremor in the building. Meanwhile, two security guards dived under the desk uttering expletives.

"It's not my fault!" I said, for people say the silliest things under duress. The police and fire services came within five minutes. No one was hurt, although I heard one of the firemen say, "It could have been the next Putney Hill!" (He was referring to a block of flats where there had been a massive gas explosion).'

At around this time, there were actually three explosions. Mrs Maw was removed because of complaints from the Tenants' Association, and a temporary manager, Gary Hopkins, took her place. He was extremely concerned, as well he might be ... for one morning, on the occasion of the third malfunction, an engineer was repairing one of the boilers, when suddenly part (or all) of the boiler door flew off, hitting the man in the face and causing horrific injuries. He was hospitalized for about six months, and needed skin grafts. As for our tough old building, the damage was contained within the basement. A resident, Derick Mallett, completes the gruesome story for us:

'In 1991, I was in hospital being treated for a gall bladder complaint, and found that the man in the bed next to me was the engineer who had been injured in the explosion. He was comatose, and had to be moved as he was only placed in the gastric ward temporarily. But I retain no visual memory of him.'

I do not know if the unfortunate man was at all culpable, but if there was a claim, it would probably have been ours to pay through the service charges. Either way, the whole episode was kept very quiet. Even Jay Patel of Wandsworth Borough Council told me (circa 2000) how surprised he was to have no record of the event.

Some Years Later: A Tour of the Boiler Room, and Beyond

After the third explosion, all of the heating and hot water had to be run from one boiler. Some time elapsed. Then, in about the year 2000, Andrew McKeer kindly took me on a tour of the Boiler Room, and so I was able to assess the current state of affairs.

'There are now two smaller boilers and one large one,' he explained. 'The hot water pipes are lagged with a quilt matting, and are also insulated with a thin layer of aluminium. The cold water goes straight up to a tank on the roof, whereas hot water travels on a circuitous route to every flat. There are many thermostats and pressure gauges. If the pressure rises above a certain level, everything shuts down. There are also sensors present which will detect a gas leak.'

The system seemed to be well organized, and safer than it had been. I was shown the original control panel from the 1930s, complete with the switches for every flat, which I thought was pretty remarkable. Also in the basement were a new locker room, and an exercise area for the grounds man! Then we visited the huge water tank on the roof, and Mr McKeer continued:

'The tank is 30 tons in weight when full. Unfortunately, an explosion split it in 1998, and it had to be dissembled piece by piece - then transported from the roof by helicopter. The tank has since been replaced by much lighter plastic vessels.' Once again, the building had survived virtually unscathed; and, once again, practically no one had any idea what had happened.

At Home with the Pharaohs – And other Pests

An apartment block as expansive as Du Cane Court is bound to attract scavengers of one kind or another, and my curiosity on this subject was not disappointed. I have learned that there was once a colony of feral cats in the basement; and a cheeky fox who would sit on the garages in full view of the Closed Circuit Television cameras. One resident I spoke to had the basin removed from her bedroom when it became overrun with mice. Even her saucepans were full of mice dirt!

Then there are the insects. A friend of mine told me of the night when a cockroach scuttled over her, although this was probably a case of mistaken identity, for Mr McKeer once said, 'I have never seen a live cockroach in the building, although I have seen plenty of dead ones.' The carpets in the corridor and in reception are sprayed for moths and carpet beetles. I have myself observed silverfish and weevils; and an interviewee of mine once noticed a cone-shaped object hanging inside her garage. She was told that if the problem was not treated, in just 24 hours there would be 2000 wasps flying around!

On January 10th, 1991, planning permission to turn a storeroom under block B into a launderette was refused by the council; and there were 31 letters opposing the idea on grounds of environmental health, for cockroaches and mice proliferate in warm, damp conditions – and, to exacerbate the matter further, the storeroom had a small window and little ventilation, and sat right on top of the dustbin sheds! In any case, a launderette already existed directly opposite Du Cane Court. But the desire to 'make a mint' is not easily tempered with common sense, and soon afterwards there was another proposal for the same facility – this time under block K! (That said, blocks B and K meet in the corner of one of our courtyards; and so the whole saga may be a single trunk with two branches.)

Naturally, there is ongoing pest control in the building, for vermin may make an appearance at any time - if disturbed by maintenance or manual labour. As we have seen, they are many and varied, but the stars of the show are definitely the pharaoh ants. In 1991, a resident might have a biscuit or a piece of cheese in his hand, and, lo and behold! Running around beneath it would be the tiny foot soldiers of an invading army, each of whom was just one or two millimetres in circumference, and wearing a light yellow to reddish colouring. The infestation was reported in the national press, and Rentokil, who have been on our books for some time, came to the rescue. Danny Ashton, the Branch Manager, kindly told me all I needed to know.

Pharaoh ants are not native to the United Kingdom, but can be introduced by holiday-makers returning from tropical and semi-tropical areas, particularly in North Africa and Mediterranean Europe; although they originated in Asia. Because of their association with toilets and drains, the ants may be rife with disease. Unfortunately, they like protein, and so are drawn to meats, cheeses ... and to organic matter, feeding upon blood, or wounds, or the delicate tissues of new born babies – such as eyelids and naval areas. They have also been found inside sterile dressings in hospitals.

In acute conditions there can be as many as thirty colonies in one small kitchen, but they are not very conspicuous, hiding in discreet places such as closets, wall cavities, light switches and telephone sockets. A colony consists of queens, males (who fertilise the queens), and workers (who are actually sterile females, and who forage for food). The workers are the only members of the colony you are likely to see, and people tend to kill them on sight. Yet ironically, if insufficient workers are received into the nest, a new queen could be produced - and so the problem gets worse. Effective treatment involves leaving baits, which are carried back to the queen. Formerly these would sterilize her, but nowadays they contain a slow-acting poison.

Du Cane Court – which has blazed various trails of one kind or another – was apparently one of the first blocks to experience these extraordinary little creatures. However, if what I have revealed is disconcerting to the sensitive reader who has ties to 'the Court', then I should add that the outbreak was handled efficiently; and that pharaoh ants have by now been found in a number of other buildings.

RESIGNATION STATEMENT FROM DU CANE COURT TENANTS ASSOCIATION COMMITTEE

The Committee gave a considerable amount of its time voluntarily. It received no money and no benefits. Whilst the Committee welcomed constructive criticism, it was not prepared to be reviled by those who contributed absolutely nothing to the common good and who were misrepresenting the facts.

The Committee did not manage the block; managing agents are paid to do this and so make the decisions.

Despite a request from the Committee, management neither issued a notice to clarify its decision concerning the newspapers, nor apologised for the situation which had arisen.

The Committee was appalled that porters openly and publicly abused tenants. The Committee also deplored the fact that the porters were permitted to cajole tenants into supporting a petition which directly opposed a decision made by management.

Management's apparent inability to manage, coupled with the disruptive behaviour of certain tenants, made it impossible for the Committee to continue.

The Committee had neither the time nor the inclination to defend its position when there were no substantiated charges.

Tenants will recall that in 1986, the Committee:-

1. strenuously challenged the validity of collecting £900,000 towards Phase III when it was not going ahead that year;
2. won the significant reduction of £450,000 in the amount payable in advance for Phase III;
3. vigorously queried the derisory interest earned on the Phase II fund;
4. involved the Fraud Squad and an MP;
5. spent a considerable amount of time during the weekend before Christmas with tenants who had received dunning letters which were to be executed on Christmas Eve. After discussions with management, the Committee succeeded in getting the letters rescinded.

The Committee had been investigating and working on the following:-

1. the unexplained excess charge for 1986, which the Committee anticipates could be as much as 50% of the general service charge for that year;
2. the estimated general service charge for 1987 which is higher than for 1986;
3. management's only partially complying with its undertaking that Phase III monies would earn interest;
4. the Phase III extent and starting date;
5. the adherence to the provisions of the 1980 Housing Act.

Had the Committee not resigned, a legal case would have been prepared to combat the current demands for the Phase III arrears.

Although having resigned, the Committee appreciates its duty to its members, and will hold the AGM, as arranged on the 12th March, so as to give its members the opportunity to determine the future of the Association.

THE EX-COMMITTEE. 15th February 1987

In the 1980s, the entire committee resigned in a blaze of controversy. The large service charge is mentioned, as is the involvement of the Fraud Squad, – but, in the end, it was not proved that any foul play had occurred. (Courtesy of the Tenants' Association.)

site: Du Cane Court

reg'd: 88/s/0634

ANALYSIS OF PUBLIC CONSULTATION.

Nº of neighbours consulted: 197 in response to both consultation and S.27 notice.

total Nº of responses :

responses against 34

responses in favour : 1

+ petition 161 sigs.

Reasons for support

1.
2.
3.
4.
5.
6.

Reasons for objection

1. Noise & disturbance & building work [||||||||||||
2. Eyesore [||
3. Overdevelopment [||||
4. Fire hazard [|||
5. Strain on drain [||
6. pure profit making exercise [|||
7. wish to be assured that cold water reserve storage tank no longer needed [|||
8. may affect structural stability [||
9. Possible damage to roof. [||
10. No advantage to tenants
11. loss of light [||
12. ... parking already inadequate [||

DU CANE COURT TENANTS ASSOCIATION

Du Cane Court, Balham High Road, London SW17

16th AUGUST 1988.

TO THE WANDSWORTH BOROUGH PLANNERS SERVICE
Wandsworth BOROUGH COUNCIL
THE TOWN HALL. WANDSWORTH S.W.18 2PU

WE THE UNDERSIGNED OPPOSE THE APPLICATION MADE BY BELGRAVE PROPERTIES LTD., FOR PERMISSION TO CONVERT THE COLD WATER TANK HOUSING INTO A TWO BEDROOMED PENT HOUSE.

SIGNATURE	FLAT.NO	SIGNATURE.	FLAT NO.
[illegible]	E 57	C.O.1 · S.M. [illegible]	
M. West	K 4 12	[illegible]	G15.
[illegible]	F002	[illegible]	H510
[illegible]	K04	[illegible]	K73
S. D. Say	K15	[illegible] Blackburn	C44
[illegible]	B42	Brown	K55
K.J. [illegible]	D.52	P. BROWN	J25
N. A. Watts	D25.	[illegible]	
[illegible]	G005	[illegible]	D58
[illegible]	A 4 13.	H.J. [illegible]	G.45
[illegible]	B510	[illegible]	C.62.
M. O'Connor	F 35.	[illegible]	G511
[illegible] Vaughan	B711	J.CARPENTER	K 37.
[illegible]	K54	G. A. SMITH	K.33
[illegible]	J 72	[illegible]	G49
[illegible]	D 32	[illegible]	H.64
A. J. Bartlett	E65	[illegible]	H 57.
[illegible]	B. 74	[illegible]	H 57
B.S. Davis.	F. 45	[illegible]	B.512.
B Summers Brandon	A 35	[illegible]	C.62
B. [illegible]	A 35	[illegible]	K24
[illegible]	D 46	[illegible]	P.T.O.

Objections, in the late 1980s, to the creation of a new property out of the storage tank on the roof. (Courtesy of Wandsworth Borough Council.)

Ack'd refer to Boro' Planner.

ELLIS MOXON

SOLICITORS

Partners: P. Moxon D.L. | I. Moxon. | C. A. Pickford. | J. A. Knott LL.B.
J. M. Glover. | A. D. T. Bentley B.A. | M. J. Bruce. | R. Badman LL.B.

Authorised by the Law Society to conduct investment business.

PLEASE REPLY TO: CREWE
OUR REF: ADTB/SOC/Turner
YOUR REF:
DATE: 21st February 1995

The Legal Department
Wandsworth Borough Council
DX 59054
WANDSWORTH NORTH

(CG) reply (by 8/3)

Dear Sirs,

Re: Flat GO 1A
Du Cane Court, Balham High Road, SW12

We act for the owner of the above, Gemma Turner.

This flat and next door GO 1B were apparently the subject of a division of one whole without the benefit of planning permission for residential user.

Mr King is the adjacent owner and we understand you are in correspondence with Robin F Clake & Co, his solicitors, regarding him and a lawful development certificate.

Would you please confirm that if applied for in respect of our client's case and flat GO 1A that a lawful development certificate would be granted. Our client bought her property on the 4th January 1991.

draft question!

Your early confirmation would be appreciated.

Yours truly,

LEGAL ... 22 ... WANDSWORTH

NAT Records indicate that units originally designated 2 bedsitting units undergone unauthorised rearrangement to form 2 self-contained flats.

83 Marsh Street
HANLEY
Stoke-on-Trent ST1 5HL
Telephone (0782) 202424
FAX: Hanley (0782) 208015
DX 20717 HANLEY

22 Market Place
BURSLEM
Stoke-on-Trent ST6 4AY
Telephone (0782) 577700
FAX: (0782) 575363
DX 22305 BURSLEM

Imperial Chambers
Prince Albert Street
CREWE
Cheshire CW1 2DX
Telephone (0270) 505000
FAX: (0270) 216452
DX 20161 CREWE

Controversy in the 1990s:
Flat G01 was divided into two studio flats without the benefit of planning permission, and around this time the legitimacy of other conversions was starting to be questioned. (Courtesy of Wandsworth Borough Council.)

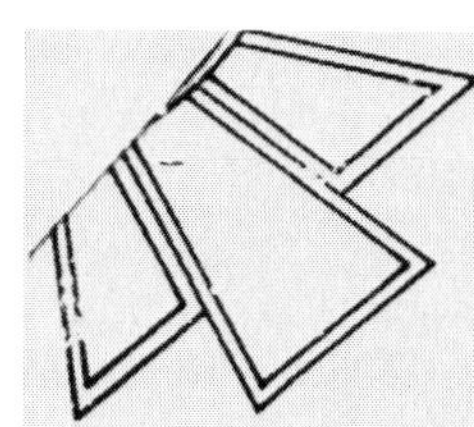

Du Cane Court Tenants Association

TECHNICAL SERVICES
RECD 24 JUL 1990

Flat C04B Du Cane Court
Balham High Road
London SW17 7JF

K R McQueen Esq
Director of Technical Services
Wandsworth Borough Council
The Town Hall
Wandsworth High Street
London SW18 2PU

23 July 1990

T ack & pass to B.P – how best to reply?
DE. 2597

Dear Sir

<u>Building work at Flat G01 Du Cane Court</u>

I have been passed a copy of Charles Jones' letter to you, dated 5 July 1990.

I was aware that Mr Jones had made a report to both the Planning Department and Building Control on 11 May 1990, and indeed on 13 May 1990 I wrote to a Mr Lewis (Planning) endorsing, on behalf of the Tenants' Association, the action taken by Mr Jones, and adding a list of further flat conversions which we felt required investigation. I copied that letter to a Mr Khosla in the Building Control section.

I was concerned to learn, therefore, that the Building Control section denied knowledge of this matter when contacted by Mr JOnes on 5 July 1990.

An A G McDonald replied (ref: BP/RL/90/E) on 4 June 1990 to my letter of 13 May 1990 to Mr Lewis. Apparently certain flats did not require planning permission for conversion. These were:

C72, C74, E55, B45, B43, E41, B31, B35, D36, J23, F17, K17.

I replied on 13 June 1990 expressing my suprise that there was no indication on the Statutory Register that Certificates of Established Use had been obtained. I have had no reply to that letter.

Nor have I had any communication about the results of investigations into other flats on the list. In addition to G01, these are:

D71, G61, A36, E37, A21, D23, E21, K27, H05.

It has since come to my attention that there are other flats which have been split in the recent past. These are:

E61, E63, E65, A51, A41, B41, A31, A32, B34, A22, A25, B21, B22.

I should be grateful if you would ensure that full investigation is made of all the circumstances surrounding these conversions.

Yours faithfully

D Watkins
Hon Chairman

Du Cane Court ◇ Balham High Road ◇ London SW17

A number of flats have been converted, over the years, into smaller units; and one or two questions have been asked. (Courtesy of Wandsworth Borough Council.)

G005 Du Cane Court.
14th April 1991

Mrs Maw,
Estate Office.

Dear Mrs Maw,

BOILER EXPLOSION.

On re reading your Circular I became very annoyed.

The fact that many residents could have sustained serious injuries or even death has been completely ignored. Many of us have seen the block of flats on Putney Hill which suffered a similar fate. We were lucky that our Security Staff proceeded calmly to take the necessary steps and a letter of thanks to them would be appropriate.

We were glad to have our services restored BUT far more concerned about the state of the Boiler House and our safety.

On this point our Tenants Association in their Press interview appreciated the situation far better than our Managing Agents.

These events cannot be swept under the carpet; a full explanation and apology should be forthcoming together with details of the steps taken to ensure that this can never occur again and full consultation with our Teants,s Association on all points.

Yours sincerely,

c.c.D.C.C.T.A.

This letter refers to the boiler explosion in 1991, which severely injured an engineer who was working on the boiler when it occurred. (Courtesy of the Tenants' Association.) The problems which led up to the tragedy had a long history, although certain managers were only here for a short time. Therefore, the present letter is ***not*** included in order to apportion blame.

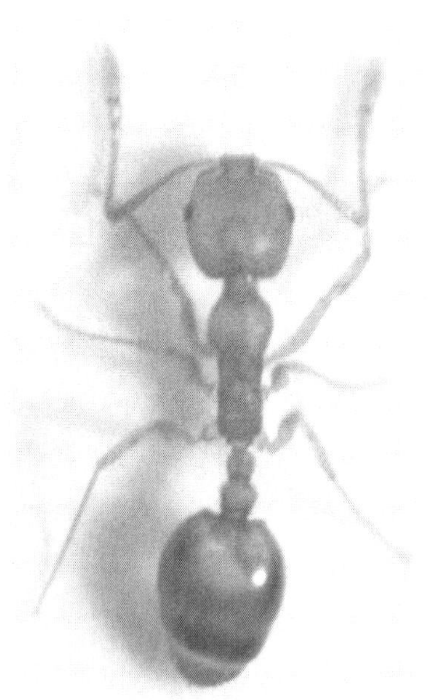

We were paid a visit by the pharaoh ants in about 1991, and Rentokill were called out to despatch them, which they did with commendable efficiency. These pests feed upon protein, and may spread disease because they are attracted to meat, or wounds, or bloody bandages. They can be a menace in hospitals. (Photos courtesy of Rentokill Initial.)

NOTICE TO ALL RESIDENTS
AT
DU CANE COURT

In the past we have issued notices at regular intervals about articles being thrown from windows.

The accumulation of cigarette ends, food, paper and other detritus is not only annoying but also now becoming a serious hazard. Lit cigarette ends cause burns and fires, they have blown into open windows fortunately to date with no major problems resulting. Food attracts the vermin, if they are attracted to the outside of the building they will find a way into it. Rubbish has to be cleared up by the staff, their time can be better spent than clearing up after the selfish few.

All the above are minor compared to the utterly stupid and wantonly dangerous incident last weekend when a fire extinguisher was thrown into the courtyard from a considerable height, it is only by good fortune that no-one was injured and no damage occurred.

May I appeal to the better nature of the few residents to not throw anything out of the windows, use your rubbish bin and use the chute and bins rooms provided. With a little effort there can be an improvement that will benefit everyone.

Andrew McKeer MRICS
Capital Property Management 27 March 2002

At Du Cane Court, anything may fall from the windows or from the roof. Apart from the above, there are a number of people who have plummeted to their deaths. (Source: general distribution.)

The base station and eight mobile phone masts on top of Du Cane Court could be affecting you or your children's health

I am not sure that you are aware that the base station and mobile phone masts on the roof of Du Cane Court, have the potential to cause numerous physical and mental health problems (see list below). Did you notice that your health declined after the base station and masts were installed in 1999; the effects will now be even worse because T-Mobile are now upgrading the system to G3 on the 15th September, 2005 (T-Mobile have not filed a prior planning application to change the technical specifications, as recommended by Part 24 of the GPPO). T-Mobile should inform all residence of Du Cane Court about the proposed upgrade: to date they have not. The current emissions from the masts will be even higher once the system is converted to the G3 system. This will adversely affect you or your children even more, and will also impact on the health of the children and teachers attending Trinity St Mary's C of E School, in Balham Park Road, and Aversham Primary School in Elmfield Road; both schools are adjacent to Du Cane Court. Furthermore, local residents in the vicinity of the base station and masts will also be affected

The physical and mental health problems associated with base stations and mobile phone masts:

1. Cancerous afflictions including leukaemia, brain tumours, breast cancer, cervical cancer, and pre-cancerous tumours
2. Brain-degenerative diseases (e.g. Alzheimer's) and epilepsy
3. Unexplained severe skin rashes
4. Unexplained low white blood cell counts.
5. Hormonal deficiencies and early menopause
6. Extreme fluctuations in blood pressure
7. Heart attacks including heart rhythm disorders, and strokes;
8. Susceptibility to infection
9. Numerous instances of headaches, migraines, dizziness, inner agitation, chronic exhaustion, faintness, tingling sensations, electric shocks, tinnitus, behavioural disorders (e.g. attention deficit disorder, ADD) lack of concentration and sleep disturbance
10. Nervous and connective tissue pains
11. Disruption to family life
12. Devaluation of property

The most common effect of phone masts/antenna are the disruption of sleep patterns, causing the breakdown of the melatonin process and subsequent immune problems leading to the inability to fight pre-cancer cells. Several post Stewart; scientific reports strongly reinforce this hypothesis, in particular:

- Saltzberg Resolution 2000
- Catania Resolution 2002
- Trower Report 2002
- Dr Helen Irvines studies Glasgow Health Board 2002
- Dr Gerald Hylands Report 2002
- Research Baconnier Lang et al October 2002 (Israel Department of Chemical Engineering Negev)
- Freiburger Appeal October 2002
- Health Protection Agency Report (UK) October 2005 (available in October 2005 through www.hpa.org.uk >Radiation section).This report gives individuals and doctors information on how to treat exposure to emissions from base stations and masts.

You should be aware that Dorrington Belgravia Ltd could be liable in civil law should you or your children have developed health problems, as a direct result of the mobile phone base station/masts installed on the roof of Du Cane Court. You are no doubt aware from the media that large numbers of people adversely affected by cigarettes are now seeking compensation through the courts, and it is in

Some concern has been expressed about the masts at the top of the building. The claims regarding ill-health are not to be taken lightly, although the mention of T-Mobile weakened the argument, since we have no masts from this manufacturer!
(Source: general distribution.)
Curiously, a company named B.Richardson & Son, which maintained television aerials at Du Cane Court, left in 2002 because people weren't paying the yearly fee. In fact, the company weren't very good at self-publicity, and many residents may have been unaware that they were receiving the said service!

Statement of expenditure incurred in the maintenance and management of Du Cane Court, London SW17

	General £	Boiler £	Lifts £	Garages £
Staff Costs				
- Sundries	3,210.73	-	-	-
- Wages	367,197.62	-	-	-
- Telephone	997.35	-	-	-
Cleaning				
- Contracts	5,425.08	-	-	-
- Material	4,696.97	-	-	-
- Pest control	10,318.84	-	-	-
- Refuse removal	21,170.66	-	-	-
Boiler				
- Maintenance	-	8,998.88	-	-
- Fuel	-	219,760.42	-	-
Lifts				
- Electricity	-	-	23,777.64	-
- Insurance	-	-	5,171.31	-
- Maintenance & Repairs	-	-	17,007.96	-
Electricity: common parts	29,061.56	-	-	-
Insurance	111,100.53	-	-	-
Gardening	18,928.14	-	-	-
Repairs, renewals & redecoration				
- General	29,404.04	-	-	-
- Fire extinguishers	4,384.75	-	-	-
CCTV	(5,706.25)	-	-	-
Security	52,500.20	-	-	-
Water hygiene	11,717.10	-	-	-
Fees				
- Audit and accountancy	2,410.74	737.33	141.93	-
- Management	108,080.44	33,056.51	6,363.09	-
- Legal	232.06	-	-	-
Major works				
- Waste pipes	5,000.00	-	-	-
- Boiler & plant	-	31,392.20	-	-
- Lifts	-	-	4,120.00	
- External decorations	125,000.00	-	-	-
- Fees	17,450.64	-	-	-
- Roadways and paths	2,500.00	-	-	-
- Fire escape stairways	35,000.00	-	-	-
- Wiring to plant	17,706.25	-	-	-
Bank interest received	(16,713.72)	-	-	-
Totals	961,073.73	293,945.34	56,581.93	-
Total expenditure				1,311,601.00

The general expenditure for 2006. (Source: general distribution.)

Wellington Road, Cressex Business Park,
High Wycombe, Bucks HP12 3PR
t 01494 897600 f 01494 897630
e info@hazlemere.co.uk w www.hazlemere.co.uk

Ref: DCC15

Dear Gregory Kieran Vincent Esq

Further to our recent letter regarding the proposed window replacement scheme we are looking to undertake at **Du Cane Court**, we enclose further information relating to the scheme.

Please note you will not be forced to change your windows by the Landlord or any other Party. Neither will the Landlord be contributing to any costs involved.

Initial levels of interest from those contacted have been encouraging and lead us to believe our enquiries could result in a working project. We are therefore now in a position to provide quotations for apartments in Blocks F, G, H, J and K.

In order to provide an indication of the costs involved we have calculated a guide price for the various apartment types at Du Cane Court, these are outlined below. Please note that prices for 1, 2, 3 and 4 bed apartments will vary depending on the quantity of windows required.

Guide Prices

Apartment Type	Guide Price
Studio Flat – 1st Floor or Below (2 Windows)	£2,900 incl. VAT
Studio Flat – Above 1st Floor (2 Windows)	£3,250 incl. VAT
1 Bed Apartment	£5,700 incl. VAT
2 Bed Apartment	£6,850 incl. VAT
3 Bed Apartment	£7,285 incl. VAT
4 Bed Apartment	£9,800 incl. VAT

If you are interested in this scheme we ask you to indicate the styles and numbers of windows for your apartment on the enclosed sheet. To obtain your exact price you can then choose from one of the following options:

a) Bring your sheet with the necessary information (window style and sizes) to the Reception area at Du Cane Court on **Saturday 9th, Sunday 10th, Saturday 16th or Sunday 17th April 2005** between **10am and 4pm**. A colleague will be available to provide prices and answer questions.
b) Return your completed sheet in the enclosed Freepost envelope. We will then send prices back to you.

Note: We will have samples of the windows together with copies of the specification agreed with the Landlord on display in the reception area during the weekends of 9th/10th and 16th/17th April.

Hazlemere
group
FENSA
Part of the Hazlemere Window Company Ltd.
Company Registered in England.
Hazlemere Window Company Limited, Wellington Road,
Cressex Business Park, High Wycombe, Bucks HP12 3PR
Registered No. 2185969 VAT No. GB 442 3633 68

This is a notice regarding the cost of replacing windows in the block in 2007. In addition, the annual service charge was higher than normal because of certain major works. Indeed, the two bills combined would have made someone with a lease on a two-bedroom flat almost £11,000 poorer. (Source: general distribution.)

A view of the roof, showing an important structure on the top of B block, which contains the motor rooms for the lifts in the foyer; and, above them, the main water tank. There are about ten storage tanks at the top of the building. Cold water travels down from the roof. Hot water, on the other hand, is heated in the basement, and pumped up to each of the flats. (Photograph taken by the author.)

On the top right are the controls for the heating and hot water system.
The other two pictures show equipment which is now obsolete. Top left, we see some original fuse boxes; and below, some on-off controls for the electricity supply. (Photographs taken by the author.)

Two pictures of the basement. The first shows the gas room, containing, among other things, the groundsman's exercise equipment! The second shows the huge hot water pipes, insulated by lagging. (Photographs taken by the author.)

In the first picture, Andrew Mckeer, former manager, stands beside the largest boiler. (There are three boilers today, in 2008.) In the second, we see an original collection point for the output from one of the dust chutes. (Photographs taken by the author.)

THE TENANTS AS A PRESSURE GROUP IN THE LOCALE

*

The residents of Du Cane Court have been politically active on many issues beyond the confines of their estate. When there was a lot of noise and commotion emanating from the Paphos Restaurant just across the road, one vociferous person got the Tenants' Association involved in legal action. Most probably the bill for this was covered by the service charge, and, when the money ran out, the case could not be pursued; although soon after, the restaurant was sold anyway. Then another establishment, Bucci's, came under the spotlight, and, in the proactive words of a well-seasoned campaigner of ours, - written on 17th July, 1995, - 'tenants have had to endure the banging of saucepans, [and] shouting and singing in the early hours of the morning'. In the mid-1990s, there were letters from 'the Court' opposing a planning application to develop 222 Balham High Road. One commentator said that it would obscure views of a nearby listed church, and reduce sunlight to the adjoining garden.

The standing within the local community of our massive residence is well illustrated by the fact that Wandsworth Council should care to correspond with the chairman of our committee, on a subject of general concern to the neighbourhood. The letter, on 13th November, 1995, read as follows: 'street cleaning is quite intense and specialist equipment is now being used to remove chewing gum and the resulting staining, and is ideal for removing pigeon droppings.' Indeed, the issue of pigeons nestling under the nearby railway bridge has caused some controversy, and a businessman who passes through may hasten his steps for fear of yolk-yellow or egg-white effluent landing upon his freshly-pressed suite - or poisoning his chicken take-away, whilst being mistaken for mustard or mayonnaise. Chrissie True from Du Cane Court was quite upset about it, although both Railtrack and Wandsworth Council protested their innocence. Finally, after a two year battle, in July 2000 the Appeal Court Judges found Railtrack liable, ruling that the owners of a property must tackle problems which arise from that property: which is a fairly obvious conclusion, if you think about it, although the proceedings must have been a terrible drain on the public purse. Pigeon proofing called 'Glide' was introduced, and the pests – unlike the legislature's bank balances - now find it difficult to perch comfortably without sliding downwards.

Some renown settled, like laurels, upon the heads of our conscientious committee, when they were photographed for an article in the Evening Standard (Wednesday, 5th September, 2001) on the subject of the Residents' Association. Meanwhile, they were busy with yet another challenge: how to police the infamous New World Club, which is just a stone's throw from our block of flats. Again, the issue was one of disturbance, late at night or in the early hours of the morning; and the feelings which it arouses in some are especially venomous, as if this small institution were full of rank matter, like an infected wound. A newsletter from our committee in May, 1999, shows that there was support from the residents for a proposal to convert the premises into flats, although unfortunately this was rejected. The owners of the club appealed to the Secretary of State, but the place was never properly licensed and was eventually shut down. Since then, it has re-opened, and, from time to time, the patrons of this bedevilled haunt continued to squeeze through the modest pimple of its front door beyond the 'witching hour'. Incredibly, they even stand accused of threatening an innocent bystander at knife point, who is not so lucky as to live in the quiet recesses of our own building; and of mimicking the local wildlife, by using our grounds as a public convenience and for sexual frolicking. If the second of these three charges is true, there are no doubt some misanthropes who would swap our friendly carp for that freshwater fiend, the Amazonian candirú fish, who has a reputation for swimming upstream and lodging himself in a small, dark aperture where the sun doesn't shine ... Anyhow, enough of that. In 2006, the application to extend opening hours to 4am in the morning was refused: and this achievement may, in some measure, be credited to the political activists of Du Cane Court.

Now Balham High Road has been regarded as a commercial thoroughfare since the 1930s; even if Balham Park Road was labelled 'residential'. Therefore it is only natural for the owner of a property upon the high road to want to maximise any available profit; and, to be fair, it seems to me that everyone has a personal *bête noire* of some description. For many, it may have been the ongoing programme of structural alterations which I have previously described. But try raising this issue and the reply you will get is: 'Oh! You can't do anything about *that*!' Yet if we are powerless to affect the management of the place where we pay substantial sums of money to live, then why should we have any influence over some other building which we do *not* live in and pay *nothing* for? I sometimes wonder if our self-contained populace and committee have delusions of grandeur, when they so liberally flex their muscles beyond their obvious remit. I envisage Du Cane Court as a kind of empire which explores other realms, while seeming, at its core, to crumble and implode. Is it a metaphor for hyperactive nations ...? Are we so energized abroad because we have no mastery at home?

Yet I should also pay homage to this homely beacon of ours on the Balham skyline, which, after a peculiarly saintly fashion, absorbs all manner of punishment, whilst retaining a spirit which is calm and congenial.

NOTABLE PEOPLE OF RECENT TIMES

*

Persons of Title

Across our multifarious population, there are few members of the peerage, or persons otherwise decorated by royal occasion. However, on the 13th January, 1987, Lord Orram, the Labour Peer, wrote to say that he had recently purchased J001 and wished to join the Tenants' Association. As far as I know, he left in the early to mid-1990s. A Frederick George Leighton once lived here, but was he related to Lord Leighton? When I asked our new manageress, Noella Morton, if she could shed any light on this, she surprised me with her reply: 'I don't know,' she said, 'but I can tell you that I befriended a girl in my schooldays who was Lord Leighton's stepdaughter.'

Viv Nnoka and Molly Tillman of Du Cane Court have both received MBEs: Vivian for her work in Nigeria, and Molly for her services to the Foreign Office. And I understand that a certain Mrs Blake, of K04, was also honoured by the Queen.

Music and Publishing

Perhaps the successful occupants of Du Cane Court no longer make the headlines as readily as their predecessors in days of yore. Nevertheless, a range of gifted and notable people continue to grace our mighty residence. We've had the first computerised astrologer living here. Then there was Mr Agate, who was the racing tipster, 'Pegasus', for the News of the World; and Mike Sarne, the composer of that popular number from the 1960s, 'Come Outside'. One lady I spoke to even remembered him practising it. And a recent (possibly contemporary) occupant is a member of the 'Dogs', a musical band which is popular with teenagers. Clive Pollard, who lives on the fourth floor, also deserves a brief tribute, for he is an amiable soul who has occasionally suffered from penury for his art. He has been a pianist for the Royal Ballet Company at Covent Garden, and succinctly summarises the pros and cons of his working life: 'I like to provide the piano accompaniment for songs, as they are very intimate, but I do find that there is a lot of backbiting between ballet-dancers and choreographers.' Clive has been composing all his life, and he would have felt a sense of achievement when one of his compositions was finally performed by the students of Kingston Polytechnic, at St Mary's Church in Balham. He has also played for BBC Radio 4, and for the Icelandic Opera Company in Reykjavic; and he recently composed a five-minute piece for the Icelandic Symphony Orchestra.

Clive Pollard is a cousin of Robert Harris, the famous author of such thrillers as 'Archangel' and 'The Fatherland' – a novel about what would have happened if the Germans had won the war. (Perhaps Mr Harris could be prevailed upon to write a sequel, describing the Fuhrer's life at Du Cane Court?) At the christening of Robert Harris's baby, Clive joined various luminaries who are often before the public eye, - including Jeremy Paxman, Peter Mandelson and Ian Hislop.

'Jeremy Paxman sat on the floor and asked me to play Beethoven's Moonlight Sonata,' Clive told me. He was transfixed throughout my performance, and at the end he clapped his hands and said, "Thank you very much indeed"'.

Geoffrey Norris, the music critic for The Daily Telegraph, lives in D block and is a friend of Clive. He specializes in Russian music and has written a book on Rachmaninov. Another man of letters who has lived here is Paul Sussman. He has been a contributor for The Big Issue and The Daily Express, and, when I last heard, he had embarked on a book himself. Success stories, both large and small, proliferate. The resident, Carol Hunt, made headlines in the local press by winning a £250 prize for her short story – which was published in an anthology. Lastly, the popular novelist, Victoria Routledge, lives here; and one day the building's favourite pensioner, May Arkell, learned of the writer's presence quite by accident, when she chanced to give directions to a member of the literary fraternity who had got lost on his way to Victoria's flat, and who was carrying the manuscript of her latest book.

Film and Television

A former inhabitant of the block, well known to many for his unique personality, and for his artistic sensitivities, was Peter Austen-Hunt. In his younger days he had an unusual job in the media, performing a little magic on the cutting room floor, by interlacing the excerpts from musical scores with moving images ... into a seamless whole; and his name is often listed in the credits of films.

Another notable character, named Eva, once shared a flat here with her boyfriend. I understand that they were both involved in the cinematic arts, she being a location sound recordist who worked for a while in the Nordic film industry. The television producer, Gary Rimmer, and a film photographer named Johnny Johnson were also here. Mr Johnson was a dapper little gentleman, who had a penchant for collecting the spare parts of vacuum cleaners from dust chute rooms. When he was dying he said, 'I've had my chips' – to which a friend responded, 'Oh! They couldn't have done him any good!'

On a more exalted level, there has been filming within the environs of Du Cane Court for two Hercule Poirot detective stories: 'Plymouth Express' and 'One, Two, Buckle My Shoe'. I can remember once seeing a 1930s vehicle on the grounds and wondering what it was there for, but a couple of my delightful neighbours recollected the events in more detail.

'There were clothes-racks on wheels in the courtyard. I felt like I was living in a second-hand shop!' Jessie Boran told me. And the whole experience evidently struck a chord with Marion Hopkins.

'The TV crew filled up one of the inner courtyards with their vans and equipment,' she said. 'In the second series, flat A11 was even redecorated for the purposes of filming. I met David Suchet, who played the leading role, and I got my picture taken with him. He was quite comical because his fake moustache kept falling off, and I recall him pausing in front of a mirror in the stairwell, in the throes of a studied gait, to peer over his shoulder at his reflection in the glass.'

With regard to actors and actresses who actually live here, we have Paul Darrow, who has appeared in the television dramas, Emergency Ward 10 and Blake 7; and a lady who has played a nurse in Casualty. Also numbered among us are one or two actors in The Bill, which has been filmed on location in flat H33. Indeed, according to our resident taxi driver, Mr Pobjoy, even Brian Blessed, Sean Bean and Bruce Forsyth have discreetly slipped in and out of our legendary premises. Whatever next?

Theatre

Keith Lundric, of the Theatre Museum in Covent Garden, has spoken to me of two brothers whom he knows: Chris Luscombe, a current resident of 'the Court', and Thespian with the Royal Shakespeare Company; and Tim Luscombe, a former resident of ten years standing, as well as a freelance director and playwright. Tim has been involved in many productions of Noel Coward plays, and several years ago he wrote and directed a televised tribute to that esteemed dramatist and wit, broadcast from the Savoy Hotel. In an interview with Phil Wilmott in 2006, Tim commented jocularly, 'When [my brother, Chris,] was acting I was directing, and about three years ago, weirdly, we both switched over, he from acting to directing and me from directing to writing. Look out, in about 10 years' time he'll move into writing and I'll become a florist ...'

Recently, I met Christopher Luscombe in the comfort of my home at Du Cane Court. He is a polite and well-spoken young man with many interesting things to say.

'A passion for the theatre has been in my blood from my earliest days,' he admitted frankly. 'Being on stage gives you such an adrenalin rush, because there's nowhere to hide. The honesty of the performer must shine through or he will fail, whereas – contrary to popular belief - the camera *can* lie. Also, in cinematic art, any excitement is diluted with a great deal of tedium. A two-minute shoot might be succeeded by a whole day of waiting around. I have no desire to be involved with film, although it is a shame that we have no permanent record of great theatre. In theatre, as in life, the magic is transient – but that is part of its charm.' Evidently, 'the ephemeral' is also apparent in other ways ...

'The acting fraternity have traditionally been gypsies at heart. They must go where their vocation takes them, and buying a house was something to be avoided at all costs.' From the way he said this, I wondered if there was even some underlying superstition. Nowadays, however, Chris Luscombe is settled in himself. Perhaps Du Cane Court gives him a sense of continuity in his social life, which his cultural predecessors would not have enjoyed; as well as providing a peaceful retreat away from the prying public eye, for even his neighbours may be unaware of the presence of a celebrated actor-come-director living near them. He is, at any rate, happy with the new challenges in his career.

'At the moment, I am directing A Midsummer Night's Dream in the open-air theatre at Regent's Park. I don't think I'll go back to acting. Being a director gives me far more control over the finished product – although I never acted in a role which I disliked.' I think that, being a creative soul, Christopher will seek out the deep meaning in whatever comes his way. He will not passively wait for it to be revealed to him. There are also many talents he admires. Among their number are Nigel Hawthorne - and Dame Judi Dench, whom he has directed. He says of the playwright, Alan Bennett:

'Now there's a disarmingly modest man. Once, when asked if he minded a play of his being cut, he replied, "Oh! Cut as much as you like. All my plays are far too long anyway!"' And Chris has worked with Sam Mendes, who made his mark with that astonishing film, American Beauty.

'Sam is very down to earth, and has a sense of humour to match. He is firm and knows what he wants, yet he made a remarkable admission to me: that an actor on stage could be unable to conjure a particular effect in rehearsal, even though, miraculously, he may get it right on the night. As for myself, I believe that no performance is ever truly complete. It is always *work in progress.*'

Many people will also have heard of Arthur Smith, who owns a maisonette at Du Cane Court. He is a stand-up comedian, and star of the television series, 'Grumpy Old Men'. He has a keenly developed sense of humour, and can certainly take a joke, - witness his unusual association with Tony Hawks (a man who gained notoriety when he walked around Ireland with a fridge on his back). I refer, of course, to the outlandish premise of Tony's recent book, 'Playing the Moldovans at Tennis'. Apparently, Arthur had wagered that this was a game at which his friend could beat the entire Moldovan football team. The forfeit for poor Arthur, if his friend failed, was to strip naked and sing the Moldovan national anthem – which he duly did one day, whilst standing on a chair outside the Balham branch of Sainsbury's! A large crowd gathered to see the spectacle; and, for posterity, the story was even covered by the local press.

An Evening with Arthur Smith

One evening, I was fortunate enough to interview the man who is perhaps the best known of our current crop of residents.

'Sorry I'm late,' said Arthur. 'I had to do a voice-over for a KitKat commercial.'

'No problem,' I replied. 'I'm delighted you managed to make it.' I had spoken to Arthur several times, and I very much wanted to know him better. He is often on the radio, being chiefly known for his association with the programme, 'Excess Baggage'. He is also a stalwart supporter of the Edinburgh Festival, and, at the time of our meeting, was soon to make a one-off appearance there at the Assembly Rooms, in the acclaimed 'Arthur Smith Sings Leonard Cohen'.

'Commercials pay well, don't they?' I asked.

'It could be as much as £5,000 for ten minutes work,' he replied. 'But this is only an audition. I don't know whether I've got the job yet.' I offered a glass of wine and some juicy strawberries. He was grateful, and availed himself of them while we talked, letting the antioxidants battle it out with the carcinogens as he smoked his cigarettes.

'You know, I'm really one of the old-timers of Du Cane Court. I bought my flat in 1984,' he said.

'I came in 1987,' yours truly replied.

'So have you found out much about this block?'

'I have conducted many interviews, some of them with very old ladies who have been here since the 1940's.'

'I suppose you've heard the old chestnut about Hitler having designs on the place? My father told me that one when I was ten years old. It seemed highly unlikely to me at the time - but the legend keeps rearing its head, as if it must have a grain of truth in it.'

'Yes, I have ... although the evidence is hard to come by.'

'Well. Balham was badly bombed during the war, but Du Cane Court escaped unscathed, so maybe the rumours were born of resentment or jealousy. You know, I've even heard from a woman in the stationery shop that, before the war, Goebbels's sister used to visit a friend here for tea!'

Arthur started to reminisce. What interests did he have when he was young? It emerged that he was enterprising and highly sociable.

'I played in the football and cricket teams at school. I was Head Boy, and Chairman of the Philosophy Club. I even edited the school magazine - and an underground publication which opposed it!' One senses that Arthur likes to put the cat amongst the pigeons.

'I studied French to A-Level, and my grasp of it is still very satisfactory. I always thought I would end up teaching. In fact, I spent a whole year in Paris teaching English as a foreign language. And, at the University of East Anglia, I took a degree in Comparative Literature, and became very aware of Linguistics.' My ears pricked up.

'I remember Chomsky from my own undergraduate days, with his superficial and deep language structures ... So,' I asked Arthur, 'when did you get your first break?'

'Well, I didn't really become a professional entertainer until my late twenties. Before that I sang in a band, and I did stand-up comedy - at hundreds of venues, in fact, over a period of six or seven years. I was often the compère.'

'I'm impressed. The compère is surely the most versatile man in a comedy club.'

'He also tends to be the most handsomely paid,' Arthur confessed.

'Did you ever appear at the Banana Club in Balham?' I asked.

'Yes ... in fact I may have performed there on the opening night.' I felt a little praise was appropriate, and said:

'Standing up in front of a group of complete strangers and attempting to make them laugh must be very difficult.'

'Oh, it is ... and it's especially scary when you're delivering new material. But no one is effective to start off with. You have to perform hundreds of times, and gauge different human responses to particular jokes. Eventually you get to know what works.'

'I suppose it's a bit like market research?' I ventured.

'In a way.'

And has he done much acting?

'Not much. I was in two plays which I wrote - and The Bill. They call live acting "Doctor Theatre". You get an adrenalin rush which cures virtually every ailment. If you were a cripple before a show, once the curtain goes up you are able-bodied. Then, when it goes down, you are a cripple again! It's magic really.' The conversation took a new course.

'Would it be fair to say that you are primarily a writer?'

'Yes, but with the emphasis on comedy. I have written four plays in total: The Live Bed Show, starring Caroline Quentin, which ultimately transferred to the West End; Trench Kiss, which played at the Edinburgh Fringe but never really took off; Sod, shown in both Edinburgh and London; and An Evening With Gary Lineker, which was adapted for TV. I go to Edinburgh every year. The people there are very receptive to new talent. I also occasionally visit the Hay Festival.' In fact, Arthur does an alternative tour of the Royal Mile every year for the Edinburgh Festival, - and his friend, Rory Ford, from the Edinburgh Evening News, has told me that the year he joined him, the tour finished up in a courtroom, with both of them standing as witnesses for the defence of a fellow comedian who was in the dock.

'You're a successful exponent of theatre and satire,' I remarked, 'so would you agree with the idea that, behind his façade, the humorist is really an unhappy man? And, if so, does it follow that a tragedian is a jovial fellow when relaxed and among friends?'

'Quite possibly ... You know, besides a Comedy Store, perhaps we should have a Tragedy Store. But would anyone visit it?'

'Well, they might,' I smiled, 'but I suspect that the audience would still think that the purpose was to elicit laughter rather than tears, - and that the name would be interpreted as a touch of irony.'

After this informal conversation at my home, Arthur invited me to go out on the town with him. But he did not have the West End in mind; rather, he wanted to go for some drinks in the immediate locality with a teacher friend of his. Sadly, she never turned up; but, nevertheless, an unusual evening awaited me. We set off for The Bedford Arms. Once there, Arthur, with effortless *joie de vivre*, introduced me to some acquaintances of his: including several charming and attractive young women, who laughed in all the right places, and generally hung upon his every word. Furthermore, the presence of a musician there gave him a chance to expand upon a favourite subject.

'Really, my taste in music is eclectic,' Arthur ventured. 'I didn't like Bob Dylan at all when he first came on the scene, but he grows on you. I tend to think that, in a song, the melody takes precedence over the lyric. Yet it is strange how even a bad lyric can sometimes enhance a good song.'

Later, Arthur introduced me to a couple of delightful French ladies, revelling in the opportunity this afforded for him to show off his grasp of a foreign language. Then we set off to Bar Interlude, and this time Arthur ostensibly knew no one.

'Whom shall we say "Hello" to?' he asked me, after we had collected our beverages. We agreed upon our quarry, but I was happy for him to be the guinea pig. To my amazement, two attractive young females made room for us at their table.

'This is the famous Arthur Smith,' I offered in consolidation, - although it was superfluous, for he was soon planning his verbal home run with the lovely occupational therapist.

'Now here is someone who works for a living. Not like me. I just enjoy myself and get paid loads of money!' His modesty was disarming, partly because it was so sincere.

After a little more banter we were off again, this time destined for a café, where - for the second time in the evening - his social skills worked flawlessly. Two more pretty girls (I'd scarcely realised there were so many in the vicinity!) became our companions for an hour or two. One was from Maidenhead, and a reference was made to 'maidens who keep their heads', although the kisses flowed as freely as the vodka.

Some time after this interview, my celebrated subject was even discovered on the roof with a young lady. Perhaps he had treated her to dinner, and she was to be the dessert? Gifted and charismatic Arthur most certainly is, and yet he is an enigma. He is not a stylish dresser, nor has he any designs on the lucrative art of male modelling. On the contrary, he regularly flees from his beauty sleep into the arms of late night parties and nocturnal shadows. Such a lifestyle must take its toll. But what an extraordinary man!

'Does he know all of these people - or is it just that they all know him?' I wondered, as we went our separate ways. One or two knew him, certainly. But to widen the issue, does fame beget charisma, or charisma beget fame?

Two Hercule Poirot stories involved filming at Du Cane Court: 'One, Two, Buckle my Shoe' and 'Plymouth Express'. Here, the resident, Marion Hopkins, is shown linking arms with David Suchet, who played the leading role. (Courtesy of Marion Hopkins.)

To: The Residents, Traders, and Motorists
Du Cane Court
London SW17

The Bill
Bosun House
1 Deer Park Road
Merton
London SW19 3TL

Telephone: 020 8540 0600
Facsimile: 020 8545 0761

2nd November 2001

THE BILL RESIDENTS LETTER

Dear Ladies and Gentlemen,

We are planning to film scenes for a forthcoming episode of "The Bill" at:
FLAT H33, DU CANE COURT.

We will be filming on:
WEDNESDAY 7TH NOVEMBER between **08.30** and **16.30**. Then in the rear courtyard from **16.30** and **19.30.**
THURSDAY 8TH NOVEMBER between **11.00** and **16.00.**

We will of course endeavour to minimise disruption to the day to day activities in your block.

During the filming we will be parking some vehicles outside the service entrance, in the rear access road, and opposite the exterior location.

I will be liaising with Andrew Mc Kerr, If, however, you are experiencing any difficulties you can contact either myself, or Andrew Mc Kerr on the numbers below:

ROBBIE RAYNER Location Manager **Tel: 07831 123480**
ANDREW MC KERR Tel: 020 8673 5841

I would like to take this opportunity to thank you for your help and co-operation in the making of this episode.

With many thanks and kind regards
Yours Faithfully

Robbie Rayner
Location Manager
For and on behalf of *Thames Television Ltd.*

Thames Television Limited.
Registered Office: 1 Stephen Street London W1T 1AL, United Kingdom
Registered Number: 926655 VAT Number: GB222715196

A FremantleMedia Company

'The Bill' was filmed in Du Cane Court in 2001. (Source: general distribution.)

Two talented contemporary residents: Chris Luscombe, actor and director; and Arthur Smith, comedian and writer.
(The photo of Chris Luscombe is reproduced courtesy of Lucia Pallaris, from Peters, Fraser & Dunlop Group Ltd. The flyer relates to a comedy evening. It is included here courtesy of Arthur himself, and of Clive Conway, who presented the evening. The third illustration is a photograph taken by the author during the opening of the Balham Festival one year, and shows Arthur standing beside a brightly-dressed clown.)

The Balham Festival procession passes Du Cane Court. (Photographs taken by the author.)

On the left is a member of staff, known simply as Bill, proudly parading his Chelsea Pensioner uniform. On the right is Charles Kay Green, son of the architect of Du Cane Court, depicted here sitting in our gardens. Charles was one of my most valuable interviewees – and one of the most charming. (Left photo: courtesy of either Alan Bartlett, or the author. Right photo: taken by the author.)

A NEW MILLENNIUM DAWNS

*

New Landlords and Management

After the boiler explosions and the pharaoh ant invasion in the early 1990s, it would seem that a new managerial direction was sought, with exclusively male managers for the next 13 years; not to say that our three lady managers were in any way responsible for these problems, but they may have been used as scapegoats. And the new millennium brought further changes. Allsop Residential Investment Management (ARIM) took over the running of the building from 1st November, 2002; and the freehold also changed hands. On 17th May, 2000, Dorrington Investment plc – a subsidiary of Hanover Acceptances Group, which also has a foothold in food manufacture and agribusiness, - bought up all of the shares in Belgrave Properties Ltd, who were previously at the helm; and the newly-constituted firm became known as Dorrington Belgravia Ltd. The portfolio was worth £31 million[Estates.Gazette], and included properties in north and west London, as well as Chesterfield.

Trevor Morass, Dorrington's managing director, said that he was delighted with the acquisition, as the supply of tenancies in decent locations is dwindling. Two of Dorrington's representatives, Duncan Salvesen and Peter Yates, attended our Annual General Meeting in the year 2000, and this gesture was well appreciated. The Chairman of the Residents' Association boldly proclaimed, 'We have, now, the most accommodating landlords in Dorrington ever.' They have 'generously donated new rooms to residents, which they have had pleasantly decorated'. These were an improvement on the old garden room, but not everyone was happy. In some quarters, it was felt that a loophole in the law had allowed Dorrington to bypass the principle of *first refusal* – whereby residents are given the first opportunity to buy their building when it comes up for sale; although I dare say the committee was ill-prepared to embark upon a constitutional revolution at short notice. Nor would it have wanted to deal with the thorny issues of limited resources, and of organizing insurance.

Pressure on Limited Resources

In a block as huge as Du Cane Court, the essential provisions for water and electricity are sometimes fully stretched, what with new flats being created, with frequent subletting, and with the ever-increasing number of time-saving appliances leaching out of the system. The situation came to a head in November, 1999, when residents were without water for more than 48 hours. Both the Wandsworth Guardian and the Wandsworth Borough News covered the story. A letter from the manager on the 12th of November asked residents to conserve water in every way possible, and added, 'To try to alleviate the situation we have organised a temporary supply of drinking water available in the foyer, and kettles and buckets can be filled from a stand pipe near the pond (no[,] it's not pond water!)' One resident said, 'In the 33 years I have been living here, there has never been any problem like this.' Jackson

The following month, we learned that Wandsworth Borough Council were offering £25 in compensation to everyone affected. Doubtless, the manager was relieved that the responsibility for the disruption was completely accepted by another party. However, that wasn't all. Within the next year or two, the water at Du Cane Court was treated to reduce the amount of corrosion in the pipe work; and the prospect of softening the hot water system was investigated. From time to time less palatable investigations must also be made: and so the day came when Ali the plumber had to crawl through a manhole at the rear of the building, and thence through a conduit conveying sewage, in order to remove a blockage from the pipes. How he must have wished the circulation had been interrupted at the front of the building instead, where a plumber can switch off the water without the trauma of entering a manhole. However, any proposal to flush out our pipes is a mixed blessing, for the grime they contain may seal minute fractures which otherwise would be the cause of leaks.

A newsletter for summer 2001 highlighted the problem with finding parking spaces, but we were told, 'It has always been acknowledged that parking, whilst difficult, is a privilege granted by the freeholder, [and] not an automatic right.' Residents may feel that they have been short changed on this one, but a blind eye will not be turned to any indiscretions: for another newsletter, on 3rd October, 2002, warned that any car found not to be displaying a valid permit, by day or night, will be clamped, and later removed to the contractor's pound if the release fee has not been paid. And the humble cyclist was also under pressure, as one of the bicycle sheds was phased out, and a new, rather unsightly storage area was allocated under the open sky.

The Issue of Insurance

Actuaries across the Western Hemisphere must have been keeping a close watch on world catastrophes – especially the attacks on the Twin Towers on September 11th, 2001. Thus a newsletter stated that between 1998 and 2002, the yearly insurance premium for the building rose from £50,845 to £156,278; while, with the energy reserves of the world fast running out, the annual cost of gas also rose from just under £87,000 to almost £127,000. But if our bank balances are depleted, at least our property is secure ... or is it?

A friend of mine once read through the entire insurance document and lease for the estate. To her surprise, she found that only the brick garages were insured, and not the prefabricated ones. On 20th June, 2001, we were informed that Independent Insurance, which covered the block, had recently gone into liquidation. Later, the building was covered by Zurich Insurance Company, but that policy expired on 18th June, 2002. Then it was the turn of Norwich Union. Finally, on 27th June, 2002, a letter to residents conceded that if you had lodged a claim (which was still outstanding) with Independent Insurance, or with Dorrington's insurance brokers, AON, relating to a loss before 18th June, 2001, then you might have to wait years before it was resolved. Even if the outcome was favourable, the first £250 of each claim would not be paid by the insurers. I have heard that there was one day when the building was not insured at all. God help us if a disaster should ever occur on such a day!

Work on the Building Continues

All maintenance, and probably most flat conversions, are instigated by management or by the landlords. During major works, we should, perhaps, prey for a downpour, for at least rain keeps the fair-weather workmen away, while a beautiful sunlit afternoon – with the opportunity to wear string vests and fake tans – hails the return of the virtual building site. The leasehold rules state that there should be no loud noise after 1pm on a Saturday, and none at all on a Sunday; and although the rules are religiously adhered to by the majority of manual workers, only a fool would state definitively that they have never been broken. In recent years, the fashion has been to enlarge the kitchenette in studio flats while shrinking the bathroom. Afterwards, the bathroom no longer has a window, and instead depends on an extractor fan to remove bad odours. As if this was not unhygienic enough, there was one case of a small flat in C block (probably a former guest-room) with a toilet-come-bathroom door opening directly into the living room, which is against planning regulations. Wandsworth Council sent round an office junior who gave his approval – but apparently he was never shown this flat!

In the twilight of the old millennium, and the dawn of the new, much work was done at the top of the building. In 1987, a material called Derbigum was used for re-roofing, but this came with only a ten-year guarantee which expired on 1st December, 1997. Fortunately, the new installation by Acclaim Roofing was guaranteed for 20 years, even if the manufacturer ceases trading or goes into liquidation.

There was also talk of damage to the roof caused by contractors (for instance, when they were maintaining mobile telephone masts), and a newsletter in March, 2001, promised that Dorrington Belgravia would pursue any culpable parties for the cost of reparation.

All advertisers of every kind are concerned with the quality of their products, and with the reasons why customers should purchase them; and when Dorrington conceived of half a dozen or so brightly designed circulars, on the rights and obligations inherent in their relationship to us, they were equitable enough. However, in the final analysis, all landlords are mostly focussed upon *our* obligations and *their* rights! So, whilst wishing everyone the best, we must defend our interests.

Once, for those whom it concerned, there was a request – out of the blue - for over £400 per capita. The reason? It was deemed to be time for a new lighting system for the garages. Yet there was nothing wrong with the lighting in either my own garage, or that of a neighbour of mine. We both protested, and the demand, like a hot air balloon, gently floated away. Then there was another request for about £400; but this one was not raised by hot air, and had to be taken seriously. Apparently, some plumbing had been done in various flats, but, at the time of the endeavour, the landlords did not realize that they could invoice the individual residents, – and so they simply added the cost to the general service charge bill. After the proverbial penny had dropped four years later, they began to send out invoices. Unfortunately, some of their records, much like the aforementioned balloon, had 'gently floated away', and so 300 letters were sent out 'on the fly' to discover, as in a prize draw, who had been the lucky recipients of their laudable plumbing performances. Even Noella, the new manageress, was rather embarrassed by the fiasco, and wished the freeholders could have borne the whole cost or let the matter rest.

Other events were also quite contentious. In the year 2000, the noisy task of electrical rewiring was reported as successful. And so, at last, we could all breathe a collective sigh of relief! And life was now easier for the meter reader, too, with just one location for the electricity meters in each corridor. But, while we are on the subject, why not accommodate all of the meters for Balham High Road in one place? If a conduit is needed for the wires, just dig a tunnel through people's private gardens. In fact, why stop there? Why not transfer all of the meters in London to one building? Du Cane Court, perhaps? Was some financial benefit for the residents ever negotiated with London Electricity, as we traded in our convenience for theirs? Of course, the current standards of electrical wiring are meant to be better than those which existed in the 1930s, and we must hope that this was the *primary* reason for the work.

However, there is good news as well. Whereas previously the manager would oversee not only Du Cane Court, but other blocks as well, we now enjoy (her) undivided attention. And some of the maintenance may be celebrated. In 1999, there was a notice for the replacement of the last of the old lifts. Looking after the lifts is an important business. A Residents' Association newsletter in May, 2003, informed us that 'the four lifts [in the reception area] make around one million journeys a year between them'. Heavy use must take its toll, and, on one occasion in recent years, a person was trapped in a lift of ours for 10 minutes.

At least one job since the year 2000 has enhanced the general semblance of the building. I refer to the ongoing replacement of the windows by Hazlemere Commercial. Whether or not to proceed is the decision of the individual, and at £2900 for a studio flat and £9800 for a 4-bedroom apartment (in addition to the annual service charge), not *everyone* wants to. But for those who can afford it, each new window is double-glazed, and no longer needs painting as the new frame is composed of a powder-coated aluminium alloy. Even those who cannot afford these novelties will have cracked window-panes replaced, and damaged metal frames repaired, - courtesy of another commercial enterprise unconnected with Hazlemere. (Or that, at least, is the principle. In reality, there are moments when one could be forgiven for thinking that labourers are breaking things as fast as they are replacing or fixing them, - and damage may pass unnoticed, until it is too late for a free remedy.) Naturally, there is some warping in the metal over time, although the atoms in a pane of glass are not entirely static either. Indeed, in scientific circles, glass may be regarded as a liquid. Therefore, a helpful workman informed me, it can flex to accommodate the strain. But a morsel of extracurricular education need not be the only unplanned benefit from the proceedings; for certain resourceful people, who are not blessed with balconies, have used the scaffolding as a platform upon which to sit and enjoy a little social intercourse with tea and cake. A long curtain, if it may be so called, affords some protection from the elements; however, with the odd shower of glass or stones, any hot beverage could end up receiving more than a spoonful of sugar.

The world of Du Cane Court has, of late, also become more ecologically aware, as we are now supplied with recycling bins for bottles, cans, paper and cardboard – in addition to the existing waste disposal facilities, including chute rooms inside the building, and a skip at the back of the garages. House-dwellers are usually less fortunate than ourselves, and will often have to drive to such conveniences. Perhaps we are rather cosseted here; and, like an island nation, our boundaries have assumed disproportionate significance. So it transpired that a rather flimsy perimeter fence became a subject for controversy; and so the lawyers, salivating at the prospect, must have unzipped the avaricious lips of their fat purses, and sharpened their rapier-like pencils for battle ... for if the wind blew the fence down, the direction of its fall could have legal consequences! Whether Zephyrus and his friends were in thrall to our manager, who can say? But the latter was taking no chances, and the fence was replaced in 2004.

The Gardens in Danger

Over the years, there have been a succession of gardeners who doubtless promised much but delivered little. At one point an assistant was hired whose competence was questioned, and who turned out to be a grave digger! This may have been faintly symbolic, as there were moments when it looked like the gardens themselves would be consigned to the grave. It is likely that some of the original Japanese features were lost long ago (and, even as I write, the lanterns are being slowly engulfed by shrubbery and weeds). Worse still, on the 6th of February, 1987, the larger of two cherry trees was found to have poisoned roots, and many of the roots of smaller trees near by were also infected. The pond base was cracking, and water was leaking into the basement of the building. To compound the issue further, the gardener threatened to walk out because of the presence of excreta deposited by people's pets. All kinds of disease can spread from this, and there is now a fine if anyone is caught with a dog fouling the grounds. One person actually *was* caught – but produced an extenuating plastic bag just in the nick of time!

Thankfully, the health and elegance of the gardens were eventually restored; and at last the time was ripe for some positive news. It came in the form of a certificate of excellence from the 'London in Bloom 2000 Competition'. The award was issued by the Mayor of Wandsworth, and, for a while, it was exhibited on the wall of the Estate Office.

The Romance of the Gardens

The green spaces of London are an essential part of its overall character, and the gardens of Du Cane Court provide a pleasant relief from the high density of population, just as the public parks and commons do in a wider context. Here, at 'the Court', are squirrels frolicking like kindergarten children. And here, at the height of summer, are the residents at their most relaxed, quaffing the soft winds and listening to the soporific sounds of their fountain – as if these elements were the ingredients of an elixir ... or gazing at the red brick buildings on the other side of the high road, when they glow at sunset with (shall we say) a strange passion; for, like a bloodied soldier, the sun emits more red rays as it goes down.

Of course there is the endless river of traffic, the sirens of ambulances, fire engines and police cars, and the scream of rubber on tarmac, produced by 'boy racers' revving up their monstrous engines; but you can watch it all from a comfortable deck-chair, set some way back from the thoroughfare, happy in the delusion that you inhabit a world apart from this madness; and then fall asleep, as the din subsides into a distant hum.

Finding some Character in Faceless Corridors

When a small living area is shared by many people, negligible aspects of their surroundings assume an unusual significance. I suppose it is similar to when a person loses his sight, and his hearing compensates by becoming more acute. To the uninitiated, all of the corridors are identical; yet a resident who has lived here for a decade or more, who by chance selects the wrong floor when he is in a lift, and so navigates to an alien corridor in the same relative position as his own, will soon realize from the immanent features around him that he has made a mistake. The carpet might be more or less worn; the light on the ceiling may flicker, or reveal an irksome crack in the wall where, in the familiar corridor, no such blemish had existed; whilst an alternative doorknob with a face reminiscent of Jacob Marley would surely give the game away. One day, I saw a door knocker which had been lowered to about three feet from the floor, so bowed was the occupant with the yolk of many years. Some corridors are distinguished by the pungent scents which linger there: one with an aroma of spice, another with the vapour of charcoal after some toast has been incinerated. Yet another may smell so musty, that if the Supreme Being had originally breathed life into the windows, they would have forgotten their primal function – through want of use - and reconfigured themselves as extensions of the wall.

One neighbour had a habit of opening his front door to let out any cooking smells, while shutting the windows in the corridor (and probably inside his flat), – as if he was some kind of demented Christian Dior, bottling the airborne remnants of his dinner for posterity. In winter, a particular window in the public domain was never opened, because it had recently been painted and was stuck fast to its frame! There was even a corridor which reeked like a decaying leg of mutton; and it is a considered opinion of someone I know that the source of the putrefaction was, indeed, a leg, although not one possessed by a sheep, but by an elderly person stricken with gangrene.

Then there is the variable décor. Some corridors have wall to wall carpeting, while the majority of them have a strip of exposed wood on either side of the carpet. Mr X once descended to his hands and knees, and vigorously polished the floor outside his front door until it gleamed. He even wondered if he could be paid £1000 for giving the other corridors his five-star treatment. (But then, this was a man who felt that 'my inbuilt wardrobe' and 'my *lovely* Italian cabinet' added £2000 to the value of the flat he lived in.)

And how do we account for the obsession with exterior door mats? Indeed! As if a visitor who wends his way betwixt front entrance and final destination would not have shed any detritus from his shoes *en route*. The mats have been described as a contagion spreading upwards through the body of the building (from the solar plexus to the brain, perhaps, or is the brain in the Estate Office?); and it is now decreed that they should be removed, as they are a safety hazard to passers-by who could trip over them.

But it is the *scale* of everything here which captures the imagination. Thus, an elderly friend of mine, tottering upon his slight and brittle legs, will commence an ascent of the broad staircase from our central reception with the words, 'I'm just going for a walk'. Yes, that's right ... up and around about; not down – and out, like others who are 'taking the air'. Perhaps he feels safer in a warm, stuffy atmosphere, with solid masonry around him. Hopefully, the aforementioned details will entertain him on his jaunt. Either way, ahead of him lies a physical challenge as great or small as he wishes to make it.

If the plates of glass at the ends of corridors were not framed by walls, and the carpets were suffused with the hue of the sky, then the floors would appear like infinity pools. Timid folk may prefer to liken them to long Victorian alleyways, sometimes dimly lit and seeming to lead nowhere. Yet they are not threatening to those who live here ...

Such is the multiplicity of small things which imbue Du Cane Court with character, and make it feel like home.

In July 2002, a newsletter highlighted a couple of ongoing problems. Firstly, we were warned that noise travels easily around the building when windows are left open. I can vouch for this myself, knowing how a former, deaf resident would leave her television on and her window open into 'the wee small hours', whilst those who were snugly wrapped up in bed, waiting to arrive in the Land of Nod, would have to endure what sounded like a series of government announcements booming around the courtyard.

Secondly, there was a startling revelation: 'Every year, we have vases, ornaments and all sorts of items being blown off window sills. Such [falling objects] could seriously injure or kill someone.' This followed a letter on 27th March, 2002, which introduced the subject of articles being *thrown* out of windows; and there was evidently a growing catalogue of such behaviours – as food, paper and even lit cigarette ends rained down upon the grounds! But all was 'nothing compared to a fire extinguisher being thrown into the courtyard from a considerable height. Fortunately no one was injured and no damage occurred.' Another note informed us that an unknown person had been letting off the fire extinguishers in C block. Yet remorse was a wallflower waiting for her first kiss; and carelessness, a dashing suitor whom she had not yet turned into a frog.

Du Cane Court has seen dangerous times. There was the case of the brave (or foolhardy) soul who would assist a neighbour who was locked out, by climbing through a window, crawling along a ledge, and thence moving deftly into the neighbour's flat, and opening the front door. Years ago, a window cleaner worked without a safety clasp. More recently, a certain Mr Rickman, father of ten children, would perform the same feat without a harness. Apparently, his only concessions to safety were the soft shoes he wore and the knowledge that he had insurance. This kind of behaviour seems to be catching. Maybe, before long, we'll have trapeze artists performing here!

At one of our Annual General Meetings, a young lady named Chrissie True expressed concerns about a cluster of aerials on the roof. In Australia, these are outlawed from schools because they have been associated with various health risks, although nothing has yet been proven to the satisfaction of English law. Nevertheless, it is a concern that will not go away, and in September, 2005, some notes from Mast Sanity were circulated, listing a host of maladies which could arise from the masts: cancer, degenerative brain diseases, skin rashes, hormonal deficiencies and fluctuations in blood pressure. The last malady to be noted was a disruption of sleep patterns, although this might occur anyway after reading the information! Unfortunately, the distributor damaged what may have been a worthy cause, by referring to T-Mobile masts even though we don't have any these.

Actually, there was a survey into the thermal effects of mobile telephone masts and base stations conducted in December, 2003, – but this did not examine the effects on human health. Perhaps to sweeten the pill, we were promised that part of a £6000 annual income from masts on the roof would be offset against the service charge, – although I'm not sure that it ever was.

A Near-Death Encounter outside Du Cane Court

The normally peaceful atmosphere of Du Cane Court was shattered on the 17th of June, 2000, by a screech of tyres and a car crashing into our perimeter wall. It was one of two automobiles which had been racing down the high road, the other having got away. Even the skid marks were clearly visible, and given the car had careered off the road and across a wide pavement before coming to an abrupt halt, it was lucky that no one was hurt. The incident attracted the attention of various people; and one resident of Du Cane Court reflected a fine community spirit, by overlooking the damage to our premises and offering the poor driver a cup of tea.

I supplied the story to a local newspaper; although – with the exception of a photograph - what eventually got published bore so little relation to my own account, that it could have been describing another accident.

A Fast Response to Unwelcome Visitors

A number of local councillors were canvassing for an election in about 1991, - and they even occupied a flat at Du Cane Court, before being unceremoniously asked to leave. A letter, dated 21st January, 2000, addressed this kind of issue, stating that cold callers may be escorted from the building. Officially, no tradesmen are allowed here; although the staff turn a blind eye to Pizza hut delivery boys, and, once a year, to the Salvation Army who drop envelopes through our doors. Perhaps we can live with this, but people with bogus identities are quite another matter. On this score, I once heard of an old lady opening her door to a stranger who asked to read her metre. The stranger then helped himself to her cash and valuables. In December 2003, a woman tried to dupe people into giving her money. She claimed to have locked herself out of her flat, and said she needed some cash to pay for her journey to a relative who held a spare key. A second claim was that she needed money for her electricity key meter. Fortunately, the response was swift. We received a memo on her exploits, and hopefully she won't be troubling us again.

Crime in the Locality: A Contemporary View

Some years ago, the police had suspicions that an IRA bomb was concealed in a garage in Balham. So, as part of their remit, they opened all of the garages at Du Cane Court. Fortunately, nothing was found and the padlocks were replaced. The incident was slightly disconcerting, although it was comforting to think that the forces of law and order were protecting us.

In May, 2002, Du Cane Court even supplied a strategic vantage point for some detective work. The news was that Balham Park Road had been the site of a robbery or a murder, - and Mary Whiteford, an affable lady from Scotland then in her dotage (or 'away with the fairies', as a compatriot of hers once put it), had been removed to a safe haven, leaving her apartment on the sixth floor of J block available for accommodating a huge surveillance camera, which could keep an eye on proceedings. The camera was a secret, and it may also have been a secret that the flat was empty. Thus espionage, the once-popular subject of boys' own periodicals, and of the chattering classes who have promulgated folklore about Du Cane Court over the decades, once again came home to roost.

Of course, crime can take many forms. During Christmas, 2002, an airgun was fired randomly at the windows of four different flats. Andrew McKeer commented, 'The police are not very amused'. I thought to myself, 'I shouldn't think the residents are either!' Worse still, in December, 2003, a carol singer was injured on our grounds by an airgun. The wound was fairly superficial, although it still merited a visit from the armed police. And, in the late months of every year, there are some tremendous reverberations from explosives being detonated, as if we had all passed through a time warp and were back in World War 11 ... but never fear. They are only fireworks bursting hundreds of feet above the ground.

It seems we are also powerless in the face of 'progress', for there are now proposals from the Home Office to relax the laws on the sex trade. In a paper published in 2006, a former manager named Andrew McKeer posed the question, 'What resident wants the flat next door to be used as a licensed brothel?' He also wrote that there could be a fall out in terms of antisocial behaviour; although the free spirit who was twice observed streaking across our grounds in 2006 would probably not object. While I am on this theme, I should say that I once heard a story about some Tamils sharing a small flat at Du Cane Court, which one person reckoned was possibly a 'place of ill repute' where a woman was being 'passed around like an After Eight Mint'. Quite a lot of noise came from the flat; and a friend of mine, who is familiar with this ethnic group, tells me they have a gift for imaginative abuse – and that, after a lovers' tiff, a girl might threaten to put her after-birth fluid into her man's rice.

Actually, this unusual group of individuals left a nasty taste in *our* mouths too, refusing to pay their electricity bill until they finally got cut off. But where there's a will, there's a way. They ran a connection to the common electricity supply in the corridor, until that link was also severed. Then, they ran a lead out of one window, up the wall, and thence through another window, - eventually tapping into the common electricity supply in the corridor above! They have left now. Apparently they were quite polite; and, I hasten to add, there are said to be many Tamils in Balham who are upstanding members of the community, some of whom own local businesses.

Above is the car that crashed into our perimeter wall one day. Fortunately, no one was injured, and a resident of the block showed her good nature by overlooking the damage, and offering the driver a cup of tea. (Photograph taken by the author.)

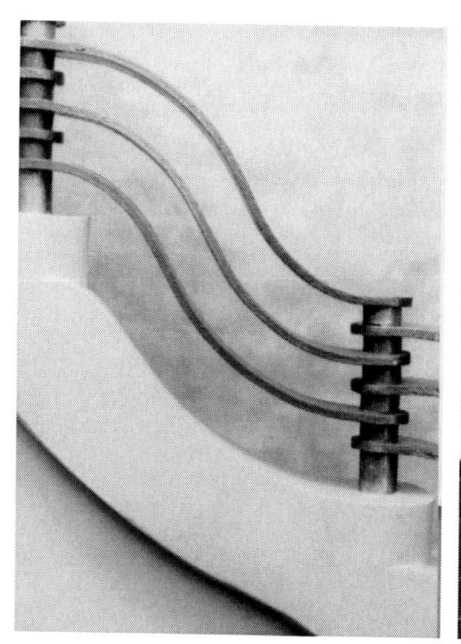

Some views of the attractive reception area. (Courtesy of Estate Office.)

Here is the onsite mini-supermarket. It was originally an Express Diary and grocery store. (Photograph taken by the author.)

A view of the front of Du Cane Court. (Photograph taken by the author.)

The outer gardens at Du Cane Court. The lower photograph shows one of the Japanese lanterns, and a water feature bordered by rocks. (Photos taken by the author.)

Above: The front-facing Japanese garden, with the water feature.
Below: On the left, a close-up of a lantern at Du Cane Court. There are four of them in total. On the right, a path leads out of the estate and towards the high road.
(Photos taken by the author.)

The two rear courtyards. The bicycles were moved into one of them, after the closing of the bicycle shed. The other picture was taken when the windows were being repaired or replaced in 2007. (Photographs taken by the author.)

The top picture shows one of the inner courtyards, when the windows were being repaired or replaced in 2007. The picture below was taken at the back of the building, but in front of the garages. It shows the lodge, which was turned into a luxury two-bedroom home in the 1980s. (Photographs taken by the author.)

Two views of the so-called ‘secret garden’, which nestles behind the garages. (Photographs taken by the author.)

Using Balham High Road as a line running from north to south … above is a view from the back of the building, facing north-west, with a surreal reflection on the glass; and below, a view facing north. (Photographs taken by the author.)

These panoramic views from the block face south-east.
(Photos taken by the author.)

CARTOON TIME AT DU CANE COURT

The designated electoral area for Du Cane Court has changed a few times over the years. (Cartoon created by the author.)

It's that Hitler legend again! (Cartoon created by the author.)

A small dilemma – in the 1930s, and even latterly. (Cartoon created by the author.)

Work on the building is not always constructive. (Cartoon created by the author.)

The landlord milks his fixed asset to the full. (Cartoon created by the author.)

A reference to the boiler explosion of 1991. (Cartoon created by the author.)

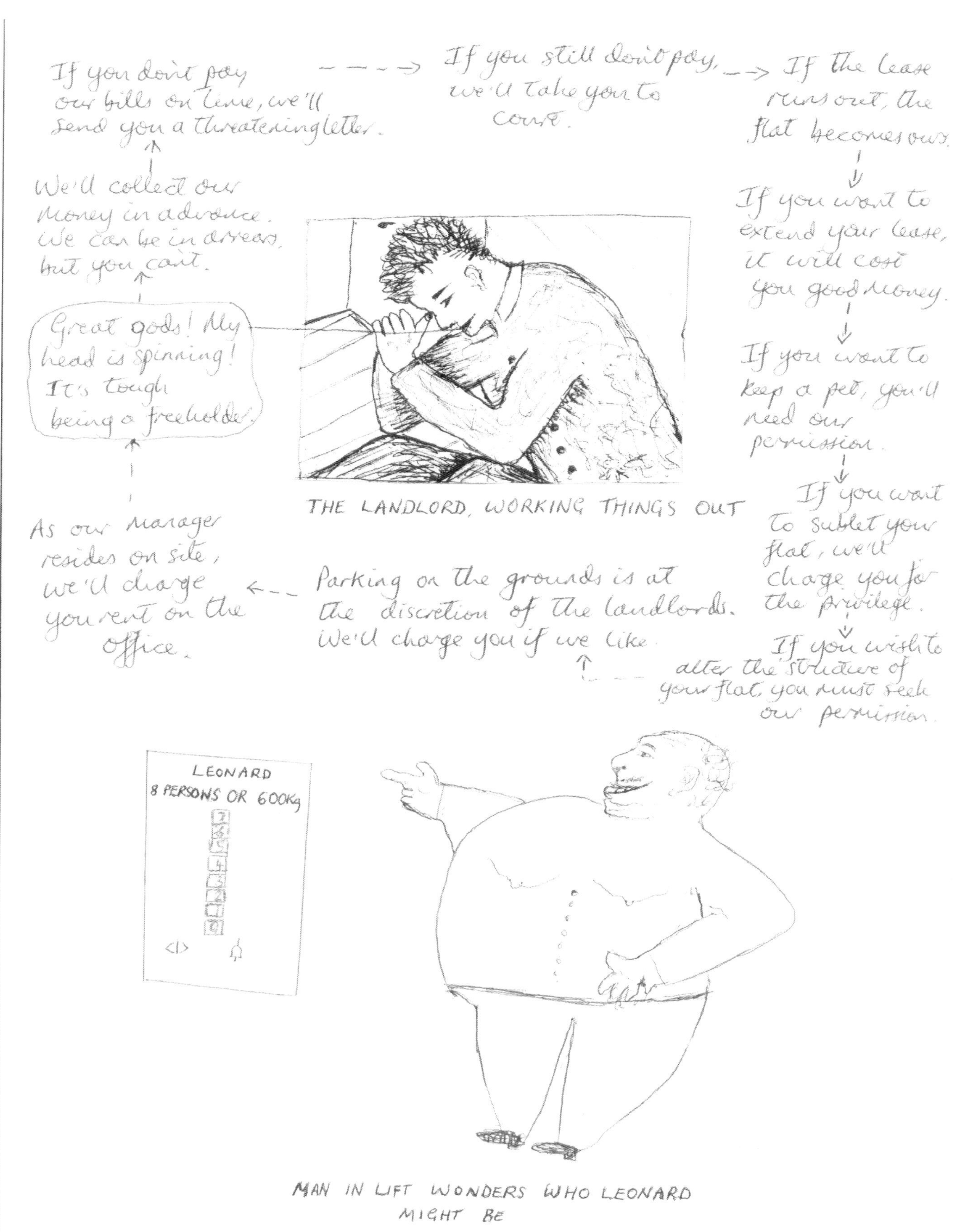

If you don't pay our bills on time, we'll send you a threatening letter.
If you still don't pay, we'll take you to court.
If the lease runs out, the flat becomes ours.
If you want to extend your lease, it will cost you good money.
If you want to keep a pet, you'll need our permission.
If you want to sublet your flat, we'll charge you for the privilege.
If you wish to alter the structure of your flat, you must seek our permission.
Parking on the grounds is at the discretion of the landlords. We'll charge you if we like.
As our manager resides on site, we'll charge you rent on the office.
Great gods! My head is spinning! It's tough being a freeholder!
We'll collect our money in advance. We can be in arrears, but you can't.
THE LANDLORD, WORKING THINGS OUT
LEONARD
8 PERSONS OR 600Kg
MAN IN LIFT WONDERS WHO LEONARD MIGHT BE

In the first drawing, we see that there are rules about most things at Du Cane Court. The second drawing alludes to a small notice in a lift. (Cartoons created by the author.)

You know, the day Job's Killing me .... what with Transporting blocks of cheese back to the nest all the Time.

TWO PHARAOH ANTS STRIKE UP A CONVERSATION IN THE LOCAL LIGHT FITTING.

Yea? Well come and Join us at the restaurant tonight. It's called, 'The Bandaged Wounds'. They say the blood there is delicious. You can have it fresh, congealed, or oven-baked (if the subject faces south); marinaded in tears and with an optional side order of sensitive membranes.

In the early 1990s, we had a pharaoh ant invasion. (Cartoon created by the author.)

There was some difficulty in obtaining suitable insurance cover at the beginning of the new millennium. (Cartoon created by the author.)

The service charge is often a hot topic of conversation. The second cartoon refers to a friend who bought herself a new shredding machine one day, and accidently put it to use on her service charge statement. Oh, well … that's one way to deal with it! (Cartoons created by the author.)

Here we have references to the bills for some plumbing work, which arrived four years late; and also to post-operative planning permission, and to increased charges in 2007. (Cartoons created by the author.)

CHANGES AND PATTERNS IN COMMUNITY LIFE

*

The Gentrification of the Area

The image of Balham has changed over the years. In the nineteenth century they used to say, 'Balham, brothel on the way to Brighton' [Smith]. The Bedford was once the most depraved bar in Britain, but is now a warm and jovial venue which stages comedy nights - the so-called 'Banana Cabaret', - and many successful comedians have passed through its ranks, including Arthur Smith.

One writer [Stern] comments upon how gentrification is always moving south. Many years ago, people spoke of the 'man on the Clapham omnibus'. Then it was 'Bal-Ham', and then citizen Smith's 'Tooting Popular Front'. In June, 2000, we were told that, soon, five new bars will have opened in a period of just 18 months, among them: The Lounge, Bar Interlude, The Point and The Exhibit ('surround yourself with art and become part of the exhibit'). Besides these amenities, local residents have My Back Pages (named after the Bob Dylan song), which is one of the few independent bookshops left in London. In fact, articles charting the improvements in this part of London have been appearing in the press for some years now; and they often note how strategically placed Du Cane Court is for those tenants who wish to take advantage of it all. Yet each time, the buoyant mood of the writer mistakenly implies that the transformation has only just occurred.

Du Cane Court has always been blessed with lively people who are naturally curious about the world around them; and there is much for them to be curious about. Immigration from Africa, Asia and Eastern Europe has added a touch of spice to the national heritage, - although the changes in this part of London have been particularly rapid, and hard for some individuals to come to terms with. The locality is peppered with exotic shops and restaurants, and, at Christmas time, with lamps dedicated to the main religions of the world. One of the lamps was a gift from the Residents' Association of Du Cane Court, although this fact is not widely known.

The various cultures co-exist peacefully enough; but let's not become complacent, so that, having reached the proverbial mountain top, we unwittingly begin our descent. Helping towards integration is the willingness to employee staff at Du Cane Court from any ethnic group. And as for keeping up appearances, residents welcome the ruling on smart dress for staff at the desk, which was re-introduced briefly and half-heartedly in the 1980s, and has now been restored to its rightful place in the annals of professional presentation and conduct. In addition, the public transport links, which contributed to the making of Balham and of Du Cane Court, continue to be good. So everything seems positive enough, and it is no surprise that flats here continue to be in popular demand. Those on the upper floors of the block, with a view over London, are often the most sought after; yet an apartment overlooking the private gardens might be preferred by some, for the lush and tranquil outlook it affords. However, flats do not often become available, and so prospective residents cannot afford to be too fussy. For instance, in approximately one year from January, 1986, there were just 18 new lessees. This implies that only one flat out of every 35-40 went on the market. Of course, many units are rented out, some 50-70 by the landlords alone; but the aforesaid statistic speaks volumes about the desirability of the place, and the reluctance of owners to sell. In our economic micro-climate, prices have risen dramatically. In the late 1960s, one could have purchased a flat here for about £2000. By 1996, a two-bedroom apartment would have set one back £60-65,000; and in 2007, the same place in reasonable condition could be valued at about £350,000. And news of the building continues to spread, for not long ago it featured in a property programme on television.

Not Everyone Moves Up in the World

The vicissitudes of commerce, and the commerce of emotions, are like the revolutions of the planets. The extreme peaks and troughs are all part of one great process. Night follows day, and may outlast what lies between ... At about 3 o'clock in the morning of the 11th of April, 2007, a tenant was out walking behind the building, and chanced upon some dark and indefinable object slumped on the ground. Upon closer inspection, he identified it as a human body in a pool of blood. Thus was revealed the first death of its kind on the estate for, perhaps, 20 years. The young victim, if he may be so called, had lived on the sixth floor, and I have heard that he cut his wrists before he jumped in order to make the outcome certain. He owned – or ran – a café in Ritherdon Road, and one wonders if he was 'in the red', for he might have transacted little business in the midst of so many similar enterprises. Apparently, he used to while away his time by sitting on the window-ledge; and the official line is that he accidentally fell.

Several days later, the stillness of the night was broken by a series of agonized cries, like that of a toddler being slowly throttled. The noise persisted for some minutes, and an overactive imagination might have construed an unsettling theory in the darkness. At least two persons contacted the night staff. Apparently, it was a fox.

Then, on 7th June 2007, tragedy struck again. A 25-year-old died suddenly of a heart attack. Whether he had been experimenting with illegal substances and had paid the ultimate price, I cannot say. But I do know that, after his front door was broken down, his 19-year-old niece rushed to him, and was so distraught that she could not be separated from his remains for twenty minutes. Noella, for whom managing the block is at times a ghastly form of social work, attempted to restore peace where calamity reigned, as the girl's frantic screams tore through the walls, and echoed down the faceless corridors ...

Altering the Community's Arterial Road

With a decades-long exodus of people from other parts of London looking for a new life in the suburbs, what was once suburban has become urban; and, to cope with the eternal influx and efflux of cars passing by the grand entrance of 'the Court', the high road is frequently under workmen's boots and pneumatic drills ... and it seems the wise men from the council cannot make up their corporate mind. They widened the road in the 1920s. Then they widened it again in the 1950s. Then they narrowed it in the 1990s, to accommodate a larger pavement. And what, prey, will they be doing next? Why, surely, they will be widening it again? Or maybe they will be resurfacing it, or supplementing the river of traffic with another island for pedestrians, who are oftentimes left stranded in the middle of the thoroughfare. And how apt is our terminology. An *island*, indeed! For the River Falcon once flowed under the open sky, and circumnavigated the grounds which would one day be the setting for Du Cane Court.

Balham Carnival, Rio Style

The diversity of the area is celebrated each year in the Balham Festival, a local extravaganza opened more than once by our very own Arthur Smith. I recall, with fondness, the first time I attended the opening ceremony. It was held on the grounds of St Mary's Church, at 10.30 am, on Saturday, the 3rd of July, 1999. The official photographer took pictures of Arthur and Dorothy (the contemporary vicar of St Mary's Church) standing by the Mayor of Wandsworth, who appeared in full regalia.

'I am extremely honoured to be asked to open this festival,' said Arthur. 'Balham, in its own way, is famous. Jack Dee lives here, as well as Ainsley Herriot of "Ready, Steady, Cook". But the act of the opera singer in Balham Station surpasses them all.' This was an allusion to a musical dipsomaniac, who serenades everyone travelling to and from work, - and I think it raised a few smiles.

The following year, the festival was due to commence on a wet and overcast morning. No one was sure where it would all start, and I wondered comically if it had been cancelled. But, at around 11.00 am, my fears were laid to rest by the sight of Arthur Smith and his entourage in the car park of Tesco's supermarket. There was actually a good turnout, including residents from 'the Court'. And when proceedings got under way, there was also plenty of entertainment. This included delightful circus acts. Two young men, one on stilts, were juggling skittles between each other with a mesmerizing fluidity of motion; and a playful exchange occurred between a clown and a little girl, in which the clown repeatedly dropped a skittle, to make room for the one which his companion handed to him.

In a few quiet moments, Arthur delivered his usual speech, and, following the applause, a musical interlude was brought to us by a brass band containing children of mixed race, who, at one point, gave a simple rendition of the patriotic hymn, 'I vow to thee, my country'.

Meanwhile, a smoky, atmospheric barbeque in the grounds of St Mary's Church awaited the arrival of hungry visitors. All this ... and there was a mini-film festival in the Bedford Arms still to come. But before the magic of celluloid, a procession of colourful floats, and rows of dancers with smiling faces, transformed the high road alongside Du Cane Court. With the weather transformed, they seemed to say, 'Let the good times role'.

The Success of High Rise Living

Traditionally, the British have not taken to communal living as well as the Europeans [Potter]. But people in this country are beginning to see the advantages it offers, including greater security and companionship. Du Cane Court, however, has had an easy ride into public approval, because – with certain colourful exceptions - it has always attracted a middle-class, well-behaved clientele; and also because, in spite of any criticism, it is better managed than *some* other blocks, albeit at a handsome price. Other buildings which have never fallen out of favour are the 40-storey high Barbican tower blocks [Sweet] – and the good news about apartment life is spreading. Even Goldfinger's Trellick Tower, - formerly London's 'tower of terror', where a club room and hobby rooms, with washers and dryers, were all trashed, – now exudes an air of friendliness. The whole concept of 'communal life under one roof' is like the dome of St Paul's, rising triumphantly from an Edwardian smog.

Du Cane Court has been called many things over the years, some of them flattering and some derisive, although in most cases even the detractors were being humorous rather than cruel. It has been likened to a hotel, for its luxurious reception area; to a student hall of residence, for the short-term rentals which it provides; to government departments, for the clerical staff it once reputedly housed; and to a hospital, for the legions of mature folk who have grown old and infirm upon its premises. Like a schizophrenic, it has many personalities, and through them all the sense of community survives; but many residents still long for an informal place to meet. A small move in the right direction was a fund-raising initiative in 2006, held in the reception area for the Macmillan Nurses. The event was well-attended, which reflects favourably upon the people here, especially as some of them have entered the 'farewell period' of their lives with little wealth to their names, and as they may be concerned that the system of 'controlled rents' no longer operates.

Within these walls, there is always a residual air of familiarity: witness the casual attire of the masses who visit our mini-supermarket at weekends. They may even be arrayed in their dressing-gowns and slippers. The chairman of the Residents' Association is somewhat irked by this fall from grace, and has observed, 'Maybe we should have an edict against such behaviour. There really is no excuse for it. *I*, for one, have a track suit which is almost exclusively reserved for brief trips to the shop, and which I can throw on at great speed. So at least a modest sense of etiquette is maintained.'

Comparisons with Dolphin Square

In my relentless quest for information about Du Cane Court, I stumbled across stories of other blocks which have parallels with our own. The chief example of this was Dolphin Square. As in 'the Court', many of its residents had paid controlled rents since 1964 [Low]. Those who took a fancy to the place used to wait years for a flat, and then faced a stringent interview to get in. Christine Keeler, the girl at the heart of the Profumo affair, and her friend Mandy Rice-Davis, were both linked with Du Cane Court in folklore, although they were actually tenants of Dolphin Square - as was William Vassall, the Admiralty Clerk convicted of spying in 1963.

Dolphin Square has also had its fair share of profligacy: erring husbands with mistresses, and a flourishing brothel in the 1970s. But the higher echelons of society have not shunned it. Princess Anne lived there for a while, but hated the noisy neighbours, the traffic, and the sight of hookers plying their trade. A visitor once said that the corridors had 'the lingering aroma of boiled cabbages'; and, in spite of attempts to smarten up the place, we are told that there is still something 'irrepressibly drab' about it. Well, perhaps we will draw a line under the comparison there.

SUGGESTIONS FOR THE FUTURE

*

In this concluding chapter, I would like to strike a chord with readers who live in leasehold homes themselves, and who, from time to time, reflect upon the politics of their situation, and upon whether or not all things must be set in stone.

Why Not Like Parliament?

Sometimes, in blocks of flats, decisions are taken – regarding maintenance or decoration – after little or no consultation with the tenants, although it is patently their money which is being spent. It seems odd to me that we do not have a democratic constitution at Du Cane Court, which allows us to 'elect' one of a number of options available to us when major works are on the agenda. If you raise this issue, you are told that it is impractical to consult everyone. But how long would it take to draw up a list of salient choices, each with its pros and cons, and then post them through every door? Indeed, the ballot papers regarding the largest job in the forthcoming months could be sent out with the service charge requests – and then the problem of distribution simply disappears! The votes could be counted, and the popular choice acted upon. But, I hear you cry, what if the ballot papers are not returned? Well, what happens in a general election? It does not matter if the turnout is poor. In the end, the winner is the party with the most votes – regardless. Really, just consider this: how is it we can have a democracy for sixty million people, when we cannot organize one for Du Cane Court? But we can soften the voices of dissent with a small compromise. Let's put a single notice in the display cabinet, with a date by which all replies must be sent to the manager's office.

The same principle could be applied as a route to self-government. So whenever the freehold changes hands, let's have a referendum. Except that the law needs to change first. The attainment of the freehold by tenants should not be predicated upon a majority of more than 50% favouring the motion. Oh, no. It should simply specify that the winner of the 'election' is the one with the most votes – *again*, regardless of the turnout. After all, if this was not the protocol in a general election, then, with an unspectacular turnout, the party in office might govern forever!

So much for the freehold. Why not simply elect our own manager? The rule of law does allow us to do this. And if the apex of the pyramid can be replaced, then why not the lower strata? In fact, I wonder to what extent we could turn to our internal population to satisfy staffing requirements, and whether the block could therefore be self-regulating? The committee could still oversee everything, and, if they feel they are 'hard put upon', they may be paid for their time. Think of the benefits. Anyone we employed would be completely accountable and less expensive (with no commission paid to a third party). Indeed, we might save so much money, that existing staff could be offered their jobs back with salary rises! So long as there is a chain of command, we'd have nothing to fear. After all, how do the freeholders get things done? Why, they delegate, of course! When was the last time any freeholder of ours ran around like a headless dodo, coordinating all and sundry on the premises? If you catch sight of one, please inform the curator of the Natural History Museum; for such a rare, flightless bird could be sacrificed and stuffed for his collection.

An Audit Trail with Full Transparency

I have asked for a list of flats currently being worked upon, on account of the fact that work may occasionally exceed the hours when it is permitted; and, when it does, even loud sounds can be difficult to locate. Regrettably, this has been refused on the grounds of privacy, but the right to privacy is not greater than the right to peace and quiet. We might, at least, have a list of the freeholders' flats being worked upon at any given time; especially as the freeholders, themselves, do not live here, and are exempt from the environmental impact of their actions.

And what about the impenetrable documentation which we receive? Fellow leaseholders, unite! Let us lobby for a clearer breakdown of our service charges. In Du Cane Court, there was a total management fee of just over £147,000 in 2006, whilst a figure for salaries is listed separately. Yet surely the manager gets paid a salary? And since when did accountancy records list only debits? Surely credits are also required for the books to balance? Yet apparently Du Cane Court is an exception. How our money is spent is itemized - but not how it is raised, flat by flat. We should remember that if the accounts are both fair and transparent, then there is no privacy issue. Each bill is simply a function of the floor space of the flat.

Now it *could* be argued that the same charge should be levied on every flat which has only one occupant, for will the occupant of a two-bedroom flat be more likely to wear out the carpets in the corridor than the occupant of a studio? Will he ask more questions of the porters, or expect special favours from the manager? Will he make more use of the gardens? The answer, in every case, is 'No', and the argument comes with only one proviso: the number of rooms which are heated will vary. However, let us return to the first principle, which is founded upon floor space, and consider an alternative layout for debits and credits:

Income:

Apartment	Size of Flat	Owner	Yearly Service Charge
Flat W	1-bedroom	Tenant	£2000
Flat X	2-bedroom	Tenant	£2500
Flat Y	Studio	Freeholders	£1300
Flat Z	1-bedroom	Managing Co.	£2000
etc....	......	......	......

Expenditure:
(itemized under subheadings such as the following)

Electricity, Buildings Insurance, and Major Works: such as repairing or replacing the lifts or the roof, or painting (the windows, the reception area, or the corridors)

Salaries:

Manager, Manager's Assistant, Cleaners, Gardener, Gardener's Assistant, Porters, Security Staff, and Grounds Man

Personal Satisfaction, and the Aims of this Project

Writing this book has fulfilled and challenged me in many ways. There has been the research with its 'eureka' moments; the painstaking process of drawing all of my information together into a composite whole; the question of how to take the reader with me on my journey; and then, there are the people which this endeavour has brought me into contact with, thereby making it a more sociable exercise than the writing of fiction. Although fiction and non-fiction are really not so different: for, in both cases, research makes the subject credible, and imagination gives it life.

My wish is to put Du Cane Court on the map historically and architecturally, and to have the building listed. I would also like to think that I have provided a living record of the place ... and I wonder if a tribute might be arranged for each of those residents who have created a special stir in the world, even if it is only a plaque on a front door.

Hopefully, we can learn from the past, and realize what this building could have become, and (in the right hands) what it could yet be. The resident population is somewhat like an oversized family, with a need for various facilities and for social cohesion; and there has been a sense of missed opportunities, and of squandering the 'family silver': the children's crèche, the squash courts, the combined restaurant and ballroom, the bar and the games room. What else must be sacrificed to the god of mammon before we realize the intrinsic value of our heritage?

Are all of the key organizations which are dedicated to preserving and celebrating unique architecture actually aware of our block? When I telephoned The Twentieth Century Society, the respondent turned the conversation around and started to quiz me! He explained that he wished to make Du Cane Court a listed building, but lacked the information necessary to fortify its claim. If listing could be achieved, it might confer special protection from the assaults of inclement weather and the erosion of time; and prevent any more superfluous structural changes from taking place. For listing affects not only the exterior of a property, but also the interior - unless that property has undergone a 'material change of use'. On the other hand, the new status may require that only specialists shall be called upon to perform particular services, and their fees could be even higher than what we are accustomed to.

Recommendations for the Gardens

I favour the reduced employment of noisy garden machinery, and a return to traditional methods of horticulture. It would also be gratifying to have roof gardens, as originally planned, although our priority must be to render the ground floor gardens in their 'best light'. Towards this end, it is good to see our water feature has had its fountain restored. (For some time, the fountain was absent, probably because of a water shortage.) Furthermore, the lanterns we have are treasures, and ought to be maintained and displayed properly. They may gradually be eroded if nothing is done. The snow lantern by the pond has been broken and reassembled wrongly. Its large plate should sit on top, in order to protect the rest of it from the elements – and to capture an attractive carpet of snow in winter. The other three lanterns have most likely been imported from Japan, where they would have been framed by wood. Ideally, all of the lanterns should be decorated with blue-green lichens. However, don't hold your breath. Lichens grow very slowly, taking about 80 years to make a spot the size of a US silver dollar; but this only increases their value, for in a Japanese garden ancient things are revered [Gustafson].

Of course, other oriental features could be introduced sooner. One example is an 'echo chamber'. This consists of a ceramic pot, with water concealed below a surface of pebbles. The idea is that a stream seeps through the pebbles, and causes a characteristic echo as it lands on the water level in the pot. One may literally 'tune' this artefact by controlling the stream, the droplet size, the rate of free fall, and the volume of the chamber. If the whole thing is done well enough, it should simulate an underground cave with a river.

And how delightful it would be to have a little outhouse as a venue for the Japanese tea ceremony: an ancient and complex ritual which is even choreographed. At Du Cane Court, the public purse is large, but the possibilities are endless.

A Summing-up

A building such as ours lives vicariously through its associations, even more surely than an actor becomes himself through his fictional characters: for, in the end, what is this edifice without the architect who gave it life, the style of art deco to which it historically belongs, the gardens which lend to it such a pleasant aspect; and without its various people – the architect, landscape gardener, freeholders, staff and residents - amongst whom are the famous and the infamous? For all I know, each and every one of them may be a central player in some fantastical tale which fate has spun; and for every story I've recounted, my collective readership might entertain me with ten more.

And yet my critics begrudge me each inclusion by saying, 'But this is not the essence of your subject matter', – until, in the end, the body of my work has been undressed, the lifeblood syringed from its veins, and the flesh stripped from its skeleton; and then, what shall we do with its bare bones, but break them up and cast them to the general populace to chew upon, as if they were dogs that required no more? And to what avail? For they *do* require more. The tiny morsels of history about Du Cane Court - served up in the press from time to time – have set tongues wagging, and cajoled yours truly to invest living tissues and add the breath of life ...

APPENDIX

*

Construction

From The Builder, 29th October, 1937, I have garnered this list of companies (with company numbers) and people involved in construction; while Companies House provided some information on what happened to them later – as well as sending me a full microfiche history of the Central London Property Trust. ('Y' indicates those still trading when I checked, circa 2000.)

(Y) Redpath Brown and Co, Ltd*, WC2 - steelwork
According to Companies House, the name apparently changed several times in the 1980s and 1990s. Probably incorporated (since 7th November, 1996) as Redpath, Dorman Long Ltd

(Y) T Clark and Co Ltd**, SW1 – electrical installation. Became T Clark plc (119351).

(Y) Benny Lifts Ltd, SE11 - lifts. Still exists (283677).

(N) Ellis (Kensington) Ltd, SW7 - plumbing. Became Ellis Mechanical Services (UK) Ltd Dissolved in 1995.

(N) The Indented Bar and Concrete Engineering Co Ltd, SW1 - reinforcement. Patented as 'Indented Steel Bar Co Ltd'. Dissolved.

(N) Stonart Asbestos Flooring Co. Ltd, EC2 – jointless flooring. Slate slab products, such as bath panels etc. Dissolved and records destroyed.

(N) W.H. Henley and co, Birmingham - metal windows. No Trace of this outfit.

(N) Watamps Ltd (279709) - radios. Dissolved pre-1970, so no details are available.

(N) Holliday and Greenwood, Ltd, SW1 - foundations. Dissolved 1978.

(N) The Keymer Brick and Tile Co. - facing bricks. Dissolved pre-1970.

(N) Goodman Price, Ltd, E8 - demolition. Dissolved 1985.

(Y) Lamson Engineering Co, Ltd, EC2 - letter chutes. Now known as D.D. Lamson (323307).

(N) Excel asphalt Co, Ltd, W6 - asphalt. Dissolved.

(N) W A Telling Ltd, SE16 - plain plastering. Dissolved in 1980.

(N) Concrete Pump Company Ltd, SW1 - concrete pump machinery. Dissolved in 1980.

(N) Vigers Bros Ltd, EC3 - hardwood floors. Became Vigers, Stevens and Adams Ltd. Dissolved in 1993.

(N) Mendenhall Ltd, SW1 - decorations and fibrous plaster. Dissolved. No records.

(N) Pall Mall Galleries, SW3 - furnishings and show flats

(N) J A King and Co Ltd, EC4 - glascrete. became CCF

Concrete Industries Ltd. Dissolved 1996.

(N) Freeman Heating Company Ltd, W1 - heating and hot water services. Dissolved and records destroyed.

(N) McAndrews and Forbes, WC2 - doors. Dissolved 1995

(N) Hurtons Ltd, W1 - baths. Dissolved, and records destroyed, more than 20 years before my enquiry.

(Y) Shanks and Co Ltd, W1 - sanitary fittings. Registered in Edinburgh.

(N) Carter and Aynsley, Ltd, E1 - door furniture. Dissolved and records destroyed.

(N) Electroway Heaters Ltd, W1 - electric fires. Became Electroway Ltd in 1973. Finally dissolved (as Heatroe Catering Ltd) in 1994.

(N) Haskins Ltd, E17 - collapsible gates. Changed name. Dissolved in 1979.

(N) R.I.W. Protective Products Co Ltd, EC2 - waterproofing. No records found.

(Y) ICI Ltd, SW1 (1852101) – partitions.

(N) Piggotts Ltd, EC3 - flagstaffs. Dissolved and records destroyed.

(N) W. J. Furse and Co, Ltd, Nottingham – lightening conductors. Now Crown House Engineering International Ltd (152958). In receivership at the time of asking.

(N) Byron and Co, WC1 - wall tiling. No records held and not a limited company.

(N) The Accrington Brick and Tile Co, EC4 - bricks. Information is with the Public Record Office in Kew. No date as to when dissolved.

(N) The Stonehenge Brick and Tile Co, Leighton Buzzard – bricks. Not a limited company. No records available.

(N) Fitzpatrick Ltd, E3 - roads. No records.

(Y) The Adamite Co Ltd – 'Bulldog floor clips'. Still exists as as Altro Ltd (154159)

(N) Messrs Rice and Sons Ltd - general contractors. Dissolved 1994.

The architect was Mr George Kay Green, employed by the Central London Property Trust.
Japanese and roof gardens were designed by Seyemon Kusumoto, Fellow of the Royal Horticultural Society.

*Redpath Brown and Co, Ltd, is no longer listed. It is likely that:

24th August, 1987 - became Cleveland Bridge and Engineering Company.

19th October, 1990 - became Cleveland Structural Engineering Company

7th November, 1996 – presumably became, or subsumed into: Redpath, Dorman Long Ltd (incorporated 1893). However, the similarity of the company name could be a

coincidence. Address is:
PO Box 27 Yarm Rd, Darlington, Co Durham DL1 4DE

**In 1889, Tommy Clarke founded the company (which still bears his name today) as electrical engineers and contractors. The T.Clarke group comprises -
T.Clarke plc
T.Clarke electrical contractors Ltd
T.Clarke (Midlands) Ltd
Veale-Nixon (Newcastle) Ltd
Meggitt Marsh and co Ltd
Weylex Properties Ltd

Holders of the Head Lease

Du Cane Court Ltd, 8th February, 1935 – 31st August, 1985
Company Number: 297017. At some point, became Walrob Properties Ltd.

Du Cane Court Ltd, 1967-1998
(Another company of the same name)

Landlords

14th January, 1935. Charles Henry Copley Du Cane in Le Lohier Dinan. Sold a parcel of land to the Central London Property Trust, who then built Du Cane Court.
29th September, 1936. Most of the new building was transferred to the trustees of the Royal Liver Society.
27th January, 1938. Trustees of Royal Liver Society purchased the rest of Du Cane Court.
2nd April, 1967 – An article in The Times reported that Central and District Properties had just sold Du Cane Court To First National Finance Corporation for £1k. (I have no record of when the vendors purchased it.)
31st May, 1972 - Royal Liver Trustees - Nessdale Ltd (of Knightsbridge, London)
24th June, 1974. Nessdale Ltd sold to Regalian Securities
13th September, 1984 - Keston Properties sold to Du Cane Court Ltd, lessees. (The two companies had the same address: St Alphage, Fore Street, London EC2)
14th August, 1986 - Swallow Securities sold to Olayan Europe Ltd. It is rumoured that at one point Olayan owned the building, and Swallow Securities owned flats that were let.
22nd September, 1987 - Olayan Europe sold to Belgrave Properties Ltd
17th May, 2000 - Dorrington Investment Plc acquired all of the property owned by Belgrave Properties Ltd, and

became Dorrington Belgravia Ltd.

Managing Agents

Among the managing agents whom residents readily remember are:
Keith Cardale Groves
Ayrton, Hooper and Jackson
Capital Property Management Ltd
Allsop Residential Investment Management (ARIM)

Information from the Register of Electors

Divisions, Wards and Polling Districts for Du Cane Court:
1936 - Du Cane Court was in Balham Ward, Dictrict D
1947 – Balham & Tooting Division, Balham Ward, District D
1948 – Wandsworth Central, Bedford Ward, District Q
1949, 1951, 1955, 1960, 1963 – the same
1964 – Wandsworth Central, Nightingale Ward, District Q
1968 – the same
1975 – Battersea South, Nightingale Ward, District JC
1976, 1981 – the same
1992 – Wandsworth, Tooting; Nightingale Ward; District JC
2001 – the same

The following figures give an approximate indication of the building's population over time. Of course, some residents may be excluded: those too young to appear on the list; those living here but not yet registered; and those who might never appear on it because they were registered with a property elsewhere. Regarding the second of the three groups, take the following statistics as an example.

1936: Only 3 occupants listed – all members of the Swift family, and all living in E04.
1937: 379 registered electors in Du Cane Court - only blocks down to E are listed. There were still no Lower Ground ('00') flats. The rest of the building was obviously not yet completed. Also strange is the fact that the first five names are not listed with flat numbers.
1938-39: 625 electors
It would appear that quite a few of the flats were still empty (and maybe under decoration), although it is likely that the building was essentially complete.
1939: 693 electors
1939-1945 – No electoral register
1945 (June) - 961 electors: made up of two separate counts of 891 and 70, both in June, 1945
1949 (June) – 989 electors
1949 (November) – 960 electors
1951 - 962 electors

1953 – 1051 electors: made up of two separate counts of 957 registered electors and 94 to be included on the next register.
1955 – 951 electors
1960 – 901 electors
1963 – 883 electors
1964 – 870 electors
1966 – 820 electors
1968 – 833 electors
1975 – 772 electors
1976 – 753 electors
1981 – 729 electors
1992 – 731 electors
2001 – 764 electors

For the following records, I have generalized to a degree. For instance, while I would have checked that Andrew Sandham had flat B04 in 1938-39 and in 1958 – I would not have checked every year in between; and, also, just because I did not see an electoral record for someone after a certain period, this does not prove that the person had necessarily left.

B04. Andrew Sandham sharing with Kathleen Louise Sandham. He lived there from 1938-39 to 1958. At least by 1954, he was living on his own.

K36. Andrew Sandham, 1959

B01. Elizabeth M. Sellars sharing with 5 others in 1945-6, one of whom was Charles V. Dhanapala.

B11 – Derek Thomas (stage name 'Derek Roy') lived here from 1945 to 1949, with William and Marianne Thomas. I could not find the entry for 1950. By 1951 he had left, but William and Marianne were still living here.

George & Beryl Parkinson. Observed in the records between about 1945 and 1960. It is rumoured that George had his own musical quintet.

Tommy Trinder, 1939-1955.
G002 – Tommy Trinder and Violet Trinder, 1939. He was still there in 1955, but living on his own. He is not recorded against this flat for every year. For example, he is recorded in 1950, 1954 and 1955; but not in 1945, 1946 and 1948.

Ernie Bubley, 1948 – 1976.
G003 - Ernest Bubley and Jacqueline J. Bubley, 1948-51.
In 1948, they were sharing with someone called Joan Watson.

C11 – Ernest Bubley and Jacqueline J. Bubley, 1952 onwards. They were still there together in 1968. Ernest Bubley was living on his own in this flat in 1976.

Relations of Margaret Rutherford?
A41b - Cecilia F.Rutherford, 1945
A41b – Xaviere F.Rutherford, 1946
A41b – Xaviere D.Rutherford, 1983

E02 - Frank and Harriet Sarah Winn were living here in 1939. Were they relations of Anona Winn?

I also observed Lily M. Hearne was in E410. Perhaps she was a relation of Richard Hearne ('Mr Pastry'), for he is understood to have visited his mother here. And I saw Mary E. Todd recorded against F42, which is of interest as one individual told me that Richard Todd, the film actor, had possibly been seen here.

D75 – Albert and Irene Agate, 1968. The racing tipster, 'Pegasus', who was a certain Mr Agate, was known as Stan by his friends here – but maybe that was a middle or assumed name. It is possible that this was his flat.

C11 – George A. Jackson. Probably this was the same Mr Jackson who managed the block during the war. In 1948, he was sharing the flat with three other members of the Jackson family.

K001 - Margaret Whelpton, 1956 and 1957.
Margaret Whelpton was one of the managers of Du Cane Court in the early years, who is clearly remembered by older residents. I thought I also observed her name against K34 for one year – but when I looked for the record again, I couldn't find it.

G002 – Arthur and Annie Hearse, 1957. Mr Hearse was Head Porter, so probably this was his flat.

H26 Netta Verga, 1939. This was the lady who, upon her death, was found to be harbouring a mummified baby in her flat.

Interviewees

I interviewed a number of people who are, or have been, residents of Du Cane Court. Some of these had been here for a very long time, including about half a dozen since the 1940s or 1950s. See the ACKNOWLEDGEMENTS section for more detail.

Organisations Contacted or Visited

I uncovered several court cases of interest, which I should mention here: Orion Property Ltd and others vs Du Cane Court Ltd and Others, and General London and Urban Properties Ltd vs Du Cane Court Ltd and Others (both dated June, 1962); Regalian Securities vs Ramsden (1981); and Kay Green and Others vs Twinsectra Ltd (1996).

Architects Registration Council of the United Kingdom
Associated Newspapers, Reference Library, Northcliffe House, 2 Derry Street, Kensington, London W8 5TT.
For newspaper clippings on the following subjects:
Dog owners at Du Cane Court, Daily Mail, 1950;
Mr Jackson broadcasting about the dance hall;
References to plans for 20 new flats on the roof, 1973/4.
Battersea Reference Library
British Library supplied:
the article on Semi-Detached London;
the article on The Rise and Fall of Leasehold flats
British Music Hall Society. Special thanks to Max Tyler.
Companies House. For microfiche records on Central London Property Trust, and information on all of the companies that worked on the construction of the building.
English Table Tennis Association Ltd
(Spoke to Ken Muhr and Ron Crayden. Especially useful was Ron Crayden's article on Ernest Bubley.)
Everett Collection / Rex Features. Stephen Atkinson
German Historical Institute. Spoke to Mrs Klauk.
Guildhall Library, Corporation of London
Sarah Ash supplied information from the Times Index.
Japanese Garden Society
Kensington and Chelsea Public Library
Land Registry. Anthony Batho, Richard Coppin
London Metropolitan Archives. Supplied historic land transactions relating to the Du Cane family
Marylebone Cricket Club, Lord's Ground, London NW8 8QN
(Stephen Green, Curator, provided information on Andy Sandham.)
Museum of Garden History. No mention of Du Cane Court
National Heritage
National Monuments Record. Only had a photograph of the building, dating from 1952.
NHS Traceline. Debby assisted me by finding a copy of Kusumoto's death certificate.
Office of National Statistics. Information from the census for 1991. (Data for 1931, 1951 and 1971 was held at Wandsworth Council.)
Peters, Fraser & Dunlop Group Ltd. Lucia Pallaris
Proceedings of the Residents' Association

Public Record Office, Kew Gardens
Rentokil Initial. Spoke to Donna and to Danny Ashton
Royal Horticultural Society
Royal Institute of British Architects
Theatre Museum, Covent Garden. Keith Lundric provided information on theatrical celebrities.
The Garden History Society Website
The Raymond Mander & Joe Mitchenson Theatre Collection. (In the end, I did not reproduce any of their pictures.)
The Twentieth Century Society
Victoria and Albert Museum.
Art Deco 1910-1939 Exhibition – 27th March to 20th July, 2003
Wandsworth Council. Looked at microfiche records; and at information from the census for the years 1931, 1951 and 1971.
Wandsworth Museum
Wandsworth Public Record Office
Wandsworth Heritage Service (formerly, the Local History Library), Lavender Hill, Clapham. Useful for Register of Electors, some articles, and a photograph.
West Hill Reference Library
Westminster Archives Centre, 10 St Anne's Street

References

Obviously, innumerable ideas in the present work have no identifiable source apart from the author's own mind. For instance, the chapter entitled 'Some Philosophical Reflections' was not facilitated by any references.

I do not have full details of every reference used. Sometimes the information I had access to was incomplete. For example, the general category in the Local History Library, *Wandsworth Notes*, encapsulates interesting things – but does not always mention where they came from.

Brighton & Hove Bus and Coach Company Ltd Website - 'Names on the buses'. Section on Harry Leader.
Burke's Landed Gentry
Chelsea Flower Show Catalogue, 1937
Contract Law Information Network –
Central London Property Trust Ltd vs High Trees House Ltd. Uniserve Electronic Publishing Group, copyright 1995 (1947, Kings Bench Division)
Daily Mail, 9th November, 1946 – 'Mr Jackson ran a 4th Programme'
Daily Mail, June 1950 – 'Dog Owners Fight Ban in Flats'
Daily Telegraph, 11th July, 1989. Obituary for Tommy Trinder
Daily Telegraph, 5th February, 1994 – article on Anona Winn
Encyclopaedia Britannica – notes on Wandsworth (from

internet site, www.britannica.com)
Estates Gazette, 27th May 2000 – article on Dorrington Acquisition
Evening Standard, 25th April, 1931
Evening Standard, 25th April, 1973 – Re: Prices of flats here
Gardeners' Chronicle, 1937, vol. 1
HMBC Garden Register
Journal of RIBA, 30th July, 1937
Journal of RIBA, 27th June 1938. Two articles:
- 'Some Homes for Heroes 1919-1925'
Journal of RIBA, 6th March 1939 - Some information on Asbestos
Journal of RIBA, 20th March, 1939
Journal of RIBA, 8th May, 1939
Journal of RIBA, 16th October, 1939. Two articles:
- 'What Architecture can do'
- 'Emergency Legislation Affecting Housing and Building Work Generally'
Kelly's Hendon Directory, 1937-38
Register of Electors
South London News, 25th October, 1985 – 'Spinster's Tragic Secret: Baby's Body Found in Suitcase'
Streatham and Tooting News, 13th June, 1986 – 'Suicide over Move'
Streatham News, 4th May, 1928 – 'Old Balham and Tooting'
Streatham News, 27th February, 1931 - 'Andy Sandham's Parents' Golden Wedding. His First Cricketing Lessons.'
Streatham News, September, 1937 – '"Andy" Sandham Retires. Long Association with Streatham. Winter Tour in the Argentine.'
Streatham News, 30th August, 1940 – 'D.F.C for Old Grammarian'
The Builder, 1st October, 1937
The Builder, 29th October, 1937
The Huguenot Society of Great Britain and Ireland Website
The original brochure for Du Cane Court
The Tatler and Bystander, 29th March, 1944
The Times, 7th October, 1966. Re: Controversy surrounding allocation of shares in Du Cane Court Ltd
Wandsworth Borough News, 31st January, 1958 – '90ft High Road Scheme'
Wandsworth Borough News, 14th March, 1958. Re: Branch of The Writers' Club to be formed in Wandsworth
Wandsworth Notes, Volume 5, p.168. Streatham News, 1930
Wandsworth Notes - Friday, 25th April, 1958 - 'Radiation Danger in Wandsworth'
Wandsworth Society -

'Architecture: Wandsworth Society Publication no 2', 1989

Other References, by Authors' Names

Ablett, Mrs E. and Short, Mr H. – 'Memories of Balham' (Wandsworth Notes)
Atherton, Mark – 'Telling a Tale is Profitable' (Streatham and Tooting News, 21st July, 1994)
Barker, Godfrey - 'Bankers Who Hung in the Balance' (Evening Standard, Monday, 26th April, 1999)
Barry, Jane – 'Are you being served' (Evening Standard - Homes and Property, Wednesday, 20th October, 1999)
Barry, Jane – 'Battersea Freehold Fighters' (Evening Standard, Homes and Property, Wednesday, 24th May, 2000)
Blandford, Edmund – 'Target England: Flying with the Luftwaffe in World War 11'
Block, Michael – 'Ribbentrop' (1992, Bantom Press)
Bloom, J.H. – 'Bygone Balham and Tooting Bec' (1926)
Carter, E.J. – 'The Case for a Learned Society' (The Journal of the RIBA, 10th January, 1938)
Conway, Judith – 'Japanese Influences on English Gardens' (1988, Architectural Association)
Crayden, Ron - 'Ernie Bubley: A Man of many talents' (Sci. News, No. 61, June 1996)
Eade, Christine - PW, 26th May, 2000
Fishburn, Dudley – 'Improving the Lot of City Dwellers' (The House Magazine, 25th January, 1993)
Flemming, Peter – 'Invasion 1940' (1957, Rupert Hart-Davis)
Frindall, Bill - Andrew Sandham, 1890-1982 (from 'The Guinness Book of Cricket Facts and Feats', 1991)
Glancey, Jonathan and Robertson, Gael – 'Thoroughly Modern Living' (published by Hanover Acceptances Group, Dec. 2004
Gower, Graham – 'Balham: A Brief History' (Revised Edition, 1996.) Designed and produced by the Publicity and Print Section, Wandsworth Borough Council
Green, G.W.C – 'A History of Wandsworth'
Green, Margaret – 'The Abrahamic Covenant or Birthright of Israel in its National and Temporal Aspect' (1913)
Griffiths, Sian – 'Mayor gives green light to roof gardens'
Gustafson, Herb – 'The Art of Japanese Gardens: Designing and Making Your own Peaceful Space' (1999)
Hamnett, Chris and Randolphe, Bill – 'The Rise and Fall of London's Purpose-Built Blocks of Privately-Rented Flats, 1853-1983' (London Journal, volume 11, (2), 1985)

Hastings, Max – 'Not Very Funny Haw Haw'
(Sunday Telegraph, 16th November, 2003)
A Review of 'Germany Calling: A Personal Biography of William Joyce, Lord Haw Haw', by Mary Kenny.
Hook, John – 'The Angel of Death has been Abroad: The Air Raids on the London Borough of Wandsworth 1939-1945'
Jackson, Alan - 'Semi-Detached London: Suburban Development, Life and Transport 1900-1939' (1973)
Jackson, Marie – 'The Week the Taps ran Dry'
(Wandsworth Guardian, 18th November, 1999)
Jankowski, Edmund – 'Owning Your Flat: A Practical Guide to Problems with Your Lease and Landlord'
Jellicoe, Geoffery and Susan et al, editors –
'The Oxford Companion to Gardens'
(Oxford University Press, 1991)
Jenkins, Christopher Martin – 'The Complete Who's Who of Test Cricketers'
Jones, E. and Woodward, C. – 'A Guide to the architecture of London' (1983)
Jones, Rick – 'Citizens Du Cane',
Evening Standard, 23rd March, 1988
King, Debbie – 'A Step Back in Time'
Kusumoto, Seyemon – 'Gardens of the Far East: A Japanese Garden on a Bognor Estate'
(The Estates Gazette, 28th November, 1936)
Larkin, Colin Editor - The Encyclopaedia of Popular Music, 3rd Edition (1998)
Low, Valentine – 'The End Beckons for Famously Low Rents'
(Evening Standard, 7th February, 2002)
McKeer, Andrew (MRICS, FIRPM, FPRA Hon Consultant
'Prostitution Threat to Leaseholders'
(from Federation of Private Residents' Associations Newsletter, issue no 77, Summer 2006)
Orwell, George – 'The Road to Wigan Pier'
Published by Penguin Books, 1937
Paul, Samuel – 'Apartments: Their Design and Development'
Reinhold Publishing Corporation, 1967
Peel, Lucy and Powell, Polly and Garret, Alexander –
'An Introduction to 20th-Century Architecture' (1989),
Published by Secaucus, N.J.; Chartwell Books, 1989
Potter, Jennifer – 'Building Blocks'
(Evening Standard, 7th April, 2000)
Raggett, Jill – 'China and Japan - Some Garden Parrallels'
(Shakkei: The Quarterly Journal of the Japanese Garden Society, Volume 5, no 4, 1998)
Renshaw, Helen – 'The Age of Art Deco'
('Weekend', 15th March, 2003)
Robertson, Leslie E. – 'The Fall Guy'

(Sunday Telegraph Magazine, 30th December, 2001)
Scott, Thomas E. – 'Air Raid Precautions as a Problem for the Architect' (Journal of RIBA, 27th June 1938)
Shaw, Anthony and Mills, Jon – 'We Served: War-Time Wandsworth and Battersea 1939-1945' (1989)
Smith, Arthur – 'Gateway to the Sarf: Why I live in Balham' (Evening Standard, 17th March, 1993)
Stern, Stefan – 'From the height of naff to the shock of the New' (New Statesman, 5th June, 2000)
Summerson, John – 'The Great Landowner's Contribution to Architecture' (Journal of RIBA, 6th March, 1939)
Sweet, Fay – 'Why Tall Storeys are best sellers'
Taylor, Patrick – 'The Daily Telegraph Gardener's Guide to Britain' (1996), published by Pavilion Books Ltd
Thomas, Yvonne – 'Managing the Managers' (The Times, 5th August, 1992)
Troop, Robert – 'People and Property: Big deal in Balham' (The Times, 2nd April, 1967)
Wilmott, Phil – Interview with Tim Luscombe (published under the theatre section of www.lastminute.com, 9th February, 2006)